THE AMAZING BOOK OF BACKGAMMON

LEARN HOW TO PLAY THIS CLASSIC GAME OF SKILL, SPEED AND STRATEGY

JON TREMAINE

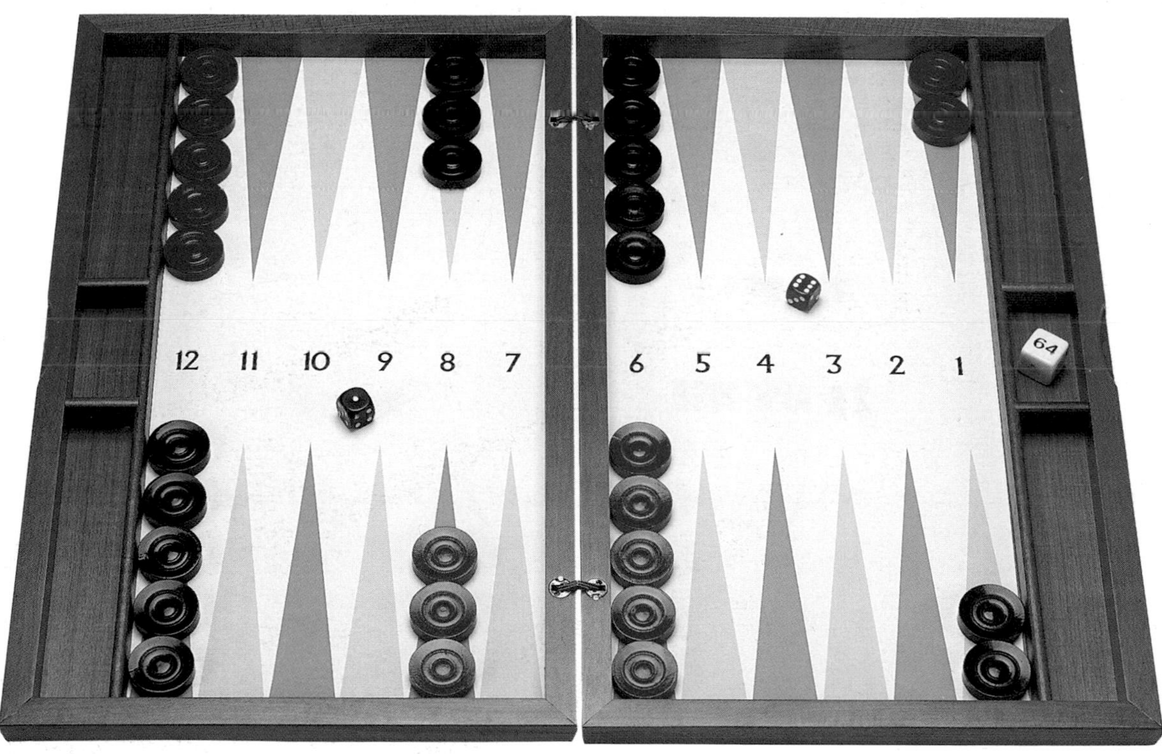

TIGER BOOKS INTERNATIONAL
LONDON

Dedication
My personal thanks to Barry Austin – publisher and backgammon enthusiast – who, thankfully, gambled on me!

Credits

Photography
Neil Sutherland

Editor
Philip de Ste. Croix

Designer
Stonecastle Graphics Ltd

Models
Adele Ladkin
Suzy Tremaine

Production
Ruth Arthur
Sally Connolly
Neil Randles
Karen Staff
Jonathan Tickner

Director of production
Gerald Hughes

Typesetting
SX Composing Ltd, Essex

Colour reproduction
Pixel Tech Prepress PTE Ltd, Singapore

Printed and bound by
Sing Cheong Printing, Hong Kong

CLB 4068

This edition published in 1995 by Tiger Books International plc, Twickenham

ISBN 1-85501-768-7

THE AUTHOR

Jon Tremaine, a professional magician for over thirty years, was introduced to backgammon while performing his act in Swaziland. He has since played the game in a multitude of countries around the world, and lectures about and teaches backgammon to groups throughout the U.K. In writing this book, he fulfils his wish to pass on to others the knowledge that he has gained while touring 80,000 miles a year and playing backgammon all the way! He is also the author of three other titles in this series: *The Amazing Book of Magic, The Amazing Book of Card Tricks* and *The Amazing Book of Origami.*

INTRODUCTION

I have two passions in life. One of them is backgammon. The other one isn't! One day I will write a book about my second passion; however, one thing at a time. Very little has been written about backgammon to date, which is surprising when you consider that the game has been in existence for over 3,000 years. That is longer than chess!

Much of what has been written for the beginner is confusing, contradictory and dull. Realizing this, I have been very careful, while preparing this book, to make my explanations clear and the illustrations plentiful. Take each chapter "as it comes" and try not to jump ahead of yourself. Most chapters end with a questionnaire section which, if you have read and digested the chapter carefully, should be well within your new-found ability to solve. The questions will, at the very least, increase your enjoyment of the book and do much to improve and accelerate your mastery of this beautiful game.

Backgammon is a game for two people. It is easy to play, but hard to play *well*! Why is this? Well, anyone can "play at soldiers" but to be a great general requires dedication, experience and study. After all, backgammon *is* a war game. It is "no holds barred" mortal combat with the total annihilation of your opponent your sole object.

An expert backgammon player can no more win all his games than a general can win all his battles. This book will teach you how to win *most* of them.

THE BARE BONES

This first chapter will give you a working knowledge of backgammon. If you study its contents carefully, you will find that by the end of it you will be able to play. After a fashion! Already you will be deriving enjoyment from this superb game. Take this chapter slowly. Make sure that you fully understand every section of it. It will give you a little knowledge about a great number of things. Each element will then be dealt with at greater length later in the book.

THE BASICS

Backgammon is a game for two people. Throughout this book the two players will be known as Red and Black. You (the reader) will always be playing Red, the text and illustrations therefore will always be from your point of view.

The game is played on a board which looks rather like an opened attaché case. The players sit facing one another across the board. Each has fifteen checkers or men, two dice and a dice shaker. Yes, backgammon is basically a dice game, a game of chance, and Lady Luck can either make or break you. It is for this reason that the greatest player in the world cannot win all the time. He will probably win four out of five; his superior skill makes this possible, but even a player of average ability can trounce him occasionally. This is what makes backgammon the most exciting, fascinating and frustrating of board games.

TABLES

The floor of the board is marked out with 24 points. The board is thought of as being divided into four sections or tables, both players having an inner and outer table. Red's inner table is to his *right*, his outer table to his *left*. Black's are the reverse; in fact Black's whole set up is a "mirror image" of Red's (**1**).

Each table contains six points – those in the inner tables are numbered 1-6 while those in the outer tables are numbered 7-12. The Red No. 7 point (R7) and the Black No. 7 point (B7) are the only points that also have a name. These are called the bar points.

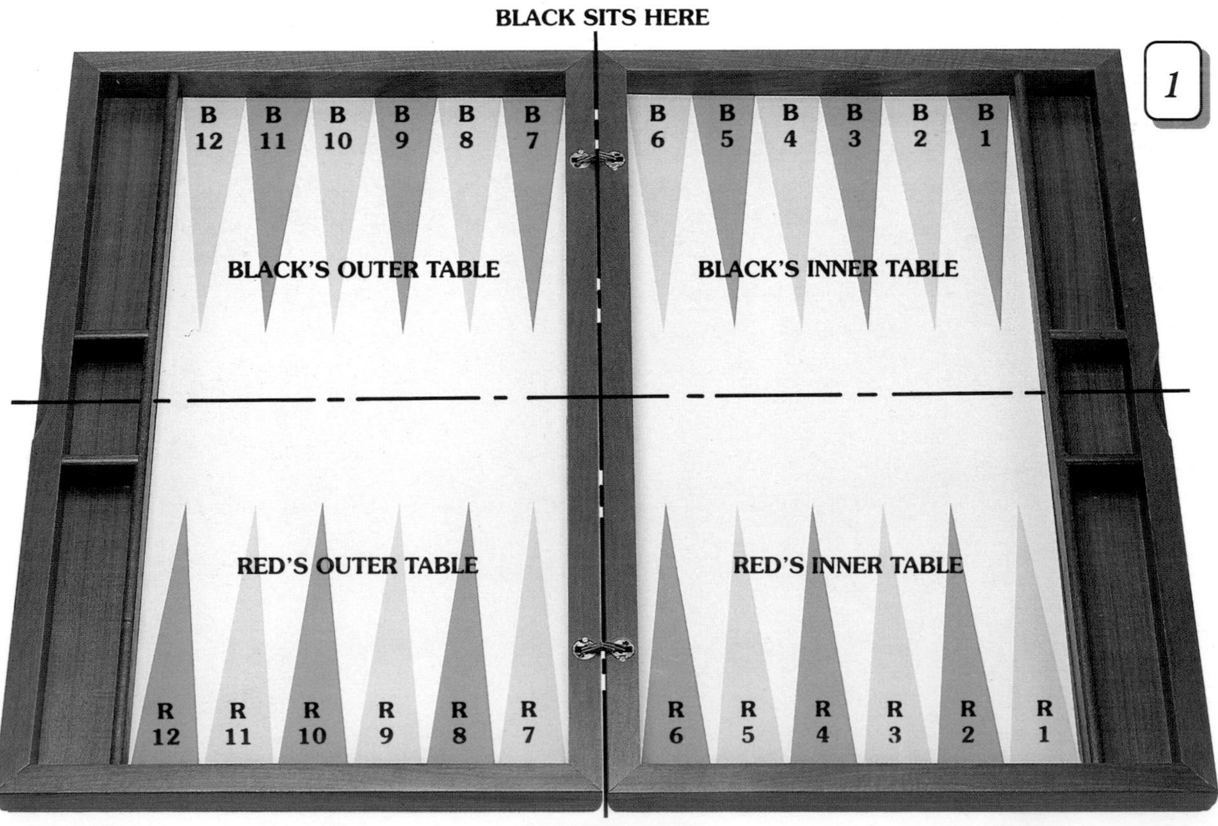

THE BAR

The bar is the raised section in the centre of the board that effectively divides the board in two and separates the inner tables from the outer tables.

Clear so far? Good.

SET UP

The board is set up with the thirty men positioned as shown (**2**). This is probably the hardest thing for the beginner to remember. Why are the men set up like this? Well, during the evolution of backgammon over the centuries, it was found that this disposition of men provided the greatest number of good (and bad) combinations of moves, making for a much more interesting game.

BLACK SITS HERE

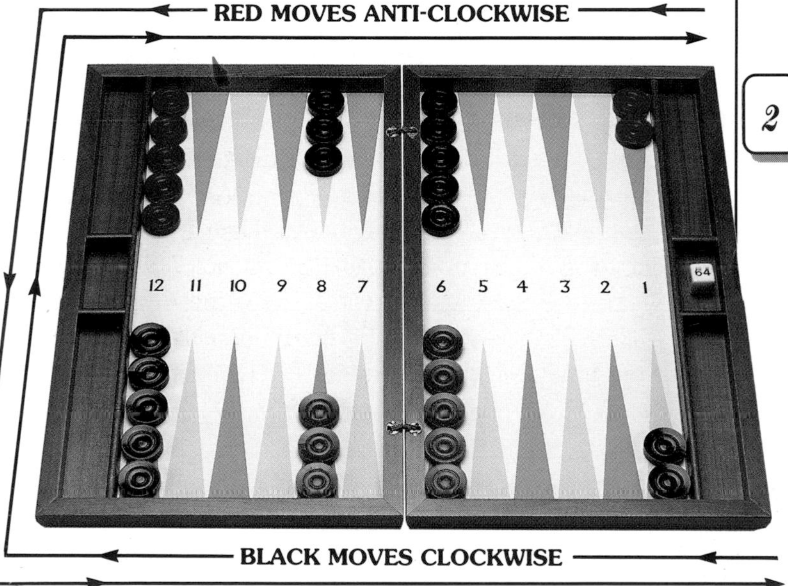

RED SITS HERE

2

You will also notice from the illustration that the players move their men in opposite directions, attacking one another.

OBJECT OF THE GAME

The object of the game is to move your men, according to the throws of your dice, around the board and into your own inner table. Once all fifteen of your men are in your inner table, you begin to remove them from the board, again as determined by the throws of your dice. Your opponent is attempting to do the same. The first player to remove all his or her men from the board wins.

Each player tries to impede the progress of his opponent by setting up blockades or **blocked points.**

BLOCKED POINTS

Any point on which two or more men rest is called a blocked point. You cannot stop on a point "blocked" by your opponent. If you get six blocked points in a row it is called a **prime** and any of your opponent's men that are positioned behind this prime will be trapped, unable to move until such time as the prime is broken by you. This is because six is the highest number to appear on a die and a prime cannot be hopped over.

You will have already noticed that backgammon has a language all of its own. We talk of bars and blocked points and inner and outer tables etc. Please do not let it confuse you. There are a few more terms for you to learn and remember. Please learn them. Not only are they used throughout this book, they are common parlance among backgammon players the world over.

NOTATION

Backgammon uses a universal notation system illustrated in (**3**). The points are each numbered. Black's side of the board contains the numbers B1-B12, while Red's are numbered R1-R12. These numbers do not actually appear on your backgammon board – they are purely for notation purposes, and for allowing us to discuss and analyse moves.

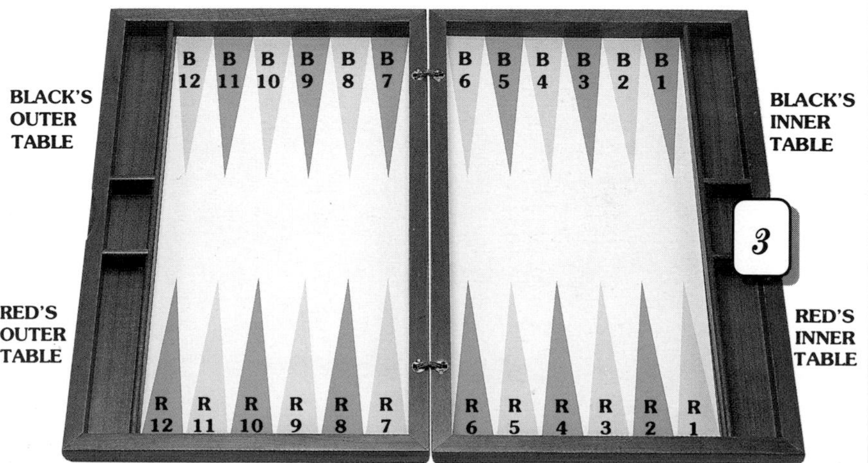

3

MOVING

Red moves in an anti-clockwise direction, while Black moves in a clockwise direction (**2**). A player moves his or her men as many points as shown on the two dice and plays *must* be made for both dice if possible. Either number may be played first. If only one number can be played, and there is a choice, the higher number must be played.

Here are some examples of play. The roll is 6-2. You may move one man six places and another man two places (**4**). Alternatively one man may be moved six places and then the *same man* advanced a further two places (**5**).

This, remember, is also two moves and each half of the move *must* end on a point that is either

- open and has no men on it
- has your own men on it, or
- has only *one* of your opponent's men on it.

Or, to put it in backgammon language, not a blocked point. You start your count from the point adjacent to the one you are moving from. You pass over and count every point whether there are men on it or not.

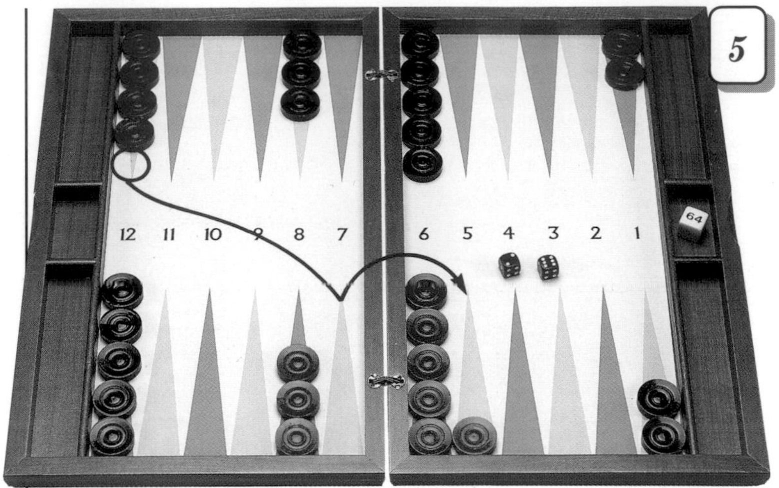

Always think of your roll as two separate moves. The 6-2 roll, for example, can be played as a 6 move and then a 2 move, or, as a 2 move followed by a 6 move. It is *NOT* an 8 move.

Do you spot the difference between (**6**) and (**5**)? Although in (**6**) the man from B12 still ends up at R5, this time the 2 (not the 6) has to be played first

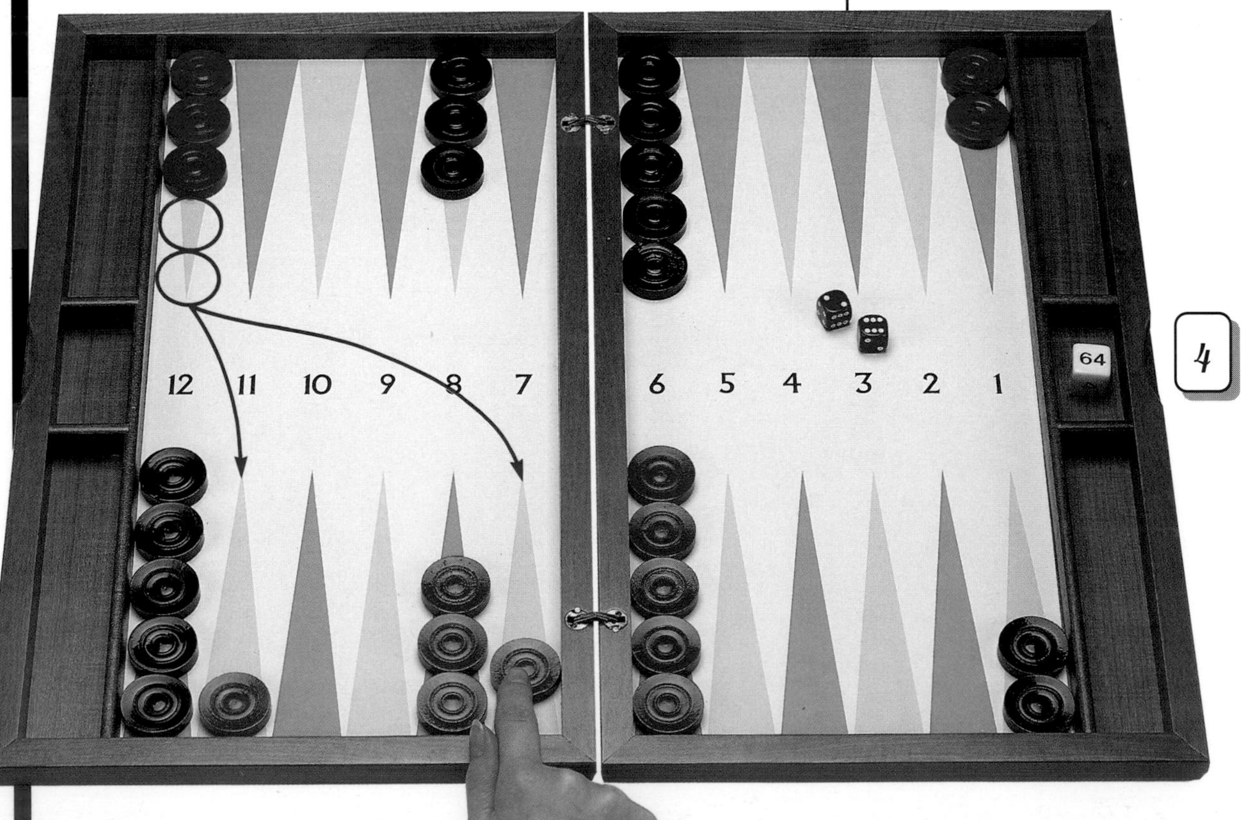

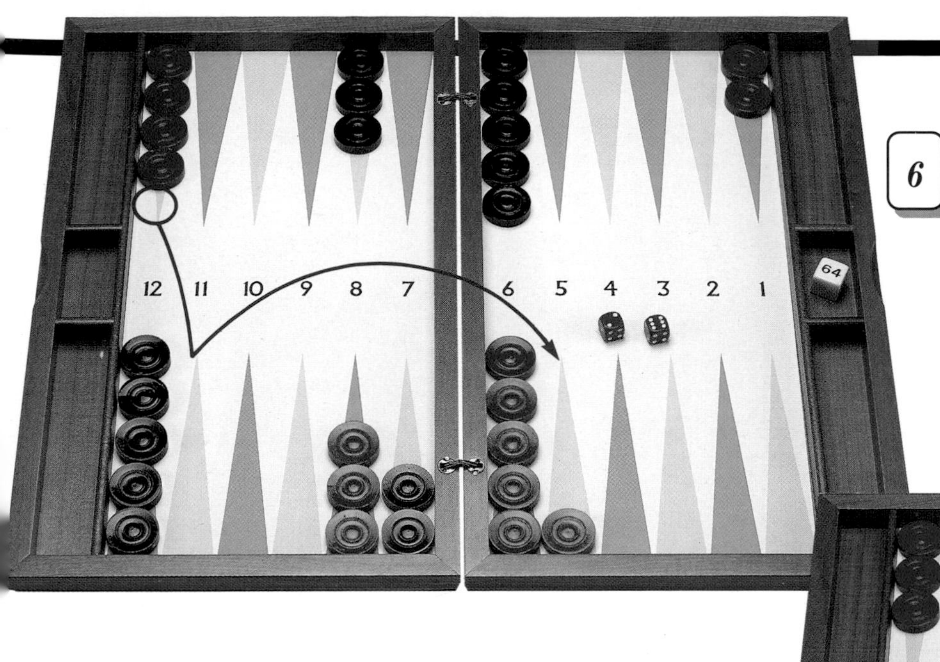

6

7

because Black has already blocked the R7 point and has to be hopped over. If Black had also blocked off the R11 point as well, the B12-R5 move would have been impossible.

ROLLING DOUBLES

When a player rolls the same number on each die he is permitted to play the roll *twice*. Example: the roll is 3-3. You may move

- One man 12 places (**7**).
- Two men each six places (**8**).

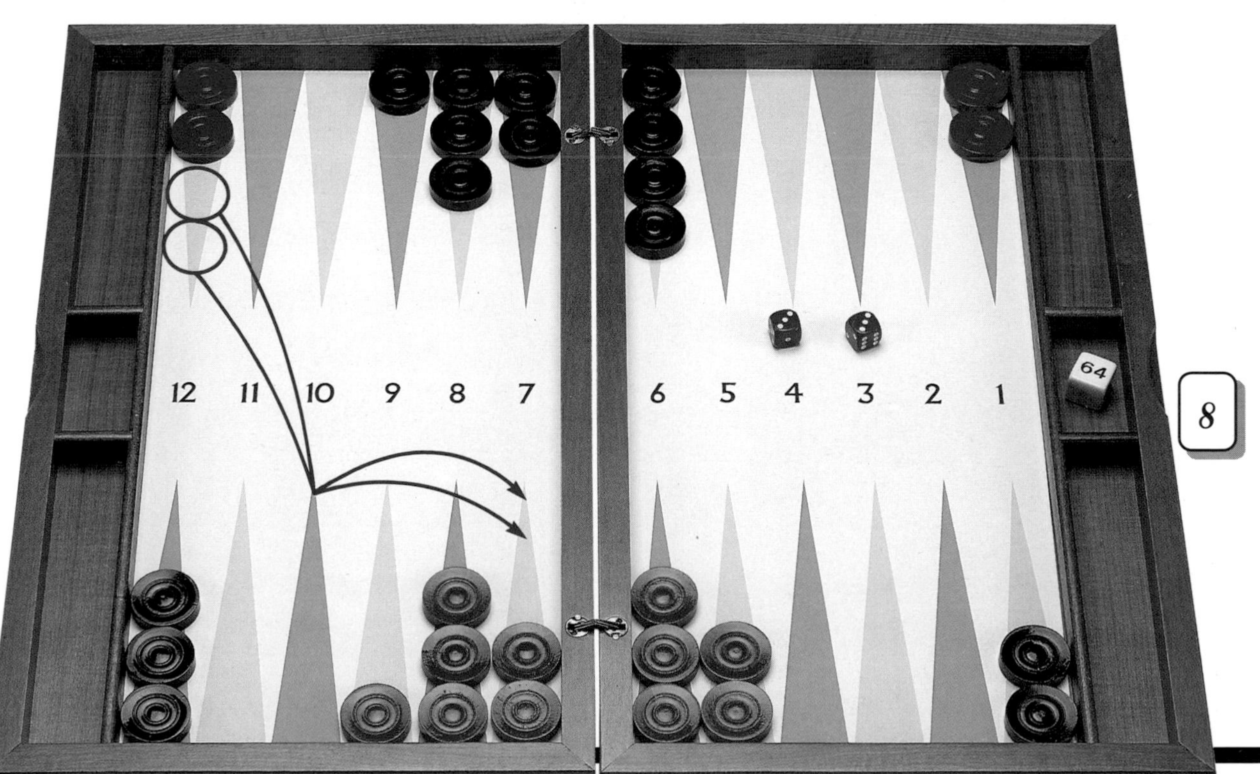

8

• Four men each three places (**9**).
• One man nine places and a second man three places (**10**).

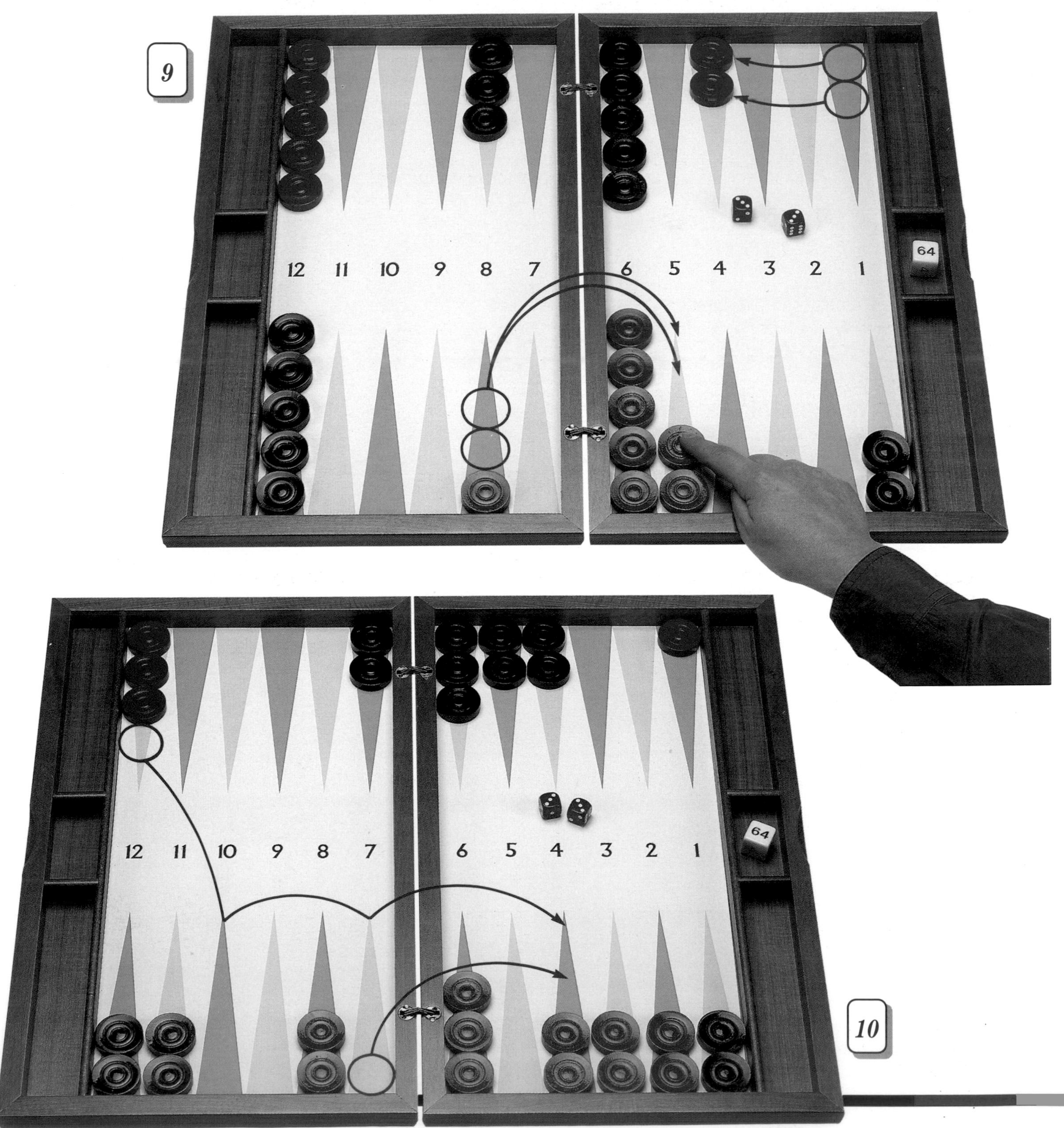

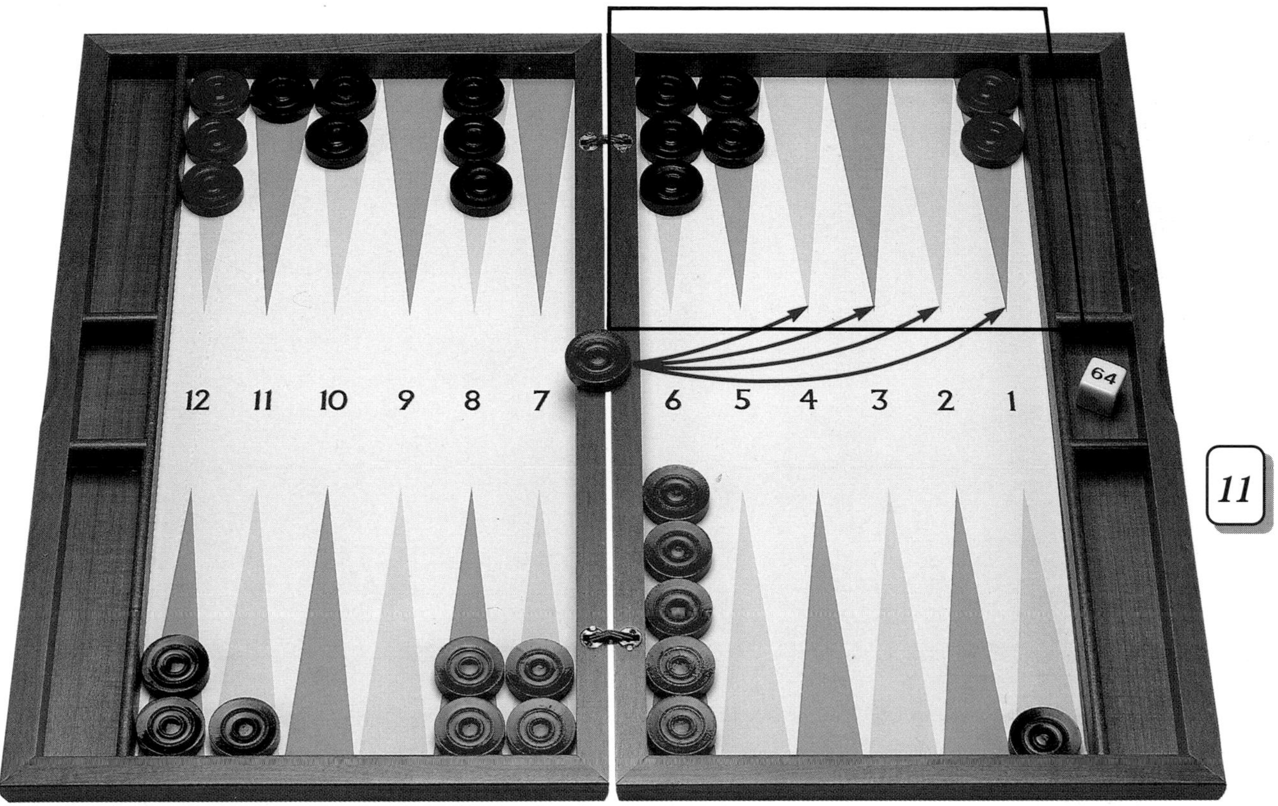

BLOTS, HITTING AND RE-ENTERING

A single man on a point is called a **blot**. A blot is vulnerable and can be **hit** by your opponent if he lands on it. If hit, your man is removed from the point and placed on the bar. It has to be re-entered at any *open* point in your opponent's inner table. Therefore, for example, if your opponent (Black) has successfully blocked his 6 and 5 points, you, Red, have to roll a 1,2,3 or 4 on either of your dice before your man is allowed to re-enter from the bar (**11**).

Say you roll 5-1. You would re-enter your man on B1 and then play the 5 somewhere else, possibly B12-R8.

If you rolled 3-4, you could either re-enter on B3 and then move the four steps, say to B7, or re-enter on B4 and move the three steps.

If, however, you rolled 6-5, 5-5 or 6-6 you would be unable to re-enter and would forfeit your turn because *all* your men on the bar *must* be re-entered before you are permitted to execute any other move.

BEARING OFF

Once all fifteen of your men are safely inside your own inner table you begin **bearing** them **off**, i.e. removing them from the board completely.

The inner table is numbered 1 to 6 and you bear off men corresponding to the numbers thrown on your dice. If, for example, you roll 3-1, you remove one man from your R3 point and one from your R1 point (**12**).

Doubles, remember, *count double* – so if you threw double 3, you would bear off *four* men from your R3 point (**13**).

If a player has no men on a point indicated by one or other of his dice, the move must be made within his own inner table if possible. For example, if you threw 5-2 and you had an open R5 point, you would remove one man from your R2 point and then move one man from R6 five places to R1 (**14**).

13

If you do not want to bear off a man for fear of leaving a vulnerable blot, you may use the throw to move within your inner table. A throw of 6-4 here (**15**) would leave you a blot if you chose to remove a man from the R4 point which Black could hit by throwing a 3. He would then send your man to the bar whence it would have to re-enter in Black's inner table and work its way round the board and back into your own inner table before bearing off may continue. And with Black controlling five of his six inner table points, Red may not find it at all easy to re-enter. You may miss a couple of throws in the attempt, thus giving Black a new lease of life. You get around the problem by playing the roll as shown. Bear off from R6 and move R6 to R2.

If you roll a number *higher* than any point occupied, a man from your next highest *occupied* point must be removed. (**16**) will make this clear. In this example you roll 6-3. The 3 is no problem – one man comes off the R3 point. But you have no 6. You must, therefore, remove a man from your next high-

14

15

est point, which in this example, means that you remove a man from your R4 point for the 6.

Great care must be taken when bearing off because if you are hit while so doing, the man has to re-enter in your opponent's inner table, work its way round the board again and into your own inner table before you can continue bearing off. Most annoying!

STARTING THE GAME

Each player throws one die to determine who has the first move. The player who rolls the higher number on his or her die starts the game using the numbers of the *two* dice just thrown. Ties are re-thrown. The players then roll in turn using their own two dice.

Always cast your dice in your right-hand half of the board. Both dice must land flat on the floor of the board. So, if one lands on top of a man, on the bar, in the other half of the board or askew, it does not count and means an instant re-roll of both dice.

Your move is deemed to be over and completed only when you pick your dice up from the board. No alteration to your move may be made after this. If your opponent, in his excitement, rolls his dice before you have completed your move, he must re-roll.

16

SINGLE POINT GAMES, GAMMONS AND BACKGAMMONS

You win a **single point game** when you have removed all of your men before your opponent has removed all of his (**17**). You win a double point game or **gammon** if you remove all of your men before your opponent has removed a *single man* yet has all of his men clear of your inner table (**18**). You win a treble point game or **backgammon** if you remove all of your men before your opponent has removed any of his men *and* he still has one or more men in your inner table and/or on the bar (**19**).

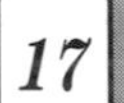

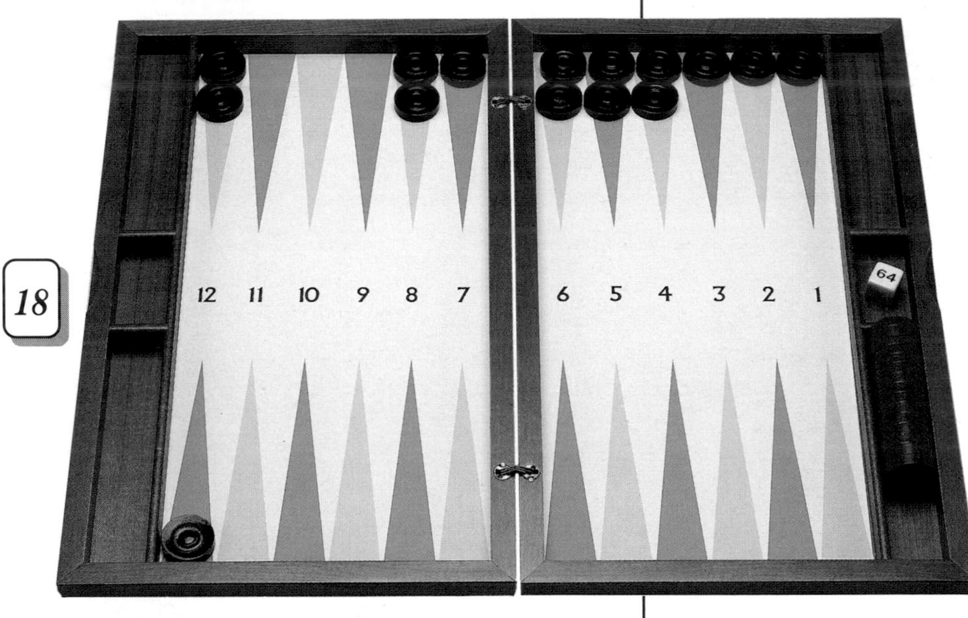

18

19

THE DOUBLING CUBE

Every backgammon set comes complete with a doubling cube (**20**). It is shaped like a die, and is usually somewhat larger than the other dice. Instead of dots, the six sides are numbered 2,4,8,16,32 and 64.

The doubling cube is used to increase the points value (stakes) of the game and must, therefore, be treated with great respect. At the start of the game the doubling cube is placed on the centre of the bar with the number 64 showing. Any player may start to double after the first roll – and may double or re-double at any stage of the game, even on the last roll. Naturally you offer your opponent a double only when you feel that you are in a favourable position to win.

To double your opponent, you pick up the cube and place it in front of him on the board with the 2 uppermost. This must be done *before* you throw your dice. He has now has two options. He can accept it or refuse it.

If he accepts your double, it means that he is willing to play on for double the original stake money. He merely picks up the cube and places it in front of himself off the playing surface. He is now said to "control" the cube and he and only he may re-double to 4.

If you now win this game he has to pay you twice the original stake. If you win by a gammon he will have to pay you *four* times the original stake (two points for the game x two points on the cube = four), while a backgammon will wrest from him six times the original stake (three points for the game x two points on the cube = six). Champagne time!

20

If he refuses your double, he forfeits the game and it is over immediately, regardless of the stage you have reached in the game. He pays you only the original stake agreed upon.

It will be obvious, therefore, that the cube should never be offered or accepted blindly. When you are in a position to win a possible gammon (2 points), it would be foolish to offer your opponent the cube even though you are ahead, because this gives him the chance of refusing it, thus immediately bringing the game to an end and enabling him to get away with only paying you the original stake (one point).

AUTOMATIC DOUBLES

Should each player roll the same number at the start of the game (when rolling to see who starts), the stakes are immediately doubled and the cube moved to 2 automatically. The cube is still not "controlled" by either player. The first double that can now be offered in the game is to 4.

QUIZ QUESTION

These then are the basic laws of backgammon. I hope that you have been following the moves on your own backgammon set. You will find it helpful to do so. As a simple test, try to solve the following problem without referring back to the text. In picture (**21**) you are bearing off. You roll 5-3. How should you play it and why?

The correct answer to this problem is given on page 86 at the beginning of Chapter Ten which deals more fully with bearing your men off.

21

THE FACTS OF LIFE

Before we go any further there are one or two facts of life that you should know about. Dice can be "manipulated". There are a handful of people around who can throw dice "to order". I am not joking . . . it's a fact. As a member of the Inner Magic Circle of London you can take my word for it! You are unlikely to come across a dice manipulator in the normal course of events; however, to be forewarned is to be forearmed. Agreed? Three simple rules can keep you out of trouble.

SAFETY FIRST

Rule One: Never allow your opponent to throw from his hands. Insist that he uses a dice cup or shaker. If he refuses . . . *do not play him.*

Rule Two: Use shakers that have a ridge inside about half an inch (12mm) from the top edge. The ridge effectively trips the dice as they leave the shaker, making manipulation from the shaker impossible. Oh yes! I know men who can even manipulate out of a shaker, but not if it has a ridge.

Rule Three: Use small dice. They "mix" better in the shaker and roll further.

Later on in this book I deal at length with the mathematics of backgammon, otherwise known as the odds. In this chapter I propose to deal with two simple aspects of this subject that you will be able to grasp easily, remember effortlessly and put to use readily.

A good player "understands" the dice thoroughly. By this I mean that he knows what combinations can be thrown and the odds against throwing any given number. It is very simple really, but it is surprising how few players bother to learn these simple and invaluable facts.

There are 36 possible rolls. The six sets of doubles: 6-6, 5-5, 4-4, 3-3, 2-2 and 1-1; plus the fifteen "combination" rolls: 6-5, 6-4, 6-3, 6-2, 6-1, 5-4, 5-3, 5-2, 5-1, 4-3, 4-2, 4-1, 3-2, 3-1 and 2-1. The fifteen combination rolls can be rolled in two different ways making a total of thirty combination rolls.

To understand this fully, imagine for a moment you have one red die and one black die. You could roll a 6 on the red die and a 5 on the black die or you could roll a 5 on the red die and a 6 on the black die. As you see the same total but two distinctly different rolls. Now look at the table below.

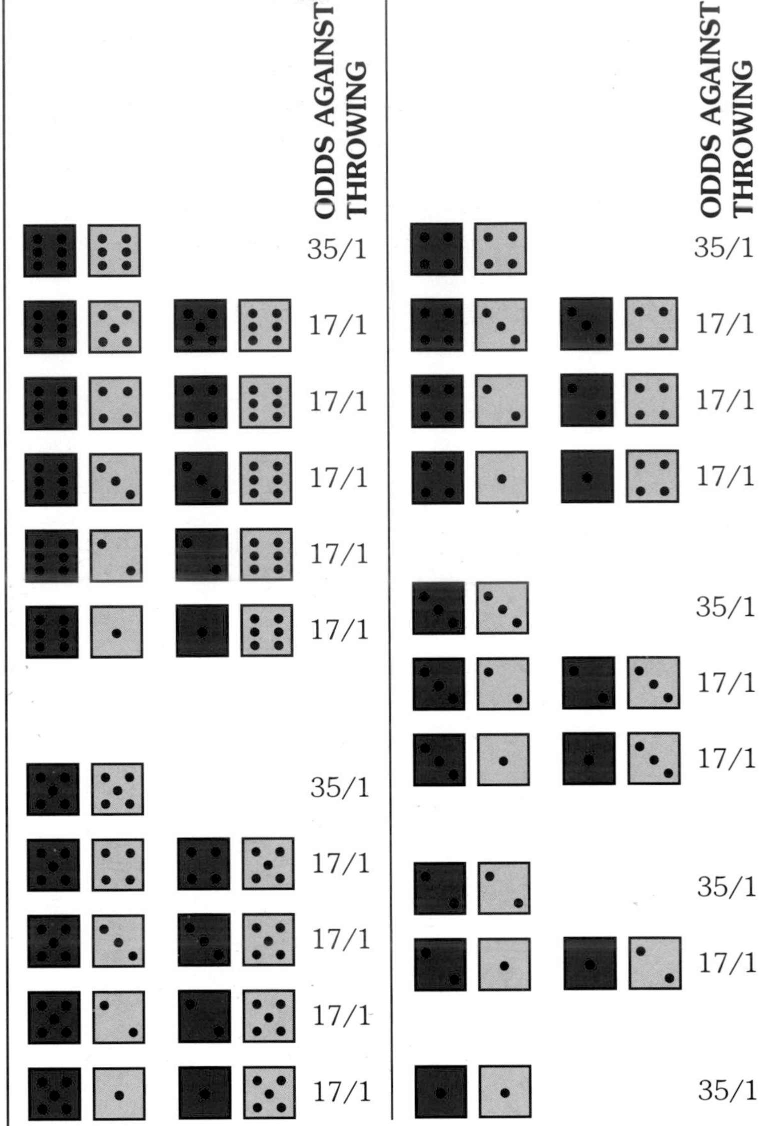

THE 36 POSSIBLE THROWS

From this you will see that the odds against throwing any *specific* double are 35/1 (one way in 36 of throwing it and 35 ways in 36 of *not* throwing it). The odds against throwing *any specific* combination roll are 17/1 (2 ways in 36 of throwing it and 34 ways in 36 of *not* throwing it). Backgammon *is* a gambling game and chances have to be taken. With the proper knowledge under your hat, these chances become merely calculated risks.

At some stage in every game you will be forced to leave a blot. Knowing *where* to leave it is very important. The odds are nearly always against your opponent hitting it anyway, but a thorough knowledge of his chances of doing so must of course influence your decision as to where to leave it. The next table demonstrates this knowledge dramatically.

This table shows us three things very clearly.

- If you have to leave a blot try to leave it a total of 7 or more points away from the attacking man, the numbers 1-6 being so much more likely to be hit because only one die is required, not a combination of two dice as for the numbers 7 upwards. So the rule is: *7 or more is better than 6 or less.*
- If you *have* to leave a direct shot (one to six points away), the closer you are to the attacking man the better (eleven ways to hit a 1 as opposed to seventeen ways of hitting a six). So rule 2 is: with a *direct shot – closest is safest.*
- With an indirect or combination shot (7 or greater), the opposite applies and the further you are away from the attacking man the better. (Six ways to hit a 7 as opposed to only one way of hitting a 24). Note that 12 is the only number where the graph rises momentarily. So rule 3 is: with an *indirect shot – furthest is best.*

These three rules will help you understand the next chapter which deals with Opening Moves, in some of which we leave blots.

ODDS AGAINST HITTING A BLOT

Number of points that blot is away	1	2	3	4	5	6	7	8	9	10	11	12	15	16	18	20	24
	11 ways 25/1	12 ways 2/1	14 ways 11/7	15 ways 7/5	15 ways 7/5	17 ways 19/17	6 ways 5/1	6 ways 5/1	5 ways 31/5	3 ways 11/1	2 ways 17/1	3 ways 11/1	1 way 35/1	1 way 35/1	1 way 35/1	1 way 35/1	1 way 35/1
Degree of risk . . . These rolls hit						6-5											
						6-4											
				4-6	5-6	6-3											
			3-6	4-5	5-4	6-2											
			3-5	4-3	5-3	6-1											
		2-6	3-4	4-2	5-2	1-6											
	1-6	2-5	3-2	4-1	5-1	2-6											
	1-5	2-4	3-1	1-4	1-5	3-6											
	1-4	2-3	1-3	2-4	2-5	4-6											
	1-3	2-1	2-3	3-4	3-5	5-6											
	1-2	6-2	4-3	5-4	4-5	5-1											
	6-1	5-2	5-3	6-4	6-5	1-5	6-1	6-2									
	5-1	4-2	6-3	3-1	4-1	4-2	1-6	2-6	6-3								
	4-1	3-2	2-1	1-3	1-4	2-4	5-2	5-3	3-6								
	3-1	1-2	1-2	4-4	3-2	6-6	2-5	3-5	5-4	6-4		6-6					
	2-1	2-2	3-3	2-2	2-3	3-3	4-3	4-4	4-5	4-6	6-5	4-4					
	1-1	1-1	1-1	1-1	5-5	2-2	3-4	2-2	3-3	5-5	5-6	3-3	5-5	4-4	6-6	5-5	6-6

Number of points that blot is away

THE OPENING MOVES

You must bear two main goals in mind as you start the game. Firstly you must try to prevent your opponent's back men on your R1 point from escaping from your inner table by setting up blocked points and even a prime if you can. Remember a prime is the impenetrable six blocked points in a row. Secondly, try to get your own back men (the two on the B1 point) out of his inner table and into safer territory. The way that you play your opening roll can do much in assisting you to achieve these ends.

THE TWENTY-ONE OPTIONS

This chapter will consider all the twenty-one opening rolls, my recommendations for playing them and a few alternatives that you may, at times, find useful. I will start with the best, most favourable roll and work down the line until we arrive at the worst. In order of preference the rolls are: 1-1, 6-6, 3-3, 4-4, 2-2, 3-1, 4-2, 6-1, 6-5, 3-2, 4-3, 5-3, 6-2, 6-4, 6-3, 5-5, 2-1, 4-1, 5-1, 5-4 and 5-2.

In the contest to see who moves first you will have already read that ties are re-thrown, so doubles are not possible as initial opening moves. However, they are possible as initial opening moves for the player who "loses the toss" and plays second. The opening set-up of the board has hardly been affected. Let us look at each opening roll now in more detail.

THE 1-1 ROLL

Move two men from your R8 to your R7 point and two men from your R6 to your R5 point (**1**). This is really a tremendous opening for you. In one roll you have captured your R5 and R7 points and with the R6 point you now have three in a row. Already you have built quite a formidable obstacle for your opponent's back men on R1. You have left a blot at R8 but for the gain in position it is well worth the risk. Besides, Black can only hit it by rolling 6-1, 5-2 or 4-3. That is six rolls in 36 or 6-1 against hitting you.

This is the only 1-1 opening worth considering.

THE 6-6 ROLL

Move two men from B1 to B7 and two men from B12 to R7 (**2**). In one fell swoop you have captured both bar points, your back men are free of Black's inner table and on their way home and you have set up a three-point block to hamper Black's back men on R1. What more can one ask of a single roll of the dice?

There is no better alternative.

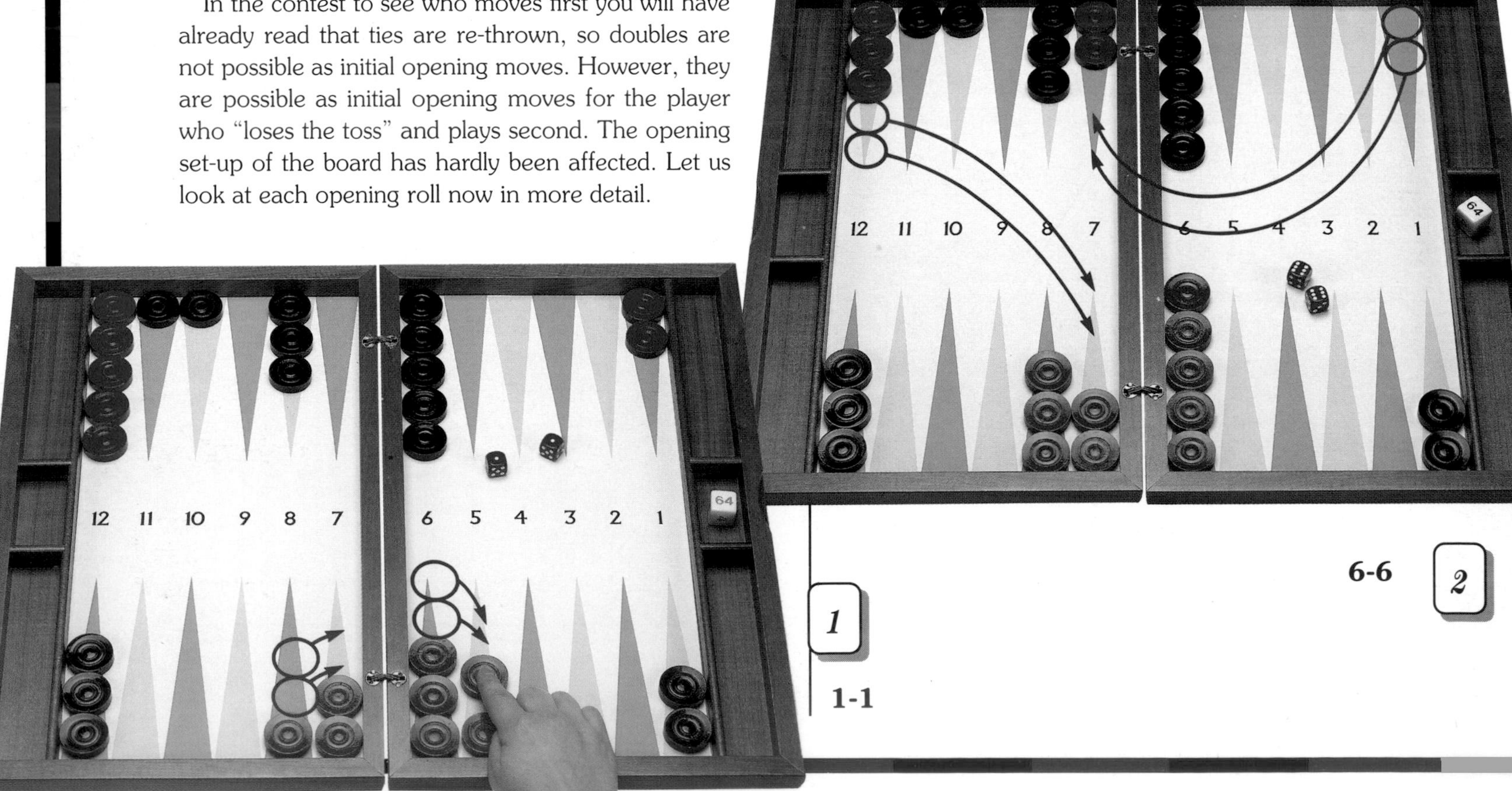

1

1-1

6-6 2

THE 3-3 ROLL

Two men from B1 to B4 and two from R8 to R5 (**3**). The longer you play backgammon the more you realize the importance of the 5 points. The way I have recommended that you play this roll achieves two goals. First, it establishes your own 5 point, an "aggressive" move. Should your opponent establish his own 5 point, your two men now on his 4 point greatly lessen its strength and usefulness as a blocking point. It prepares the way for the eventual escape of your back men.

There are, of course, other ways to play this roll. You could move two men from R8 to R5 and two men from R6 to R3 (**4**). This is an alternative but not as good as my first recommendation. Played this way, you make your 5 point and your 3 point. This gives you three blocked points in your inner table and is a very "aggressive" play. Its one drawback, however, is that it does nothing to improve your defensive position.

A very common way of playing 3-3 is B12 to R7 (two men) (**5**). The drawback of playing the roll this way is that it does not put the same degree of pressure on your opponent as do the other two alternatives. There is really no wrong way to play 3-3. It is just that some ways are more right than others!

4

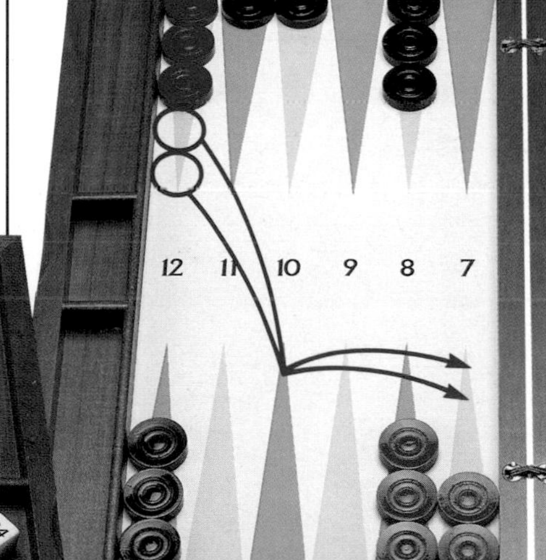

5

3

3-3

THE 4-4 ROLL

Move two men B1 to B5 and two men R8-R4 (**6**). I am very happy when I roll 4-4 at the onset of the game. The way I play it establishes my 4 point and, more importantly, captures my opponent's 5 point, thus putting a spoke in the wheel of his attack. This is another roll where there are really no bad ways of playing. My recommendation combines good attacking play with good defensive play. But what about the blot that you have left on R8? It is now vulnerable to any 7, a 5/1 chance of being hit. Not a serious risk and, if he throws 6-1 and chooses to hit my blot on R8, rather than play R12 to B7 and B8 to B7 making his own bar point, you will not hear me complaining!

Let us look at the alternatives: B1 to B5 (two men) and B12 to R9 (two men) (**7**). This is also good and most experts on backgammon recommend it. It establishes command of your opponent's 5 point and also makes your own 9 point. I sometimes play this way but, all things considered, I prefer my first recommendation. It is more aggressive.

Speaking of aggression – if I know that my opponent is a much weaker player than myself – I usually pander to my sadistic streak by playing the roll B12 to R5 (two men)! This move (**8**) is guaranteed to shake the confidence of an inexperienced player but, be warned, it is not as strategically sound as our two other alternatives. You have made your 5 point admittedly – but that is all.

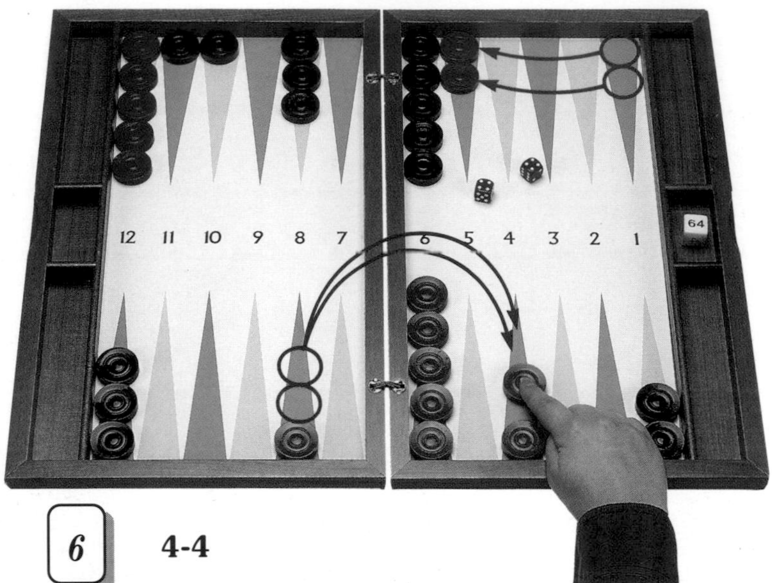

6 **4-4**

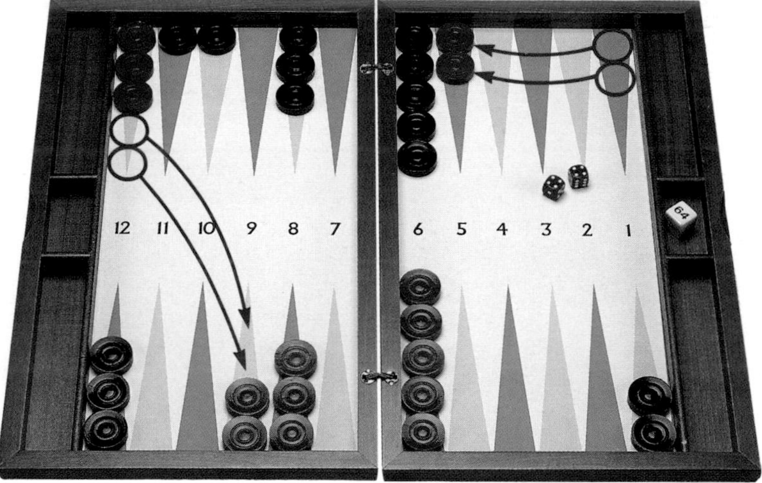

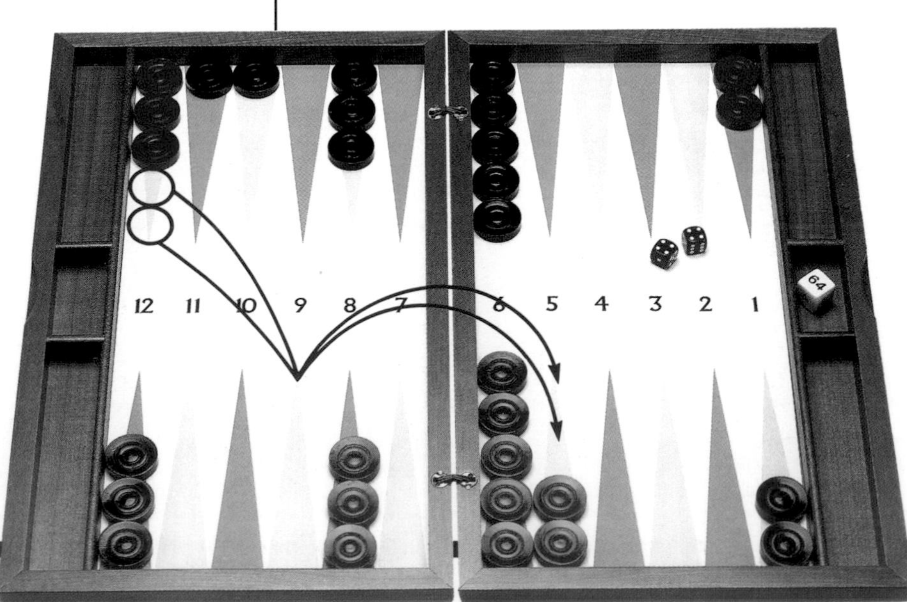

8

THE 2-2 ROLL

Move two men B12 to R11 and two men R6 to R4 (**9**). This is a useful roll. See how, on your next roll, many combinations will now fill either your bar or 5 point – which should be your primary consideration in these early stages because they are the backbone of a prime. This is sound attacking play.

Alternatives? You could have made your 9 point with B12 to R9 (two men). Not as aggressive. Or B1 to B5 (two men) would have made your opponent's 5 point. Strong defence admittedly but you have done nothing to prevent your opponent's back men from escaping.

THE 3-1 ROLL

A great opener. Play R8 to R5 and R6 to R5 (**10**). You make your 5 point. Fine play and a good attacking move. This is, barring doubles, the best opening roll and a little prayer of thanksgiving would not be out of place if you roll it. You see, the two 5 points are crucial. Whoever controls *both* 5 points also controls the game. With this roll you are half way there.

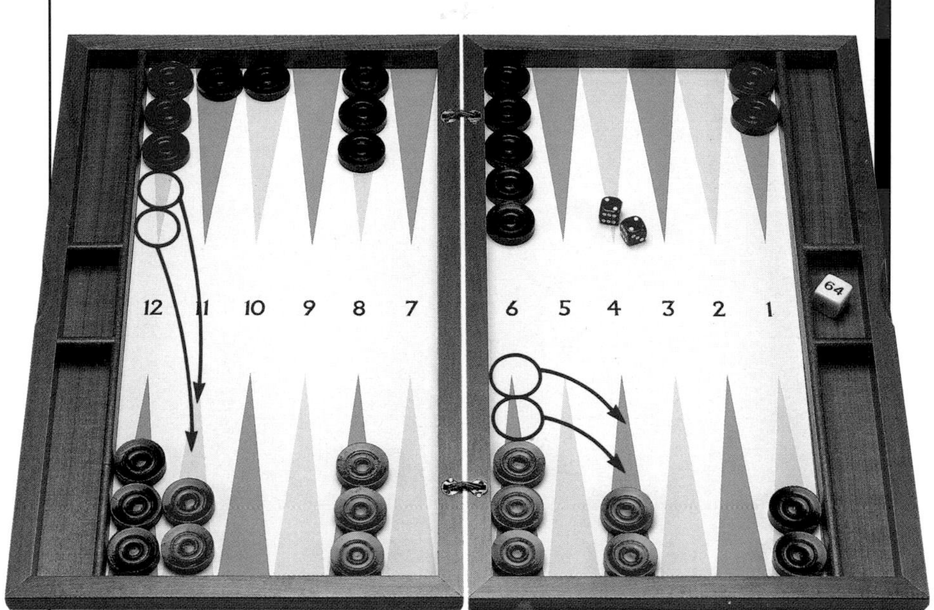

2-2

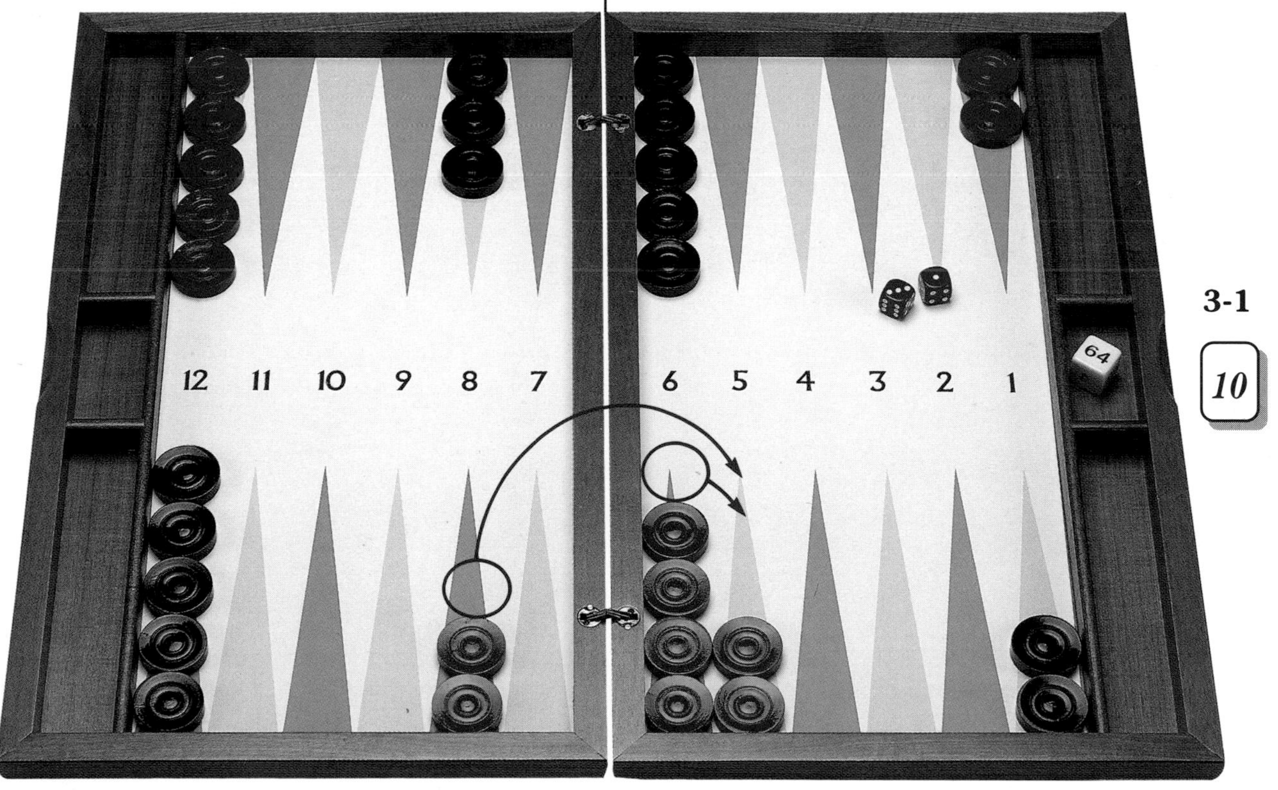

3-1

10

THE 4-2 ROLL

I recommend R8 to R4 and R6 to R4 (**11**). This makes your 4 point – the "spearhead" of your attack. You now aim to build up a prime behind this point. A very good roll.

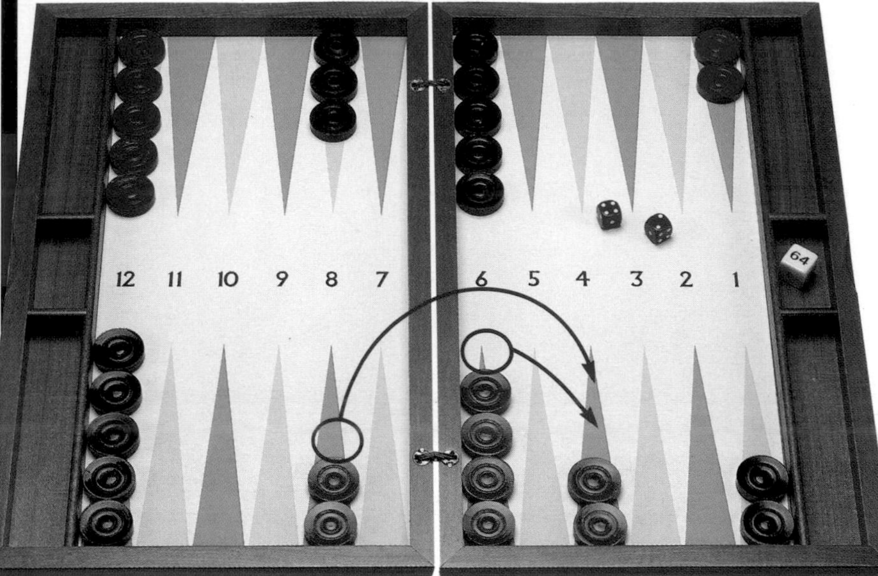

4-2

THE 6-1 ROLL

The classic move on which all backgammon experts agree: B12 to R7 and R8 to R7 (**12**). Making your bar point is the only way to play this move. It is a most fortunate roll because it establishes three points in a row for you and makes Black's exit from your inner table just that much more difficult. He must throw 4-4 to get *both* men out next roll (35/1 against) and you, of course, will be striving to extend your prime. The pressure is on.

These first eight rolls are the most favourable ones. They are all definite body blows to your opponent. The next four are "builder" moves – threats and warnings to your opponent that if he does not take action immediately something nasty is likely to happen to him.

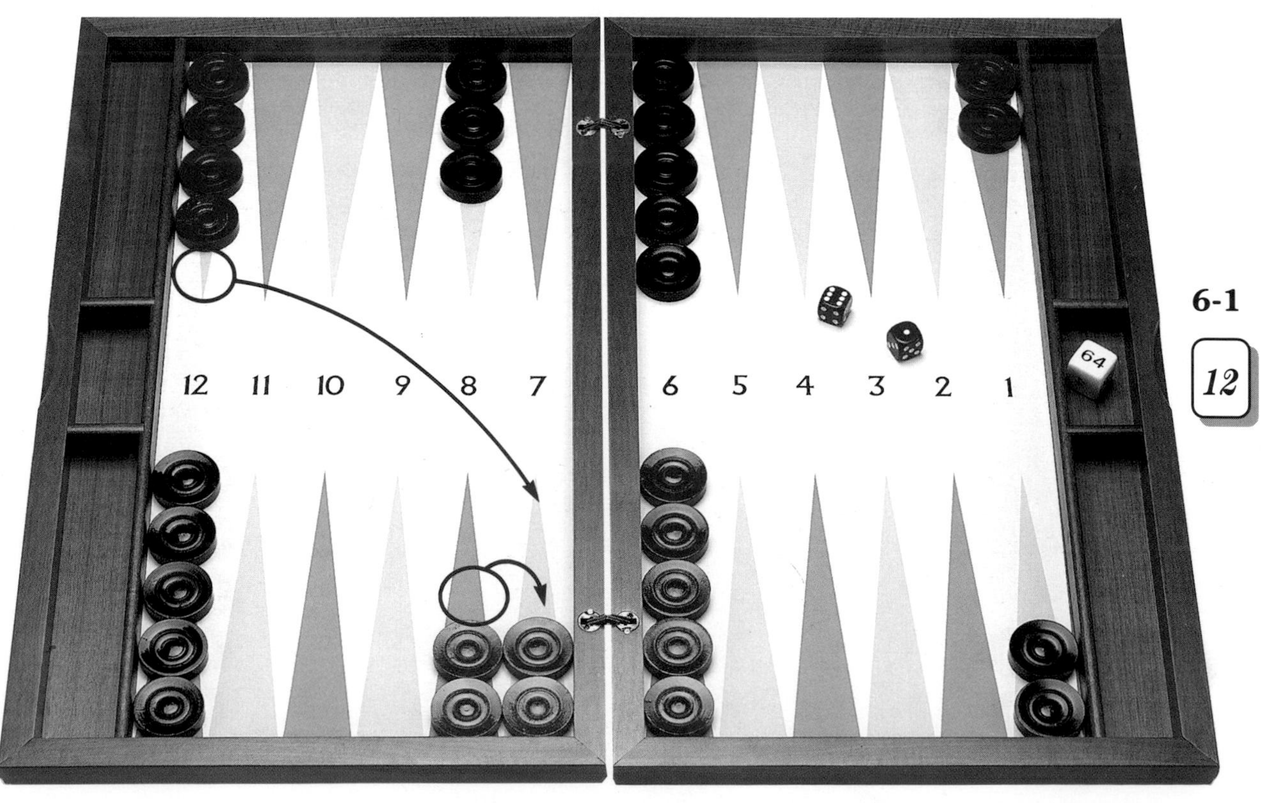

6-1

12

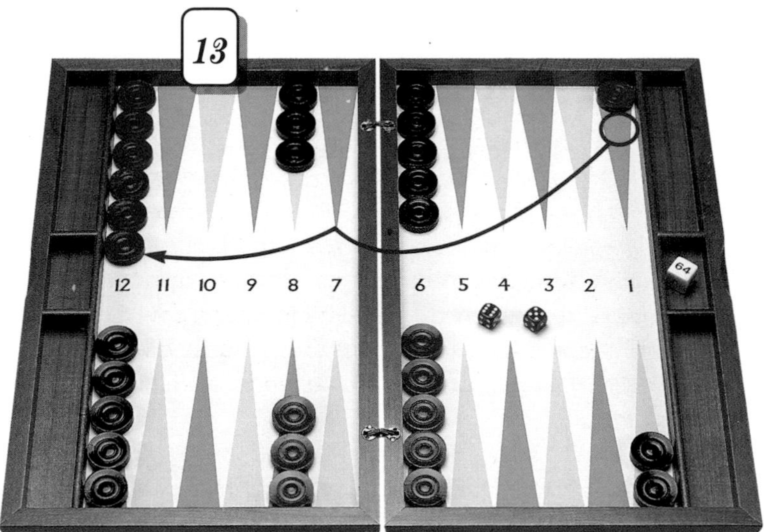

13

14

6-5

THE 6-5 ROLL

Move B1 to B12 (**13**). This move has the quaint name of "The Lovers' Leap". I can't imagine why. I thought that lovers leaped *together*! However, Lovers' Leap it is and always will be. You take the opportunity to run one of your back men all the way to the safety of B12.

I have also seen the move played like this: B12 to R8 and B12 to R7 (**14**) but I cannot really recommend this play. Admittedly it is aggressive, but it is also foolhardy. Here the hope is that your opponent will *not* roll a 6 on his next throw, and you will. If Black fails to hit it, any 1, 4-3 or 3-2 will also tidy things up for you and put you in a very strong position. You must ask yourself "Is the gamble worthwhile?" When your alternative is to move one of your back men half way around the board in complete safety, I do not think it is. Do you?

THE 3-2 ROLL

The play of B12 to R11 and B12 to R10 (**15**) puts a lot of pressure on Black's back men. The threat is that on your *next* roll it is *odds on* that you will make either your bar or 5 point and it is a whopping 17/1 in your favour that you will be able to make a point *somewhere*.

Your blots can only be hit with a 9 or 10 combination shot. The odds are 31/5 he will not hit the 9 and 11/1 he will not hit the 10. It is 7/2 against him hitting either.

3-2

15

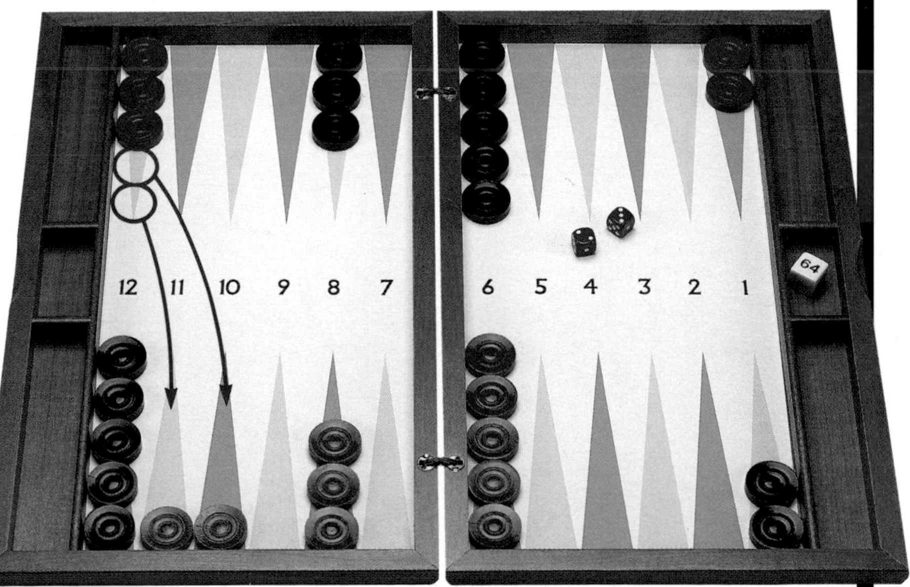

THE 4-3 ROLL

Move B12 to R10 and B12 to R9 (**16**). This play is similar to the 3-2 move, and the logic behind it is the same. There are no better alternative plays.

16

4-3

THE 5-3 ROLL

For this roll, two plays are worthy of our attention. I usually select the first example but the second is always a useful alternative.

My recommendation is B12 to R8 and B12 to R10 (**17**). Here again your chances of making a valuable point next throw are very good. Your blot is a 31/5 favourite not to be hit. I like this play because of the increased chances you have next throw of making your bar or 5 point.

The alternative is R8 to R3 and R6 to R3 (**18**). This establishes a point in your inner table. The trouble with this play is that establishing your 3 point this early in the game is a bit of a waste. Black will have little problem hopping over it. Its usefulness only takes effect when you have also established your 4 and 5 points. Until then your two men on the 3 point are, to all intents and purposes, out of play.

17

5-3

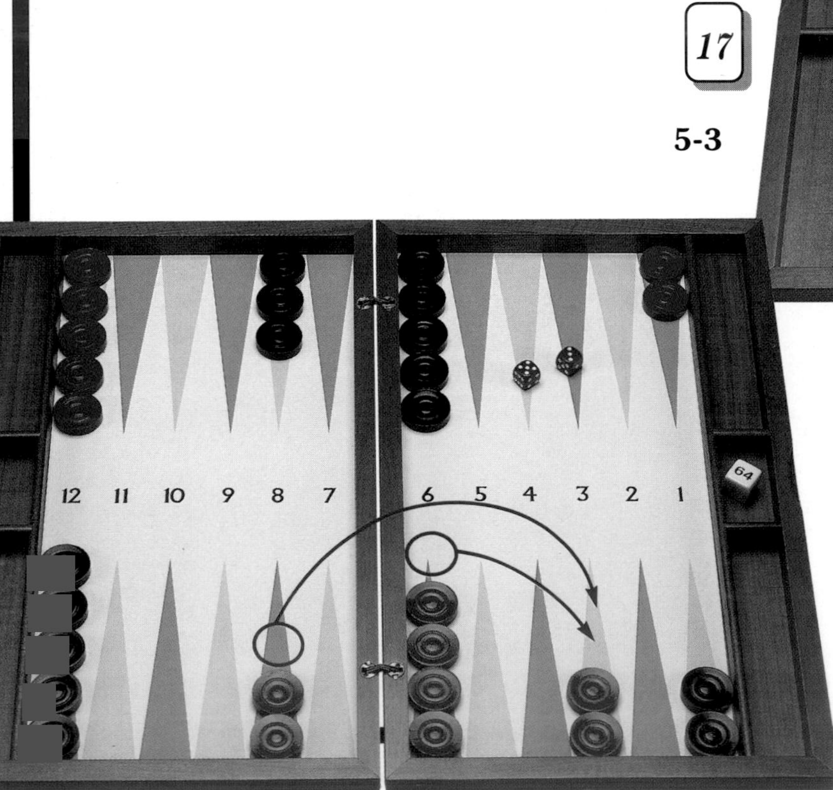

18

THE 6-2 ROLL

This is the first of the unfavourable rolls but we must play them as "favourably" as possible. So here we play one man B12 to R5 (**19**). There is a fair chance that Black will hit our blot on R5 (only 7/5 against). However, if Black fails to hit it, our chances of covering it or using it to make a point in our inner table are extremely high.

THE 6-4 ROLL

6-4 should be played: one man B1 to B11 (**20**) – the Lovers' Leap that slipped! It is not a good roll by any means, but this way leaves you only vulnerable to a 2 shot (2/1 against). If Black hits it, you have not lost much and re-entering is virtually certain on your next roll.

Making your 2 point should not even be considered, but there is an alternative that should be. Considered that is, not adopted! It is B12 to R7 and B12 to R9 (**21**). You would have to be feeling very lucky or very rich to play 6-4 this way! But I have seen it happen. If you get away without being hit, you are in a great position to make a strong point. It *can* happen, but the odds are against you. Do not give your opponent any advantage, however small!

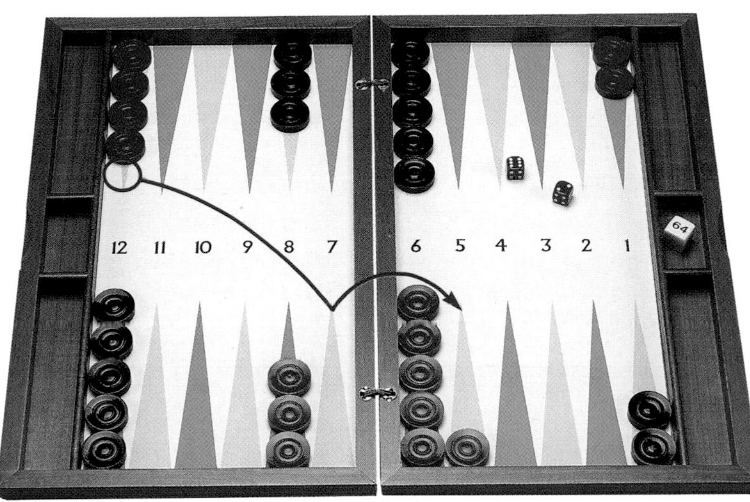

19 **6-2**

6-4

20

21

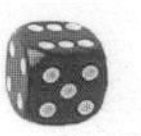

22

6-3

12 11 10 9 8 7 6 5 4 3 2 1
64

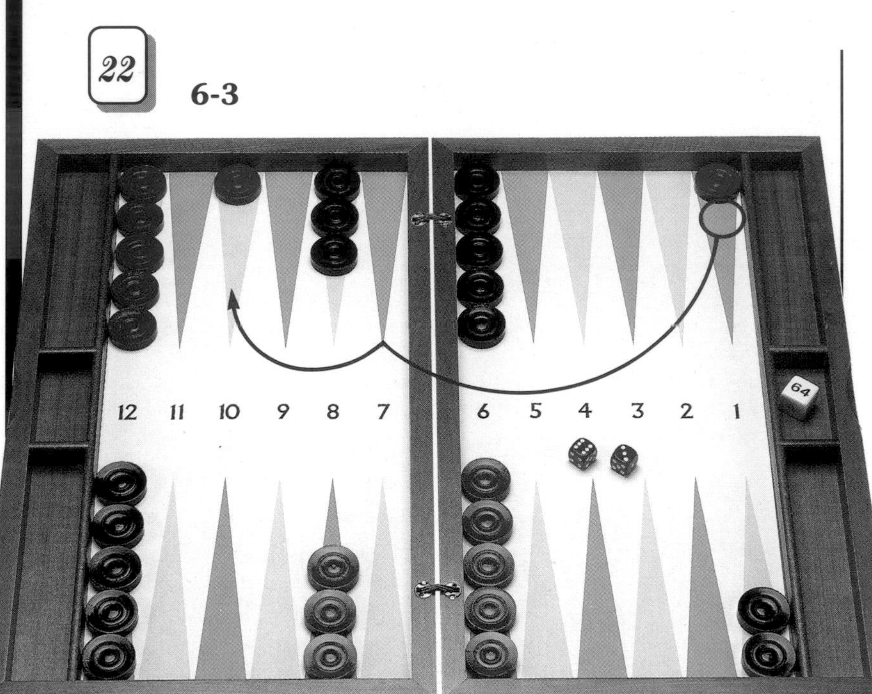

THE 6-3 ROLL

Another "nothing" roll. One of the worst. However, B1 to B10 is the best way to play it (**22**). Do not play B12 to R7; B12 to R10. You have troubles enough without going looking for more!

THE 5-5 ROLL

Here you play two men from B12 all the way to R3 (**23**). This is the least favourable of the doubles. It forces you to make your 3 point earlier than you would otherwise desire, but you have no sensible alternative.

THE 2-1 ROLL

The last five opening moves are all gambles. The first is 2-1. Move B12 to R11 and R6 to R5 (**24**). This play gives us the maximum potential if Black fails to hit us. It is the most constructive way of playing this poor roll. You stand a good chance of making your 5

5-5

12 11 10 9 8 7 6 5 4 3 2 1
64

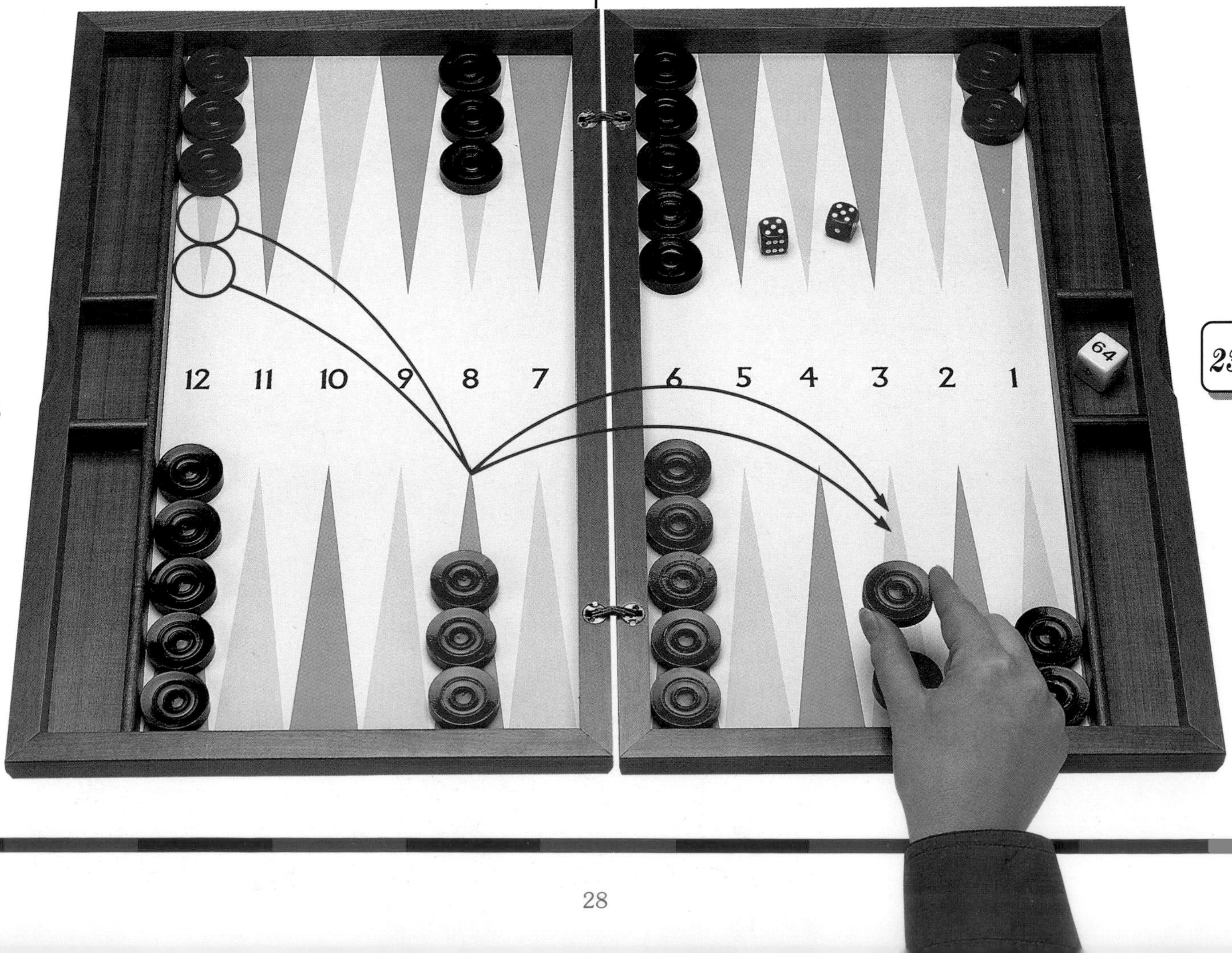

23

or bar points next throw. Do not be tempted to split your back men at B1. This will only serve to weaken your defence and is, in fact, a bigger gamble than dropping a builder onto your 5 point.

THE 4-1 ROLL

This move, B12 to R9 and R6 to R5 (**25**), is similar to my 2-1 recommendation and the thinking behind it is the same – a gamble for position.

You could play safe by moving B12 to R8 (**26**) but what have you achieved by this? Nothing. Your position has not changed. You might just as well not have had the advantage of first roll. No! Difficult rolls, as 4-1 most certainly is, must be played adventurously so that, if the gamble comes off, you will have turned a poor roll into a useful one!

25

4-1

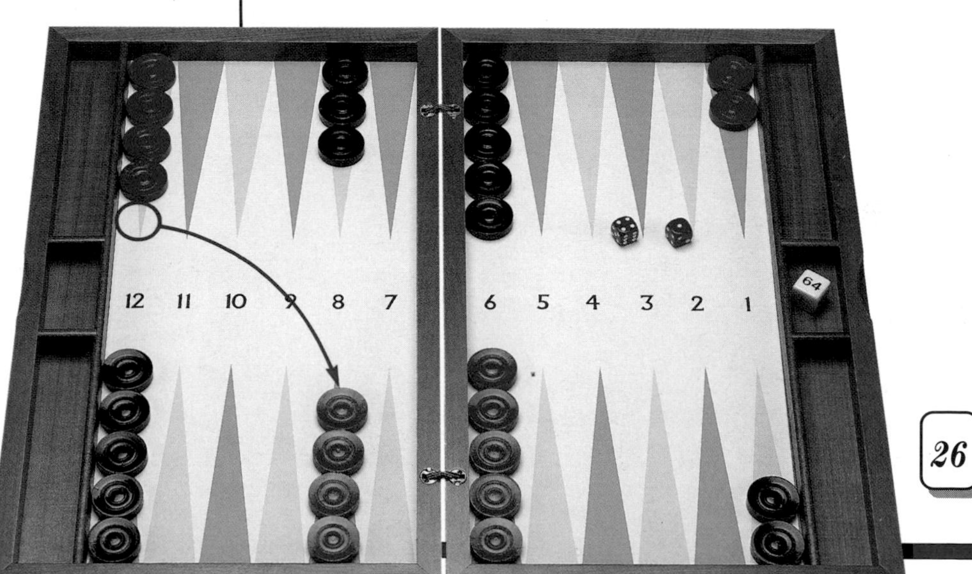

26

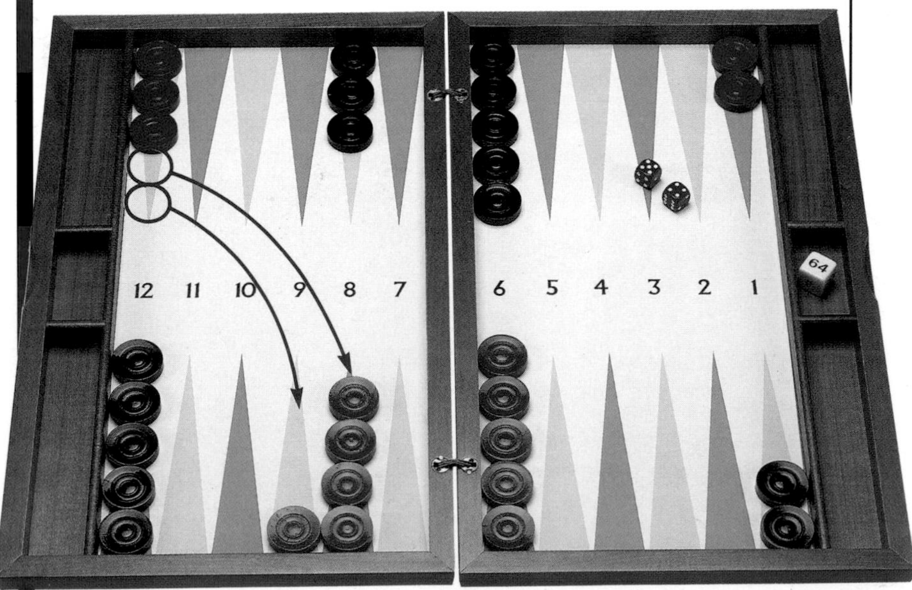

THE 5-1 ROLL

Here we have B12 to R8 and R6 to R5 (**27**). All "5" openers are ungainly and this one is no exception. The aim, of course, is ultimately to secure your 5 point by dropping the man from R6 to R5. Black may well hit it and, of course, should hit it if he gets half a chance. But if he fails . . . well, see if you can work out for yourself how many ways you can cover this blot on your next roll!

THE 5-4 ROLL

B12 to R9 and B12 to R8 (**28**) gives us the best chances here. Any alternative, such as splitting your back men, will be found to be inferior to my recommendation. Your blot on R9 is a firm favourite not to be hit and its usefulness next roll as an aid in making your bar or 5 point makes the gamble worthwhile.

THE 5-2 ROLL

This move, B12 to R11 and B12 to R8 (**29**) is the last of the twenty-one possible opening rolls for us to consider. Another "5" opener but this time the "odd man out" is on R11 – ten points away from Black's men. This blot can only be hit by a 6-4 or 4-6. That is 17/1 against being hit, so it is comparatively safe. The blot is also in a useful position to assist you in making your 5 or bar points on your next roll.

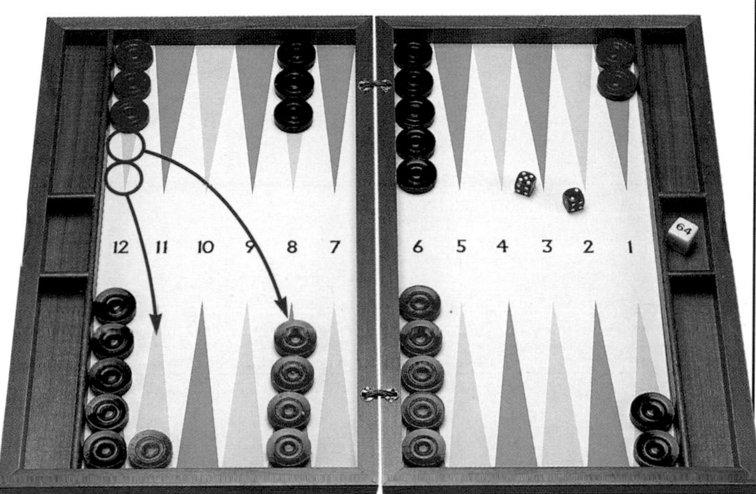

5-2

29

CONCLUSIONS

Well, there you have it – my recommendations for the twenty-one opening rolls. You will have already noticed that, in backgammon, men are never moved willy-nilly. Every part of every move is carefully considered, and the pros and cons assessed. You are fortunate that, as far as the opening moves are concerned, the weighing up has already been done for you. You only have to commit these moves to memory. So get your board out and practise these openers.

QUIZ QUESTION

Without referring back to the appropriate section in this chapter, tell me how you would play a 6-2 opener and why (**30**)? Once you have decided on your move, look back to page 27 to see if you got it right.

30

REPLIES TO THE OPENING MOVE

Suppose you have "lost the toss" – your opponent has had the first move – and now it is your turn to play. What do you do? The possibilities are almost endless. There are over 400 replies to the 21 opening rolls that I suggested in the previous chapter! You have no guarantee that your opponent will even use one of those (unless he or she, too, has read this book). Backgammon is not a game of routine. Only the opening moves are constantly played the same way. You have as much chance of winning the jackpot on a fruit machine as you have of playing two identical games of backgammon. But do not despair. Things are a lot simpler than they may at first appear.

TURNING THE TABLES

In most cases my recommendation for the opening move can also be used as the reply to your opponent's opening move as well. In fact, in most cases, it should be used. There are of course exceptions. Aren't there always?!

Obviously to write at length about every possible variation of response to the opening move would bore you silly and would take up more space than all the chapters in this book put together. So let us take a few examples so that you get the general idea, and I can expound a few more golden rules.

EXCEPTIONS THAT PROVE THE RULES

Suppose that your opponent has opened with a 6-4 and has run one of his back men from R1 to R11 (**1**). You now roll 4-2. What would you do? Would you still make your 4 point? No – the correct move here would be to hit Black's blot at R11 by playing B12 to R11 and play the 4 with B1 to B5 (**2**).

In moving to R11, Black is already making a run for it with his back man. If you did not hit his blot and Black then threw another 6-4 or a 6-5, you would be in serious trouble and would have great difficulty restraining Black. So you hit him and split your own back men in an attempt to secure his 5 point.

2

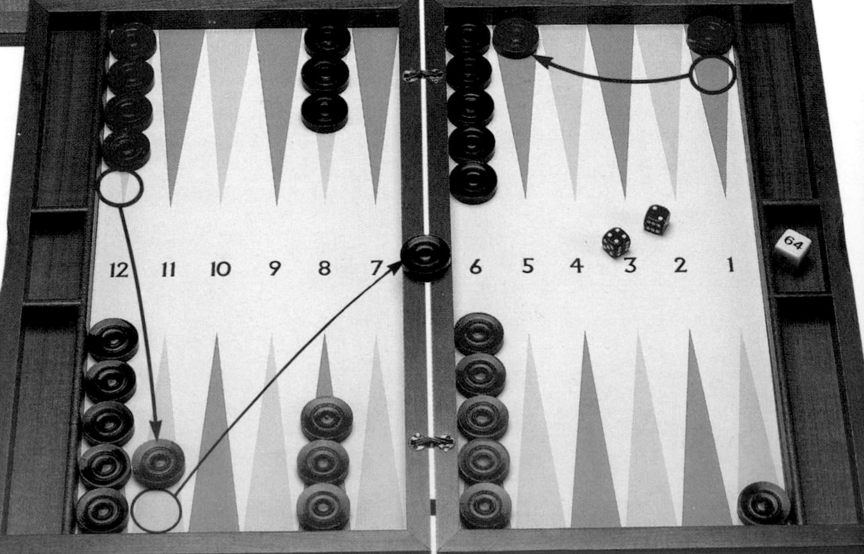

THE SECOND EXAMPLE

Here Black opens with a 5-2. Instead of playing my recommendation, he splits his back men and plays R1 to R3 and R12 to B8 (**3**). You roll 5-5. What would you do? B12 to R3 (two men)? No. The answer is to hit both of Black's blots! R8 to R3 (two men) and R6 to R1 (two men) (**4**).

Although, generally speaking, it is not good policy to make the lower points in your inner table so early, here the advantages greatly outweigh the disadvantages. You make two more points in your inner table *and* you send *two* of Black's men to the bar! That can't be bad!

Do not worry about your blot on R8. Black can only hit it by throwing 4-4 (35/1 against) and the chances are that he will not be able to re-enter both men on his first throw anyway.

3

4

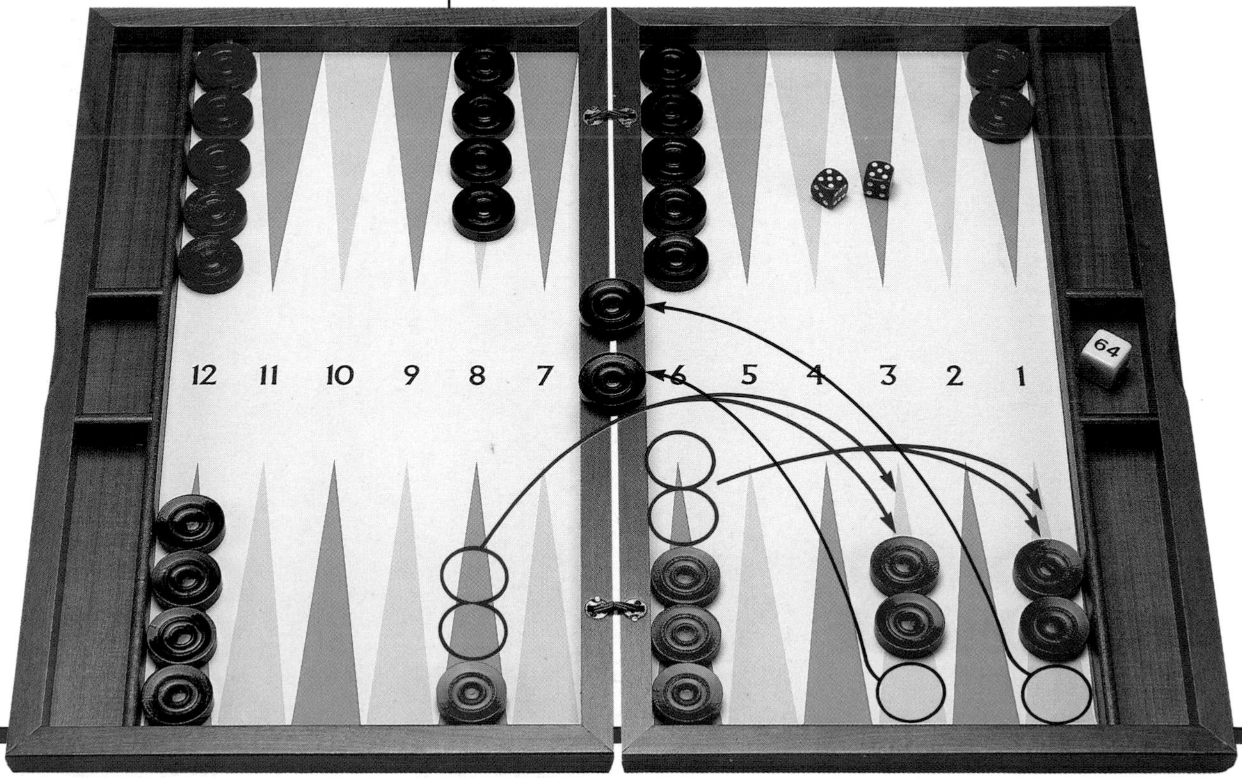

THE THIRD EXAMPLE

When your opponent has an initial roll of 6-1 and makes his bar point, you have to think twice with throws of 6-6 and 6-5. In this situation, with a roll of 6-6, some experts recommend that you play B12 to R7 (four men)! Yes, bringing *four* men down into your outer table to your bar point and leaving a blot at B12. **Do not do it!** Instead play B12 to R7 (two men) and R8 to R2 (two men) (**5**).

This is much more balanced play. It leaves you still in control of the B12 point. It is really far to early in the game for you to consider relinquishing it. It gives you an advanced point; too advanced for our liking really, but beggars cannot be choosers. It will be useful later on, so it is not a complete waste. You leave a blot at R8 which, if not hit, will be a very useful "builder" to make more inner table points.

THE FOURTH EXAMPLE

A roll by you of 6-5 in this same situation can no longer be played with the Lovers' Leap – B1 to B12. I strongly recommend that you play it B12 to R7 and B12 to R8 (**6**). If Black fails to hit your blot on R7, you are in great shape to cover it or at least use it to make a point in your inner table.

I hope you are beginning to get the idea now? Be adaptable. Do not play by rote. Try to "see" a move or two ahead. Take this next example:

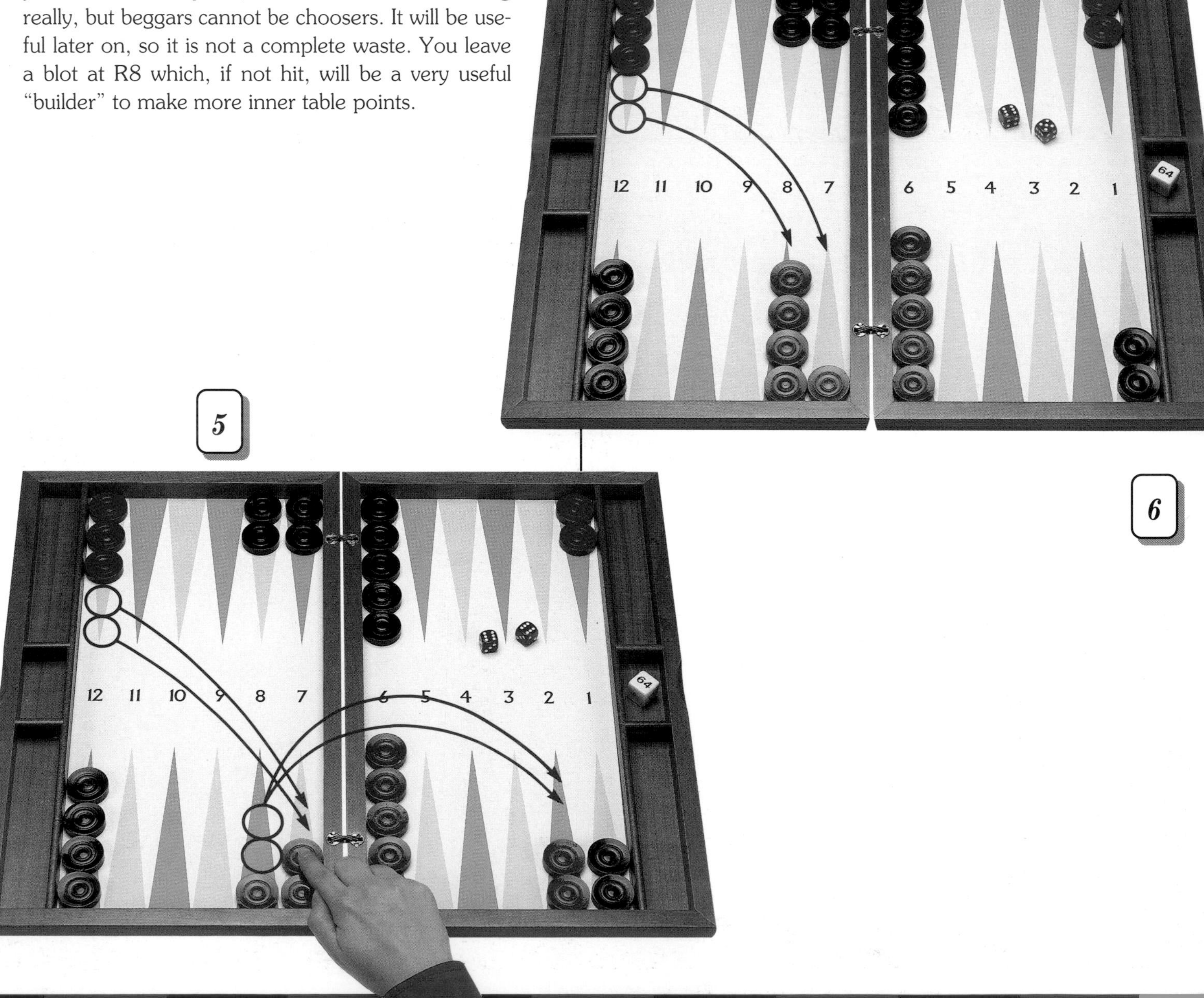

THE FIFTH EXAMPLE

Black has rolled 2-1 and has played as per recommendation R12 to B11, B6 to B5 (**7**). You now roll 6-3. To play the normal opener by running one back man B1 to B10 would certainly not be a suitable reply here. By playing his 2-1 roll in this way Black is making a concerted effort to secure his 5 point. To do this, Black could use a 6 to great effect if he is fortunate enough to roll one on his next throw. So you must offer him a red herring. You play your 6-3 by playing B12 to R7 and B12 to R10. You have placed a blot on R7, that is six points away from Black's back men. Black now *has* to hit you if he throws a 6 which successfully negates his immediate aspirations to man his 5 point. He cannot be in two places at once!

CONCLUSIONS

I could give you dozens of examples like these but it is not necessary. Just keep your wits about you – understand the reason behind your opponent's move and abide by the following golden rules:

- *If your opponent splits his back men, do not leave a blot in your outer table* as you normally would with a 3-2, 4-3, 5-2 or similar opener where you drop down two men from the B12 point. Find an alternative.
- *If your opponent makes a point in his inner table* with, say, 3-1, 4-2 or 5-3, *do not split your back men* with throws of 6-4, 6-3 etc.
- *If your opponent leaves a blot that you can hit*, generally speaking, *you should hit it*. The exceptions are blots that he may leave in your inner table on points R1 to R4 unless you can hit two, and at the same time make a point on them.
- *If he leaves you a blot on your 5 point – hit it* if you can.
- If you have to leave a blot, leave it where Black has to use all or part of a move that he would prefer to make elsewhere in order to hit your blot.

7

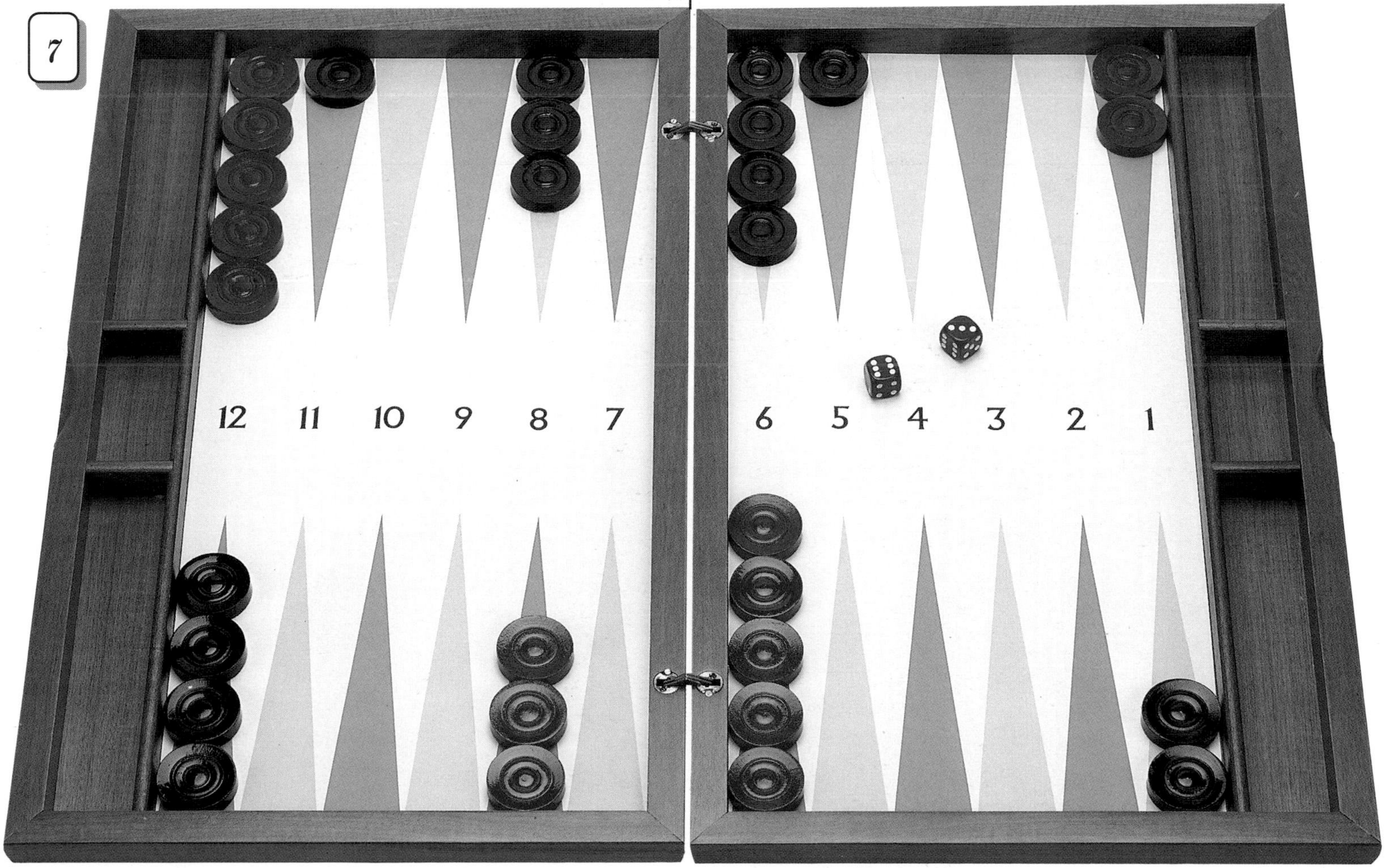

LET US PLAY

I have always thought that the best way to learn to play any game is *to play it*. In this chapter we play a complete game of backgammon – from the first roll right through to bearing off the final man. You will find most of the techniques that you have already learned put into play. Each move is explained in detail so that you, the reader, can understand the player's reason for making it. This is an actual game that I participated in and now I want you to participate in it too. Get your board out – set up the pieces and follow the game, step by step, on your own board, just as we have recreated it for you here. In the photographs we have used female models to move the pieces. Imagine that you are playing Red, as I did, and share with me the cut and thrust and excitement of this great game.

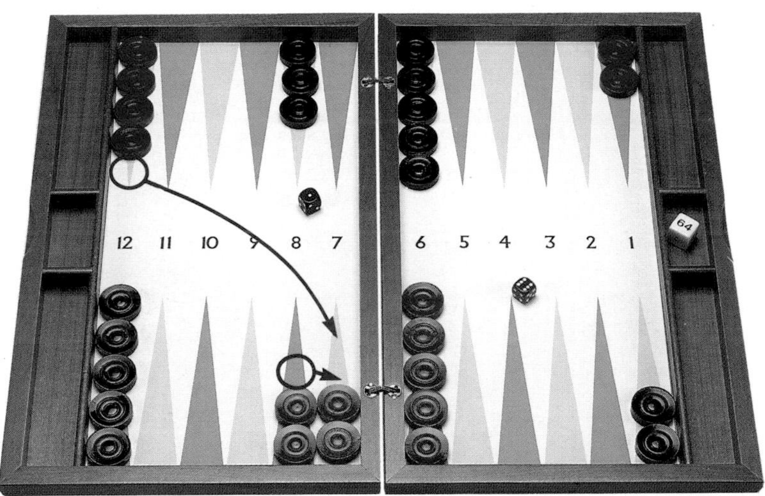

RED 6-1

PLAYING THE GAME

Red rolls a 6, Black rolls a 1, so Red is off to a flying start by making her bar point. B12 to R7, R8 to R7 (**1**).

Black, not so lucky, rolls 3-2 but makes the most of this poor roll by bringing down two builders from the R12 point. She plays R12 to B11, R12 to B10 (**2**).

Red has got a slight edge so far, having made her bar point. However, it is early days yet. She now rolls 5-2 and plays B12 to R8, B12 to R11 (**3**). This brings down two builders to bolster the blockade.

BLACK 3-2

RED 5-2

4 **BLACK 3-1**

Black now rolls 3-1, a change of luck for her, and promptly makes her 5 point. She could also have made her bar point by playing B10 to B7, B8 to B7, but considered that the capture of her 5 point should be her priority. She played B8 to B5, B6 to B5 (**4**).

Red now has a dream roll, 6-3! Immediately she snatches her chance and secures her 5 point. R11 to R5 and R8 to R5 (**5**). Red should be well pleased with this. She now has four points in a row – a formidable semi-prime – and she will be considering offering Black a double. But Black rolls 4-3, a golden roll for her! She plays B10 to B7, B11 to B7 (**6**); securing her bar point and giving her a four-point semi-prime.

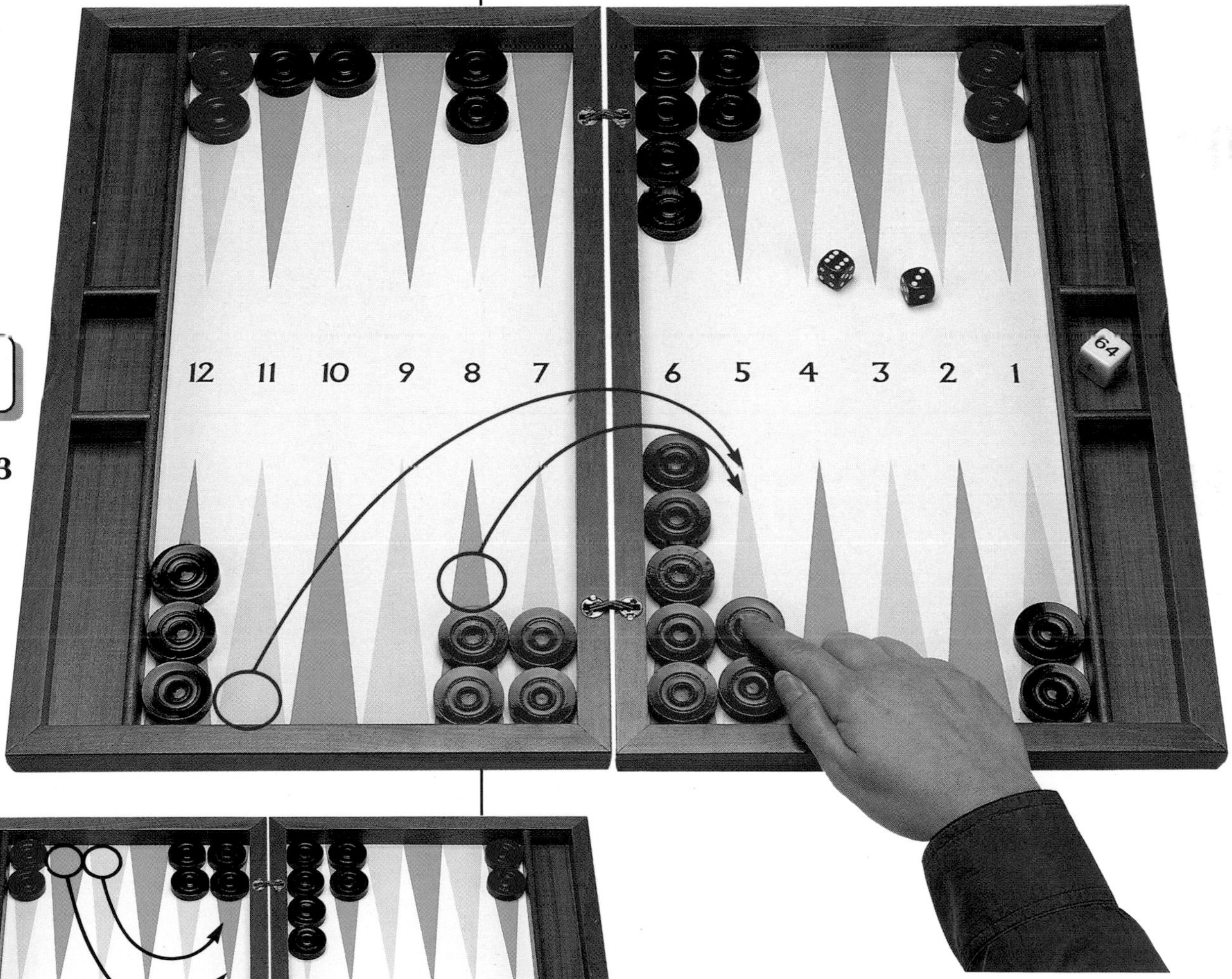

5 **RED 6-3**

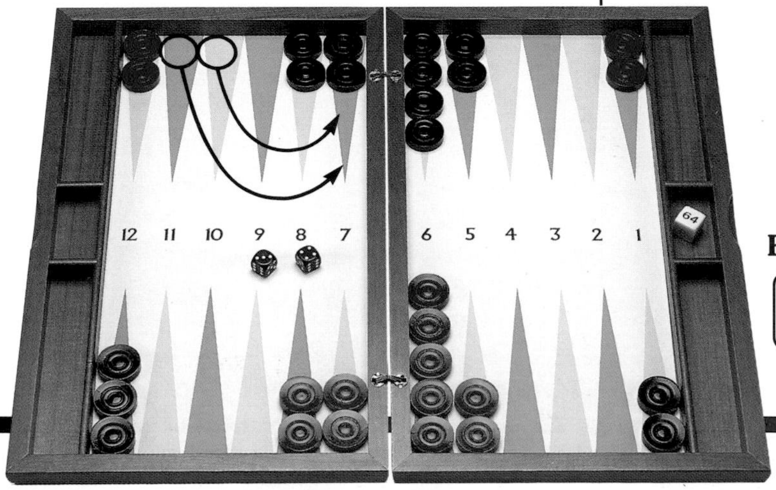

BLACK 4-3 6

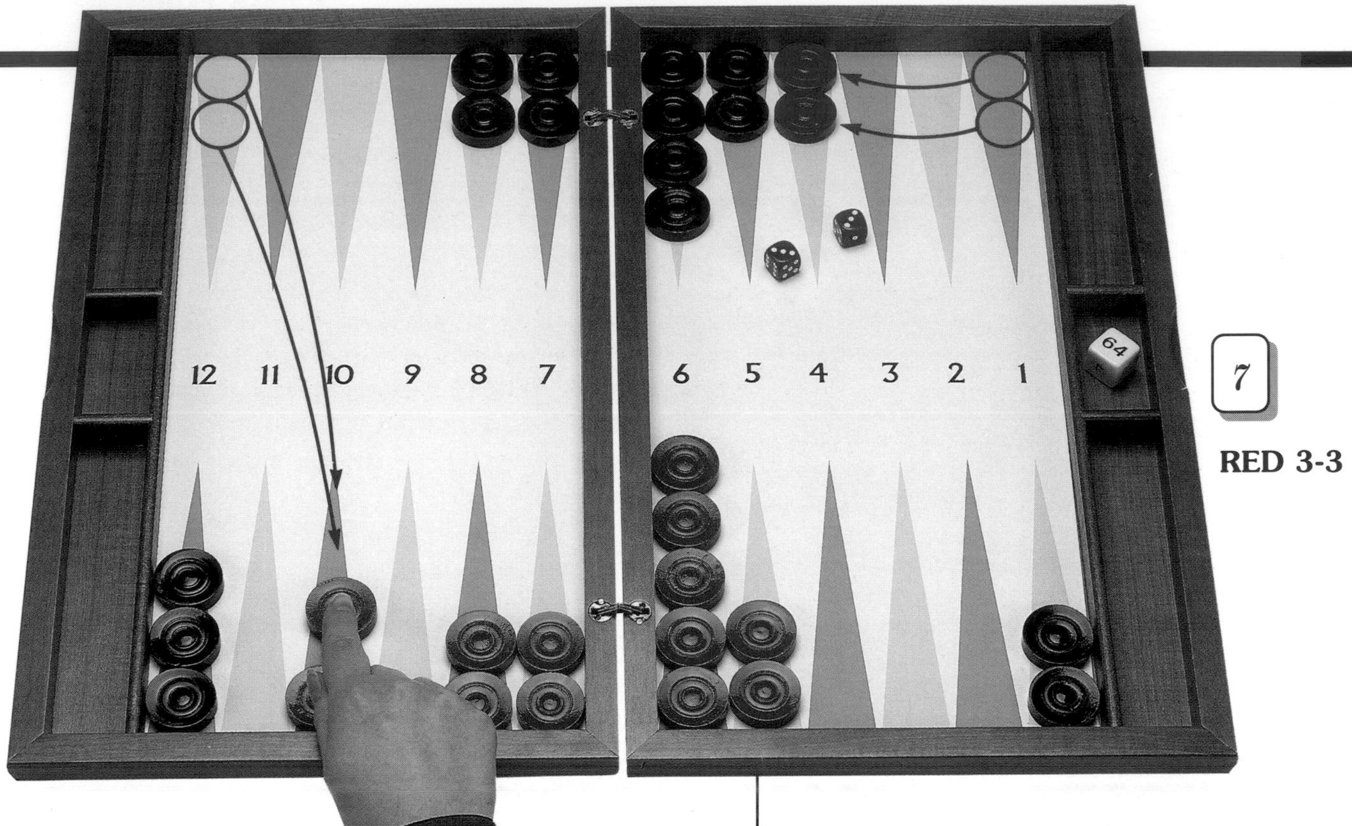

7

RED 3-3

Red now has second thoughts about doubling. She is no longer ahead, so she swallows her pride and rolls . . . 3-3. Red was obviously born with a silver spoon in her mouth. This is an excellent roll. She moves two men from B12 and two men from B1. B1 to B4 (two men) and B12 to R10 (two men) (**7**).

Of the wisdom of B1 to B4 (two men) there is no doubt. A great move that punches Black's attack on the nose. It prevents Black from advancing her prime further into her inner table. Unless she gets her back men clear of Red's trap and round to provide assistance, she just will not have enough men to form a six-point prime because two of her four men on the B6 point have now lost their potential effectiveness as they cannot build on the B4 point now controlled by Red.

Red played the second of her two threes B12 to R10 (two men), but she could also have played R6 to R3 (two men) making her 3 point. Which move is correct? I like Red's choice, B12 to R10 (two men) because I still think it is a little early in the game for Red to make her 3 point. If her back men had been clear of Black's inner table, I would have played it the other way. However, as they are not, I prefer to see the advance slowed a little in order to preserve the semi-prime. The three extra men on R6 will be useful to this end.

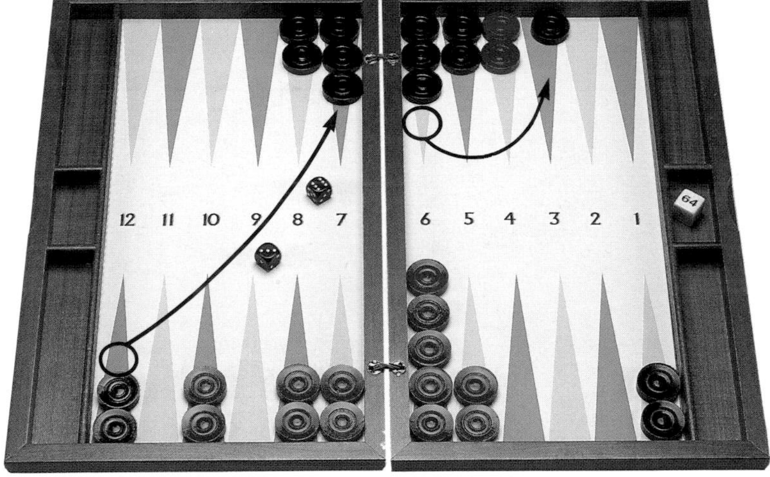

8

BLACK 6-3

Black now rolls 6-3 and plays R12 to B7 and B6 to B3 (**8**). Not a good roll for Black but she plays it very well. She cannot improve the position of her back men, so she maintains her four-point block (B8 through B5) by moving one man from R12 to B7 and one man from B6 to B3, hopping over Red's point on B4 to safety.

Red now rolls 6-2. This is how she moves: R10 to R4, R6 to R4 (**9**). Red establishes her 4 point and extends her semi-prime to cover *five* points. The blot she has left on R10 is quite safe because it is just out of range of Black's back men. Red now looks very strong.

Black also rolls 6-2 and, after some thought, moves R12 to B5 (**10**). Her alternative was B7 to B1, B3 to B1, but Black preferred R12 to B5. I think that Black made the wrong decision here because she should be slowing down her own progress in order to force Red to start breaking up her blocking points. Her two men controlling R12 are also valuable in case one of Red's back men should hop out into her outer table. Black has now left a blot on R12 unnecessarily.

Sure enough, Red rolls 6-3, seizes her opportunity and plays B4 to R12 (**11**). This sends Black's blot to the bar.

9 **RED 6-2**

10 **BLACK 6-2**

RED 6-3 *11*

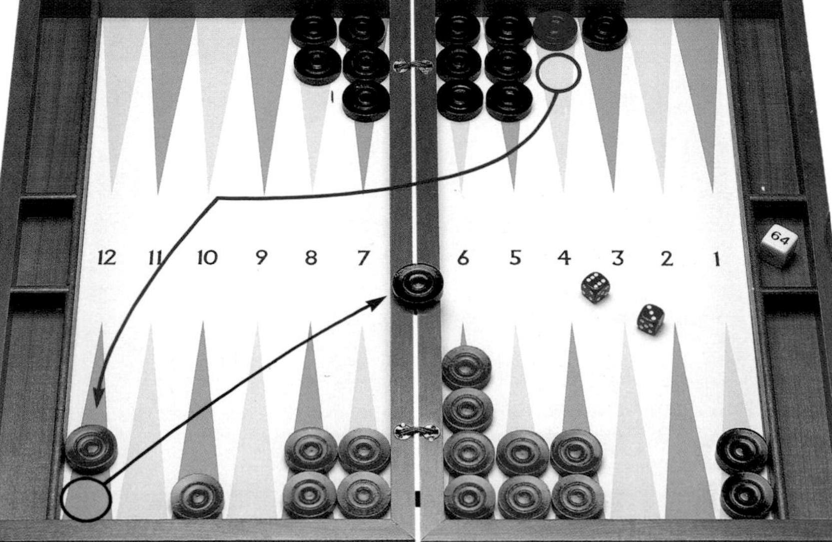

THE SECOND PHASE

Black rolls 6-4 and forfeits her turn because Red controls both the R6 and R4 points making it impossible for Black to re-enter.

Red rolls 3-3. She is really rolling well! This is what she does: R12 to R3, R6 to R3 (**12**)! Black now has real problems. Red has completed a six-point prime with Black's back men locked behind it *and* one on the bar. Red begins to smell a gammon (double-point game), so refrains from offering Black the doubling cube because it would give Black the chance to retire immediately at the cost of only a single-point game.

Black rolls 5-3 and again cannot enter. Red controls both these points.

Red rolls 4-1. R6 to R2 and R10 to R9 (**13**). Red would have liked to get her back man on B4 to safety but this is impossible for the time being – so she runs one man from R6 to R2 and one man from R10 to R9. To the inexperienced, the move R6 to R2 may seem rather strange. In reality it is extremely good play. Red, while keeping her side prime intact, is trying to slide it further into her own inner table. If Black *fails* to hit her blot on R2, any 6 and any 7 will close the point nicely, keeping the prime intact as well. Yes, Red will be odds-on favourite (15/21) to close the point.

On the other hand, if Black hits the blot on R2, Red need not worry either! She still has a prime, so Black cannot escape, and, with any luck, she will be able to re-enter in Black's inner table and work all the way round again without having to break her prime. Black will be damned if she hits the blot and damned if she doesn't, or so it seems . . .

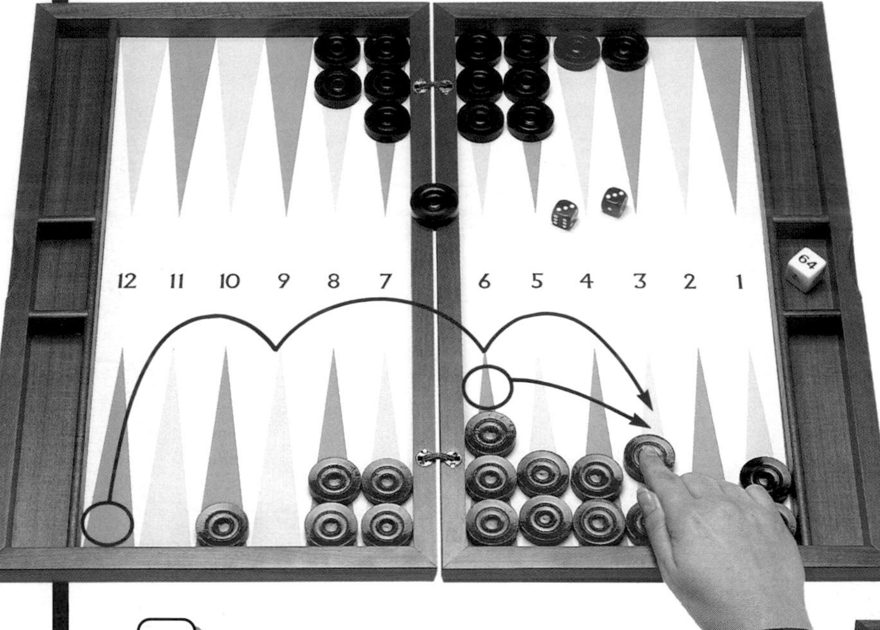

12 **RED 3-3**

13 **RED 4-1**

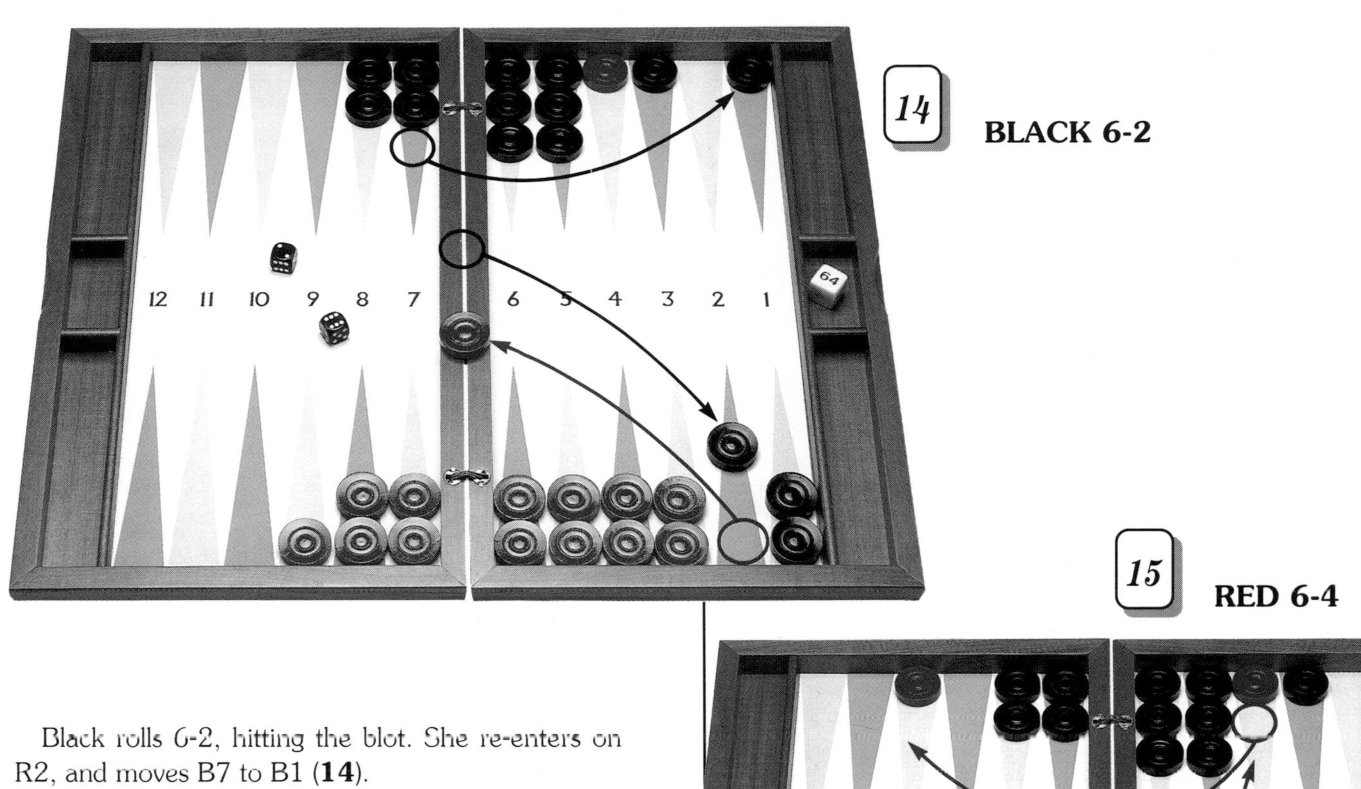

14 **BLACK 6-2**

15 **RED 6-4**

Black rolls 6-2, hitting the blot. She re-enters on R2, and moves B7 to B1 (**14**).

No comment necessary. Red rolls 6-4 and re-enters at B4, then B4 to B10 (**15**). From the bar, Red's man re-enters and jumps to the safety of Black's outer table in one fell swoop.

Black rolls 2-1. A good roll. She plays B6 to B4 and B5 to B4 (**16**), thus making her 4 point, establishing a five-point prime and sending Red to the bar again.

16 **BLACK 2-1**

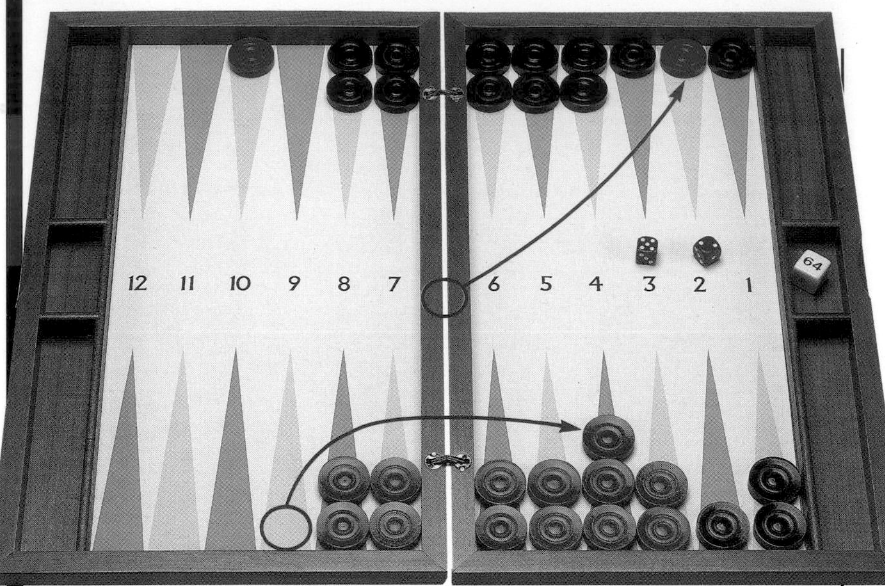

17

RED 5-2

Red now rolls 5-2. She re-enters at B2 and then moves R9 to R4 (**17**). Red is thankful that she is able to re-enter on B2 rather than B1 or B3 where Black has a couple of blots. Yes, here Red does *not* want to hit Black. Why? Well, if Black is hit and is then able to re-enter her man at R2, she will have strengthened her defence immeasurably because she would control the R1 and R2 points in Red's inner table. Red would, most probably, have great problems in bringing her men round and bearing off safely without leaving at least one blot for Black to aim at.

Black now rolls 6-6. Black has no options here. B8 to B2 (two men) and B7 to B1 (two men)(**18**). Doubles are not always favourable and here is a case in point. Black did not want to hit Red here because Red will not now have to break up her prime until after she has re-entered the man just hit. Black's back men remain trapped.

BLACK 6-6

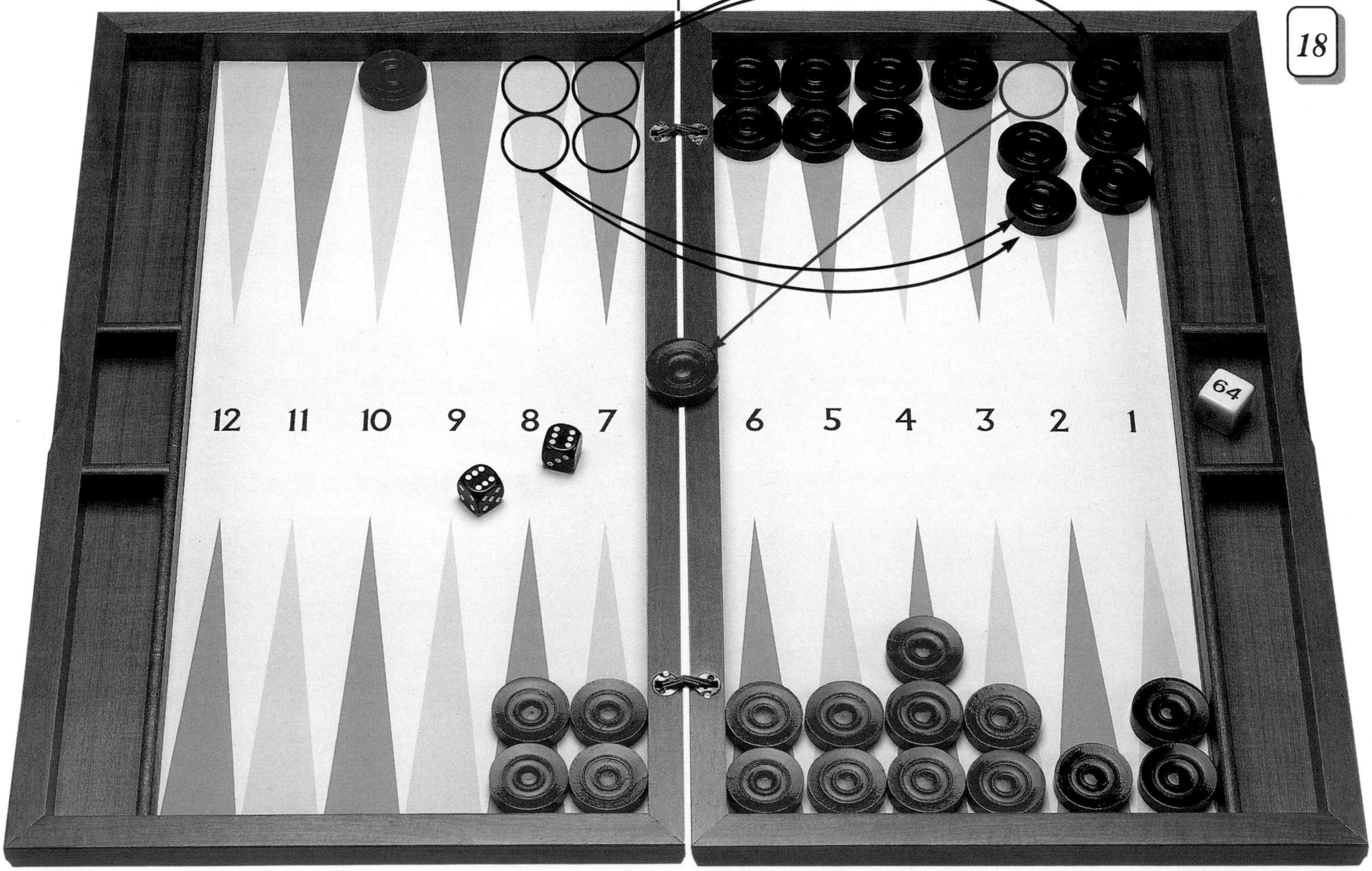

18

12 11 10 9 8 7 6 5 4 3 2 1

64

Red rolls 6-1, failing to enter, but is quite happy to remain on the bar for a while. The longer she can remain on the bar, the more damage will be done to Black's inner board – she will have to break up her points.

Black rolls 5-5. She only has two "5" moves on the board. These she makes . . . B6 to B1 (two men)(**19**). Black has to begin demolishing her inner table.

Red rolls 6-5 and is back in play with bar to B6 and B10 to R10 (**20**).

Black has got problems! She now throws 5-4. She has no "5" move and the only "4" move is B5 to B1 which is compulsory (**21**).

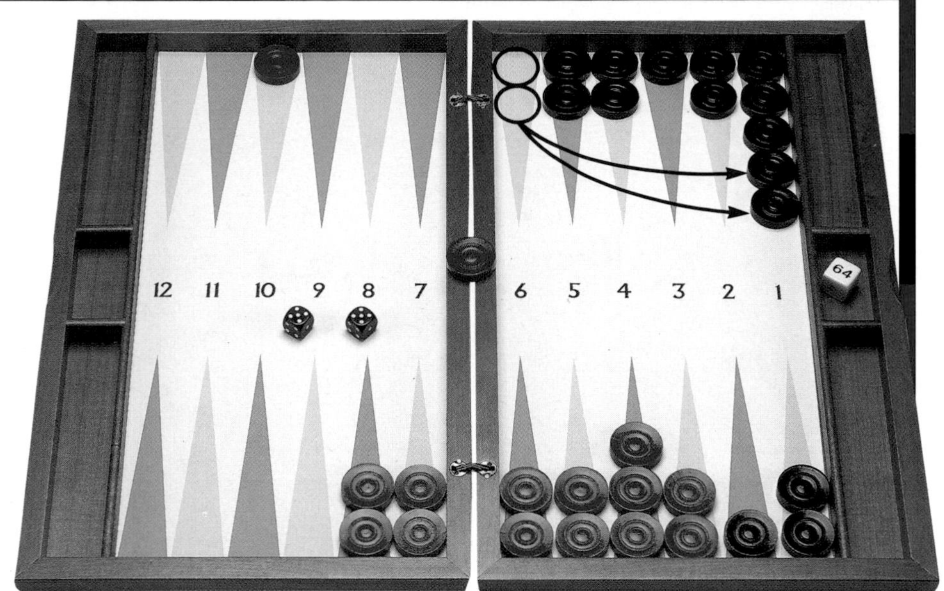

19 **BLACK 5-5**

20 **RED 6-5**

21 **BLACK 5-4**

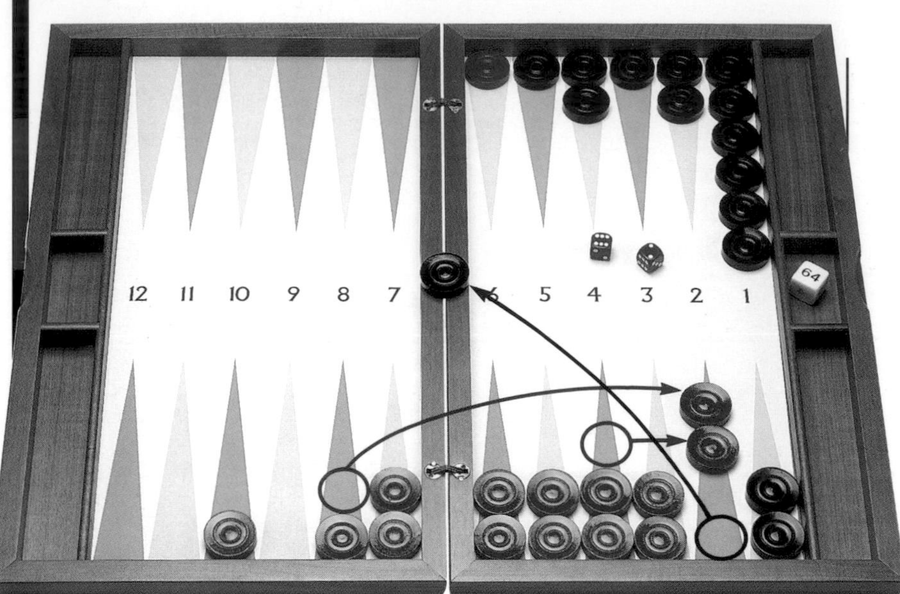

Red rolls 6-2. A very good roll. She plays R8 to R2 and R4 to R2 (**22**), so moving her prime one point further in, securing the R2 point and sending Black's man to the bar. Black rolls 4-3 and fails to re-enter.

Red now rolls 6-6 and plays B6 to R7, R10 to R4 and R8 to R2, tidying up a few loose ends (**23**). Red must now be praying that she does not throw a double 5 or double 4 on her next roll. She will be in trouble if she does. If she rolls 5-5, she will have to move three men R7 to R2 and take one man from R5, leaving a blot which Black can hit with any 5 roll. If she rolls 4-4, she can move two men R6 to R2, but she must leave a blot at R7 because two men R7 to R3 is compulsory. Black rolling a six will hit it.

22 **RED 6-2**

23

RED 6-6

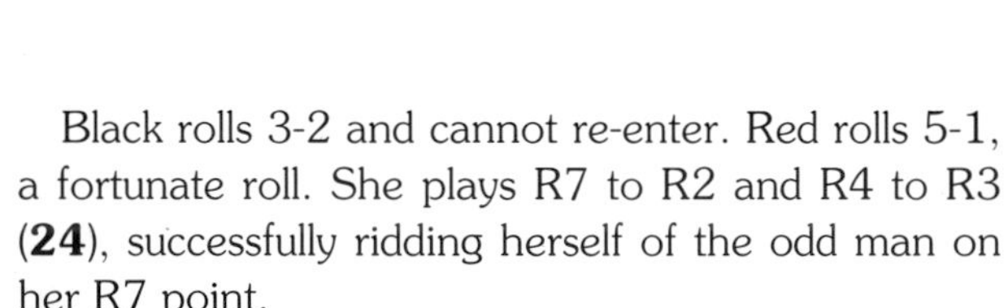

Black rolls 3-2 and cannot re-enter. Red rolls 5-1, a fortunate roll. She plays R7 to R2 and R4 to R3 (**24**), successfully ridding herself of the odd man on her R7 point.

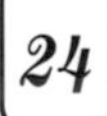

24

RED 5-1

Black rolls 6-1. She is able to re-enter at R1 (**25**) but is unable to play her 6 anywhere.

Red rolls 2-2. She plays her two men on R7 to R5 and bears off two men from R2 (**26**).

Black rolls 6-6 and now is compelled to make moves with her back men from R1. Red has already borne off two men, and Black feels that her best bet is to stay put in the hope that Red will leave a blot for her to hit as Red bears off. However, when you've got to go, you've got to go! Black plays two men from R1 all the way to B12 (**27**). She manages to keep one man back in the hope of hitting Red. Will the gamble come off? Time will tell.

25 **BLACK 6-1**

26 **RED 2-2**

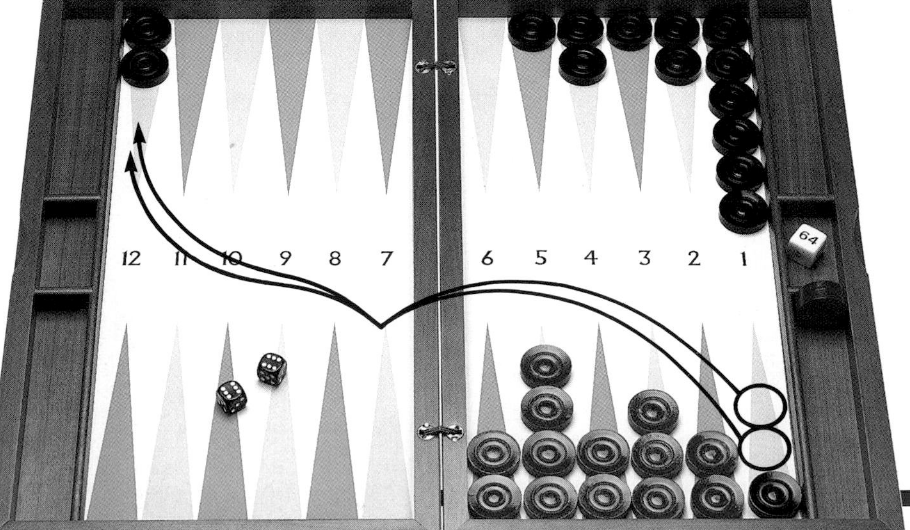

27 **BLACK 6-6**

Red rolls 6-4. She bears off at R6 and, rather than hitting Black's blot, plays the 4 with R6-R2 to avoid leaving two blots (**28**).

Black rolls 6-1 and plays one man B12 to B5 (**29**). Black has no option but to move the man from B12. She manages to close her 5 point at the same time *and* keep her back man in a fighting position.

Red rolls 6-4 and suddenly finds herself with problems. First she bears off one man from R5 for the 6. No problem. But what should she do with the 4? Should she also bear off a man from R4, or should she play R5 to R1 sending Black to the bar but leaving a blot on R1? Red decides on the latter. Bear off R5 and move R5 to R1 (**30**). She reasons this way. If she leaves a blot on R4, Black can hit it with any "3"

28 **RED 6-4**

29 **BLACK 6-1**

That totals 11 rolls that will hit it and 25 that will not. If, however, she leaves a blot on R1 – sending Black to the bar – she can be hit by Black re-entering with any "1" – that is also 11 ways out of 36 (the same odds as before) plus the fact that Black might roll a 6 and have to re-enter on R6 and thus be out of her hair forever. Black might not even be able to re-enter at all. So, hitting her opponent at R1 is much the better move.

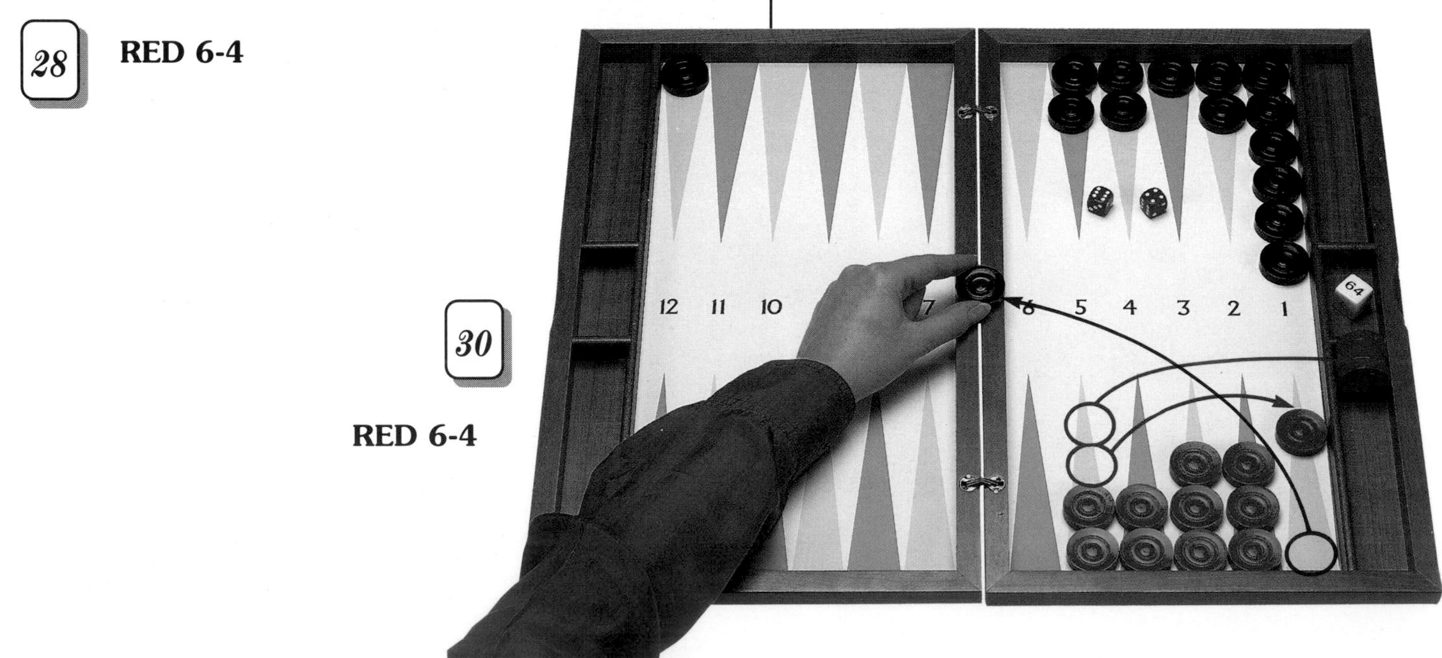

30 **RED 6-4**

Black rolls 5-1 and is happy to do so! She plays bar to R1 and R1 to R6 (**31**). Red is sent to the bar and must re-enter and come round the board before she can continue bearing off. Black controls four points in her inner table so it is by no means certain that Red will be able to re-enter on her first roll.

However, luck is with her and Red rolls 6-3. She plays bar to B6, B6 to B9 (**32**). Red enters at B6 rather than B3 to hit Black's blot because she is ahead, having borne off four men already, and she still has to bring her man all the way round and into her own inner table. Black's men already form two obstacles in her path (the men at R6 and B12). Why give herself a third obstacle by hitting the blot? The move B6 to B9 rather than, say, R4 to R1 is also good play because the odds of Black hitting the blot at B6 are exactly the same as the odds against Black hitting it at B9 (17 ways to hit). So she moves it and furthers her position by three places at no extra risk.

Black rolls 5-4. Black has to move one of her two back men for the 5. She rightly chooses the man on B12 and moves it into her inner table to B3 (**33**). She purposely keeps her man on R6 stationary in the hope that Red will not be able to pass it on her next roll; this will present her with one last shot.

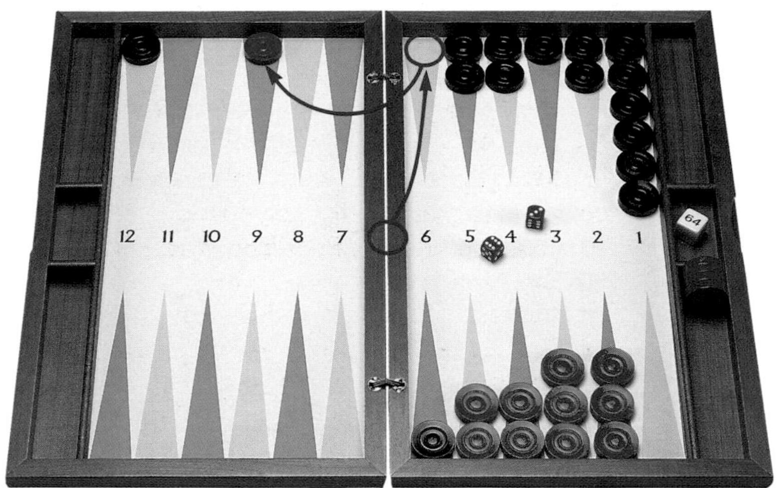

32 **RED 6-3**

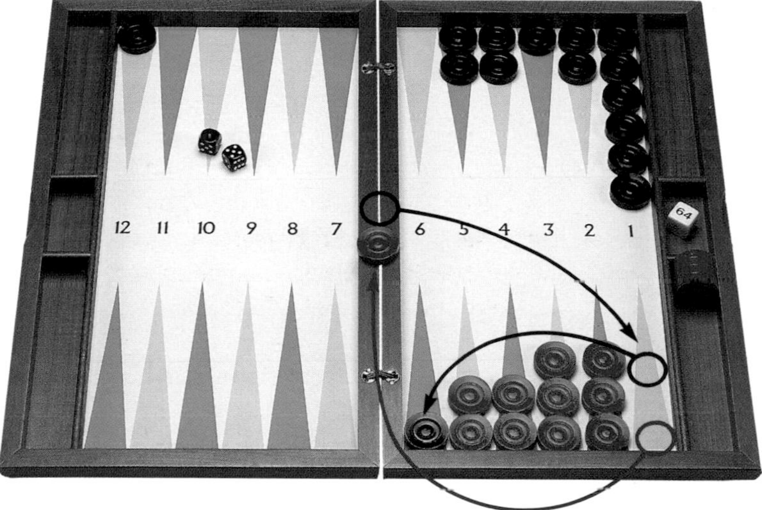

31 **BLACK 5-1**

33 **BLACK 5-4**

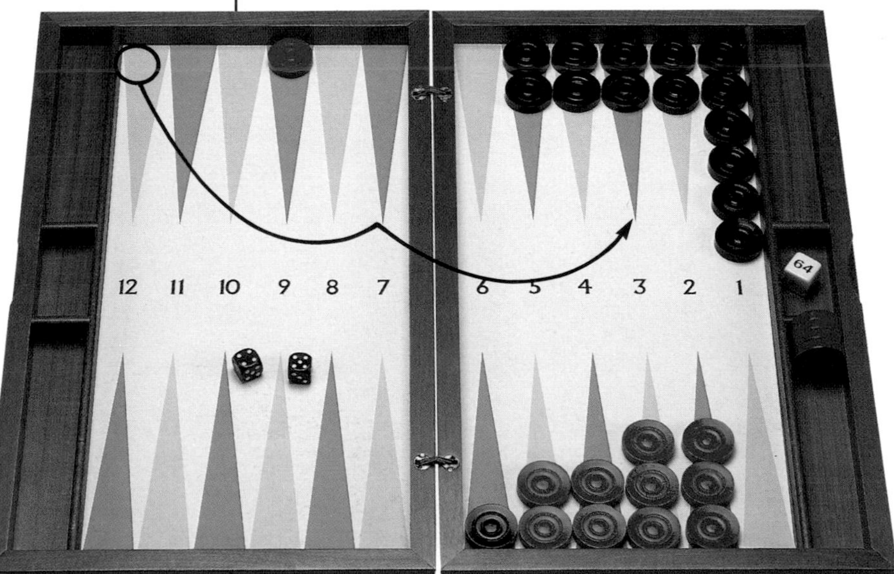

Red rolls 6-2. She plays the whole roll with her back man, B9 to R8 (**34**). She *had* to move to R10 for the 6. So knowing that if you have to leave a blot a distance of 6 or less from the opposition, the closer you are the better, she continues the man to R8. Black must now throw a "2" to stand a reasonable chance of winning.

Black rolls 6-3 and has to pack her bags and go. R6 to B10 (**35**). The race is on!

35 **BLACK 6-3**

34 **RED 6-2**

THE DASH FOR THE POST

Red rolls 2-1. She plays R8 to R6, R2 to R1 (**36**). As she was unable to bear a man off this time, Red spreads her men so that on her next roll she *must* remove at least two men. This is correct play and could be crucial.

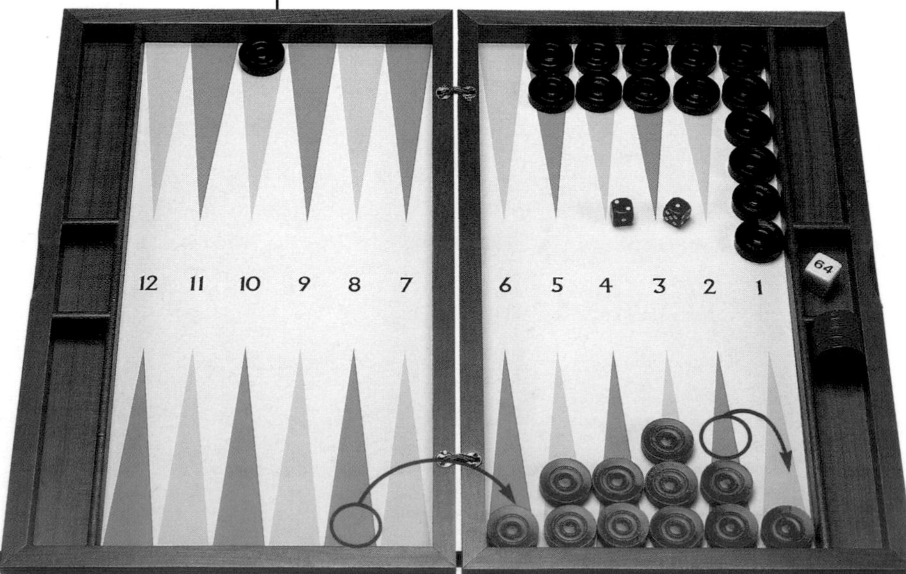

36 **RED 2-1**

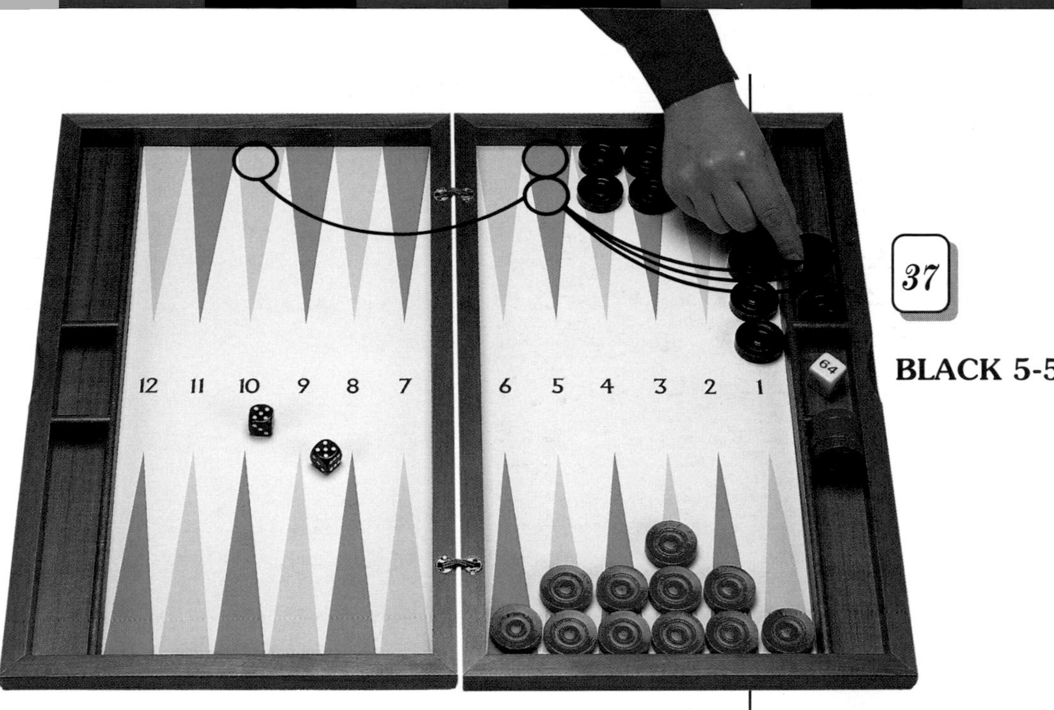

37

BLACK 5-5

38

RED 6-2

Black's turn now and a great roll for her. 5-5! She bears off three men and, despite all her previous problems, is now only one man behind (**37**). However, Red has the roll and throws 6-2. She moves by bearing off at R6 and R2 (**38**) – still one piece ahead but Black has got an excellent distribution of men for bearing off. Black rolls 6-4 bearing two men off from B4 (**39**).

39

BLACK 6-4

Red now rolls 5-1 and bears off two men (**40**).

Now Black turns the tables with a very timely roll indeed! 3-3! Wow! It is getting close! Black has caught up and is now one piece ahead (**41**).

But it is Red's roll. She throws 5-2. She bears off two men (**42**) and is grateful that she did not throw a 1. This would have cost her half a throw. With Black breathing down her neck so closely, Red just cannot afford to miss.

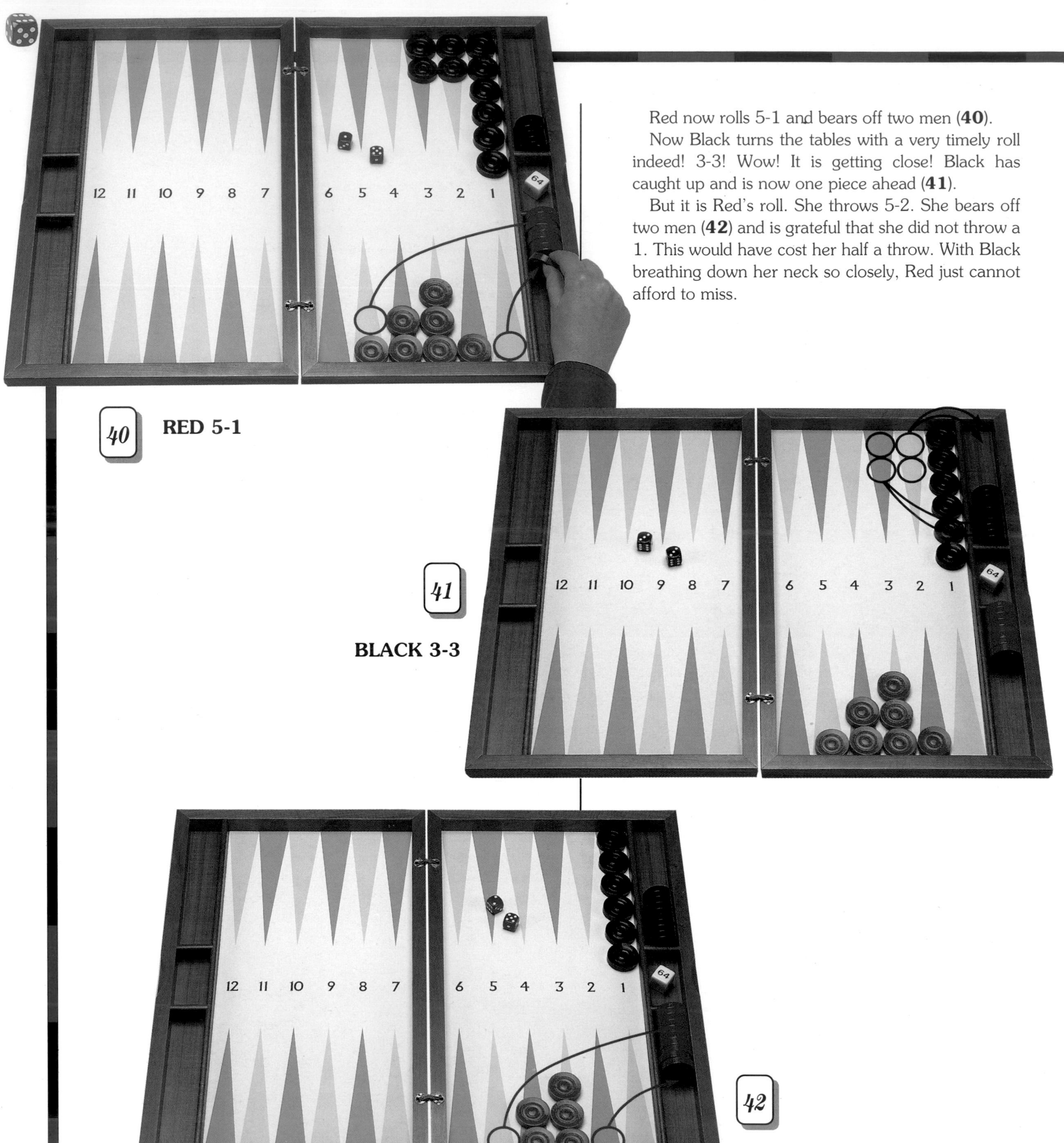

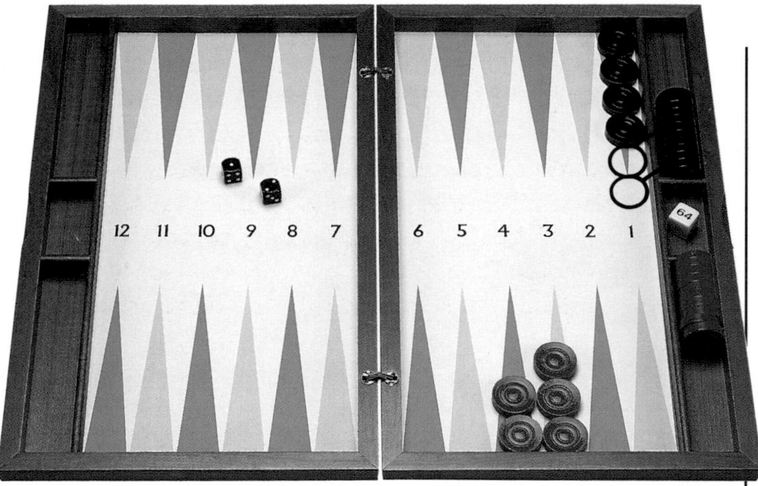

43 **BLACK 2-1**

Black rolls 2-1 and takes off two men (**43**). She will definitely be able to bear off her remaining men in two more rolls – which is more than can be said for Red! She needs a miracle . . . and gets one! She rolls 4-4! She bears off four men, leaving just one to go (**44**).

Black can still win if she throws a double. Any double will do. The odds are 5/1 that she will not – and she does not. It is 6-5 for Black. She bears off two men (**45**).

It is too late now for Black. Whatever Red throws, she must be able to remove her last man. Black loses by a whisker. A most exciting finish.

44 **RED 4-4**

BLACK 6-5 45

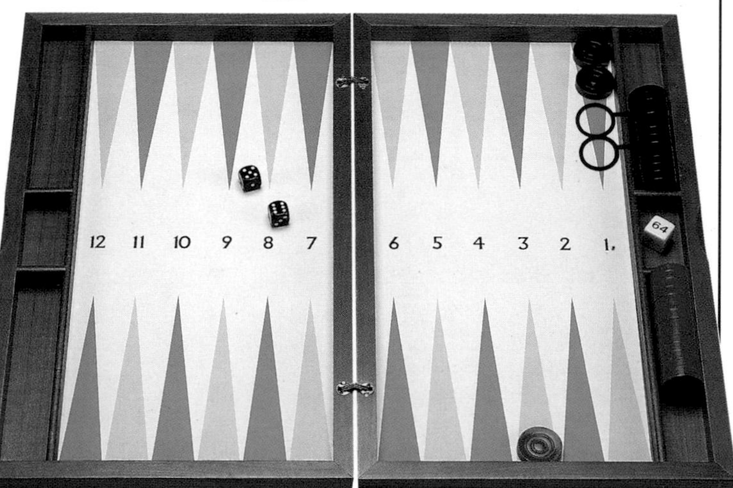

FINAL THOUGHTS

I remember how I felt when I won this game. My opponent, Mr. George Adimmou, is a superb player. George was the reigning backgammon champion on board the ocean liner the *Queen Elizabeth II*. The *Queen Elizabeth* is, quite frankly, one big floating backgammon club! Most of the officers and crew play and some play very well indeed. At the time that this game was played, the ship was cruising to and fro in the balmy Caribbean and I was enjoying two months of sun, sea and sensational backgammon. George, like many Greeks, has played backgammon all his life. He seldom makes a mistake and he is extremely hard to beat. However, this time he did make a mistake and it cost him the game.

THE PRIME OF YOUR LIFE

You should by now be aware of the importance of establishing a prime or semi-prime, if it is at all possible. In case you are not absolutely clear which is which, I will show you again. Figure (**1**) shows Black in possession of a *semi-prime*. That is, between three and five consecutive points grouped around his bar and number 5 point. In this illustration Black has four points in a row. A *prime* is six consecutive points grouped around the bar and number 5 points, forming an impenetrable block for any man caught behind it. Red is shown here with such a prime.

PLAYING A SHUTOUT

One other type of prime exists. It is called a Shutout (**2**). A shutout is in fact a prime that has been advanced until it occupies the entire inner table. It is also known as a closed board. Black's man on the Bar is "shut out" and cannot re-enter until Red chooses to open up a point for him.

Once you have established a prime, as Red did in the game that we re-enacted in the last chapter, you must systematically begin to drive home the nails in your opponent's coffin. Red reached this position (**3**), and she rolled 4-1. She played the "one" R10 to R9 and the "four" R6 to R2 (**4**). It is this second half of the move that I wish to draw your attention to, R6 to R2.

Black has a man on the bar and is waiting to re-enter. Why then leave a blot in her path in this way? The answer is simple, but seldom grasped by the beginner. It is *not* always bad to be hit! Indeed sometimes it is a blessing in disguise.

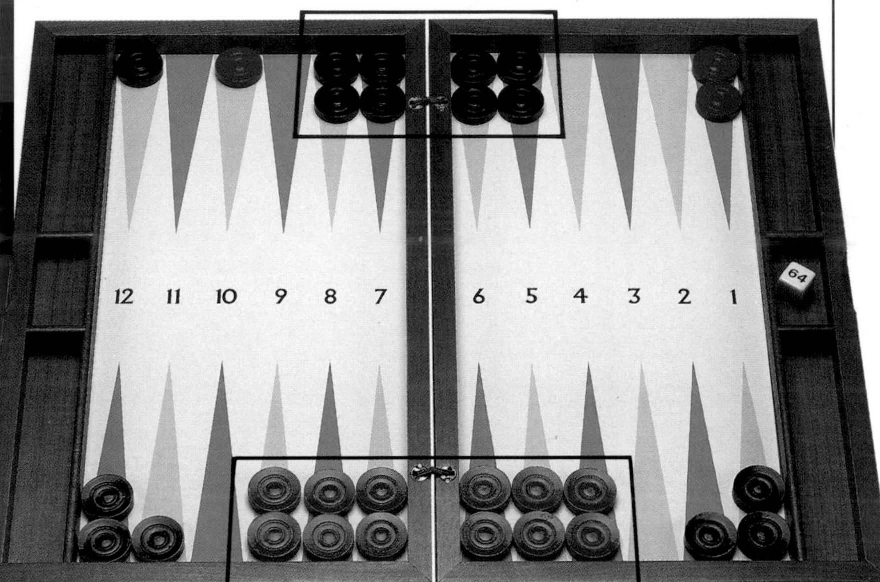

1

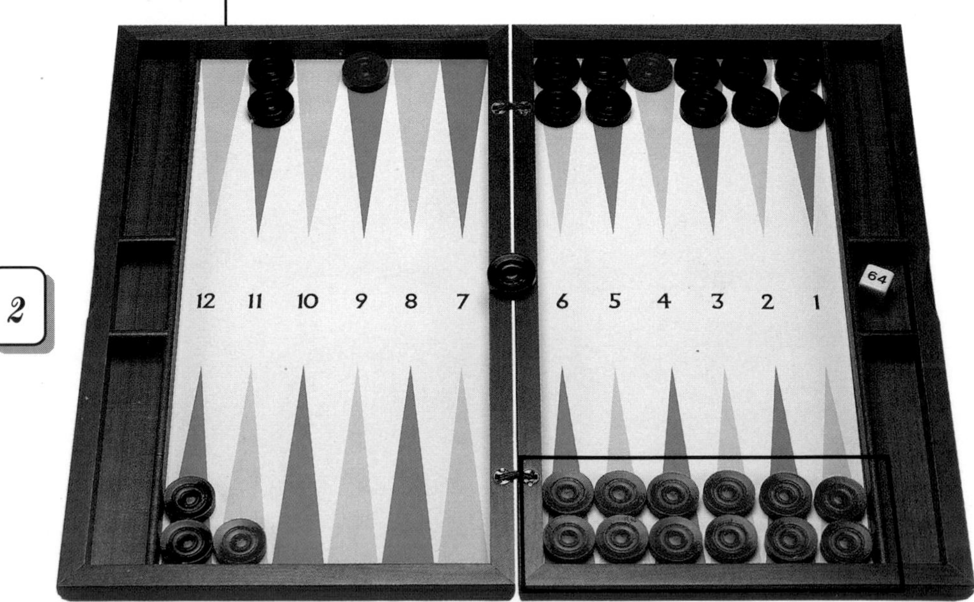

Let us first look at what happens if Black *does not* hit Red's blot on R2. Red, with any throws of 6 or 7 will be able to close the 2 point and yet still retain her prime. She will have successfully advanced the prime one point further into her inner table and, quite literally, Black's back will be against the wall. This is the whole object of the move. Only six throws will not close the point for Red.

What happens if Black *does* hit the blot. Red is sent to the Bar but Black will still be unable to escape from Red's prime. The longer that Red fails to re-enter, the worse it will be for Black because she, unable to move her back men, will have to break up her own semi-prime and other valuable blocking points in her own inner table.

So in prime play, always throw a man forward to the attacking head of the line when you are certain that by so doing you will:

- Still be able to retain your prime if your blot is hit.
- Advance your prime further into your inner table if you are not hit.

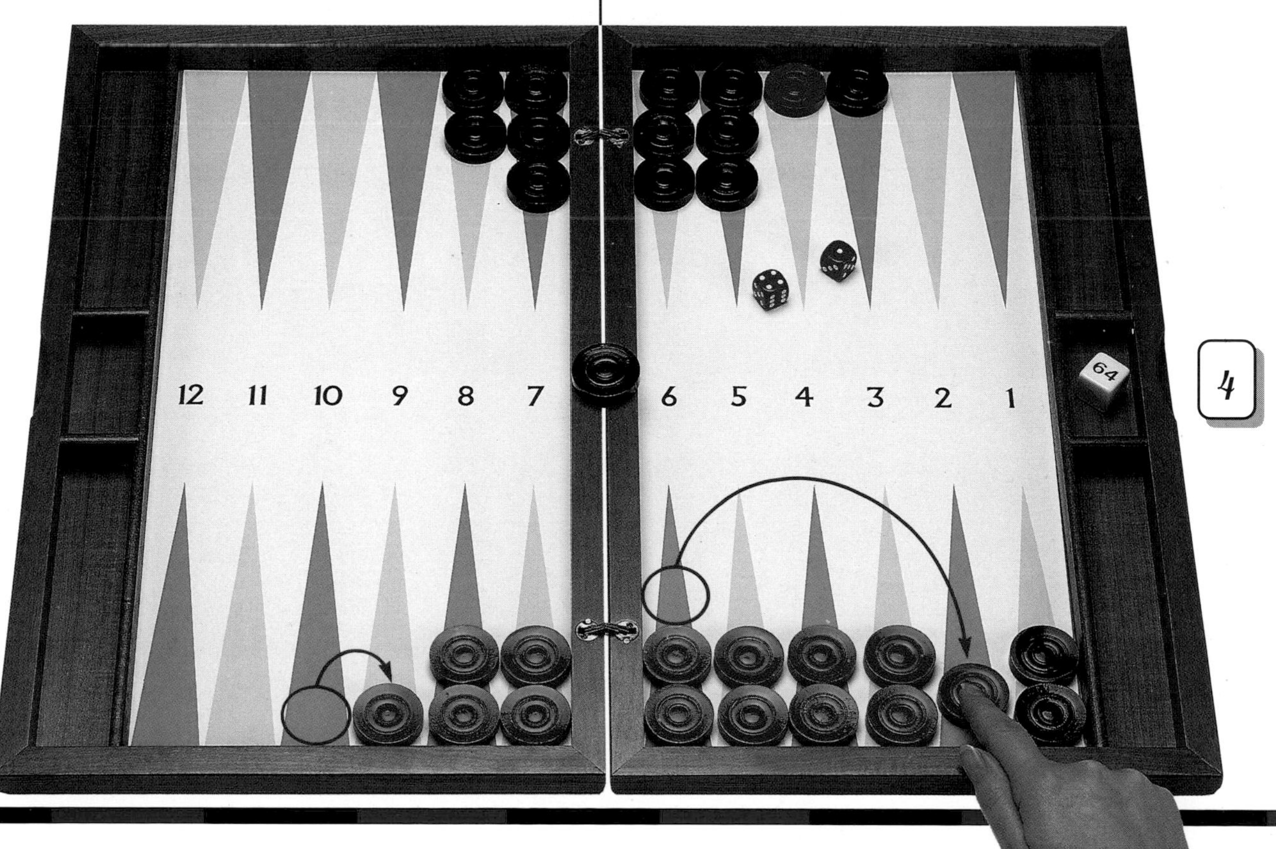

SPOTTING A WEAKNESS

Here is something else to watch out for. When you are holding a prime against your opponent, keep an eye on the distribution of the men in *his* inner table. You may get the opportunity of picking up another of his men! Look at (**5**).

You roll 5-2. Now an obvious move is to play R6 to R1 and R3 to R1, thus achieving a shutout and sending Black to the bar. However, it is *not* the best move. Look at those blots in Black's inner table. Would it not be nice to capture one of them? Let's try. Without any risk to yourself at all, the best possible move in this situation is R6 to R1 (sending Black to the bar) and R7 to R5.

Not only have you left a blot at R1, you actually hope that Black will hit it on re-entering. This would send *you* to the bar from where you would get a crack at those tempting blots in Black's inner table. If Black hits you, he cannot escape your inner table because of your prime. If he fails to re-enter, nothing is lost. You can always close the point for a shutout!

DEFENDING AGAINST A PRIME

There is one golden rule to observe if you find yourself on the wrong end of a prime:
Do not be tempted to hit your opponent's blot, should he leave one.
Sometimes, of course you have no option, the only legal play open to you being to hit it. But remember, if you have the option, always leave well alone. The next example demonstrates this point well (**6**).

You roll 6-1. *Do not* hit the blot at B3 with the 1. As things stand at the moment Black will have to start breaking up his prime and valuable blocking points with any roll that shows either a 5, a 4 or a 3 on his next turn, because although you only have a semi-prime, Black must roll 6-1 himself to escape your trap and thus keep his prime intact. So if you hit him, you defeat your own object. He will be able to sit on the shelf for a while and it will be *you* who has to break up *your* blocking points. The correct play is B12 to R12 and B12 to R7.

5

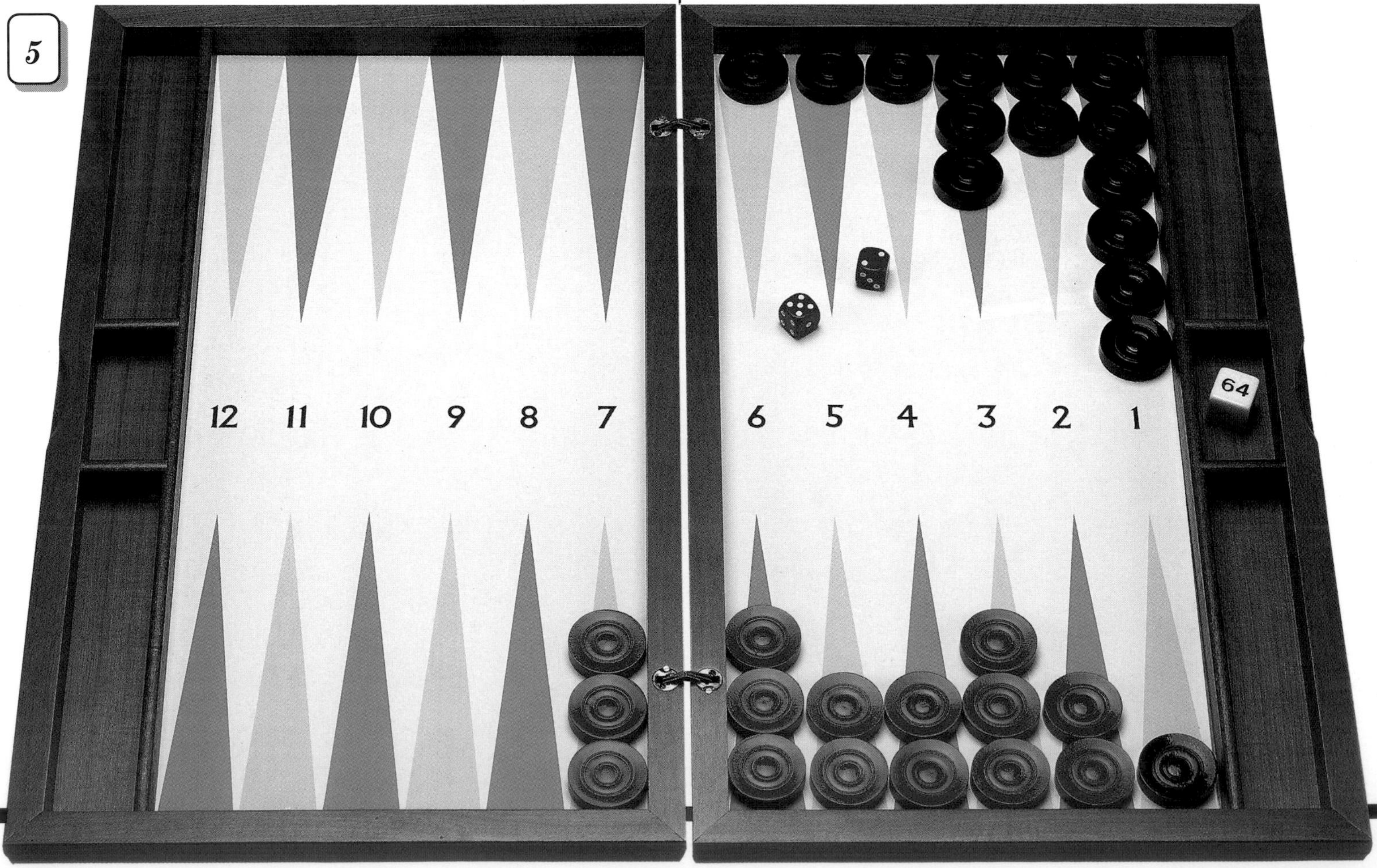

12 11 10 9 8 7 6 5 4 3 2 1

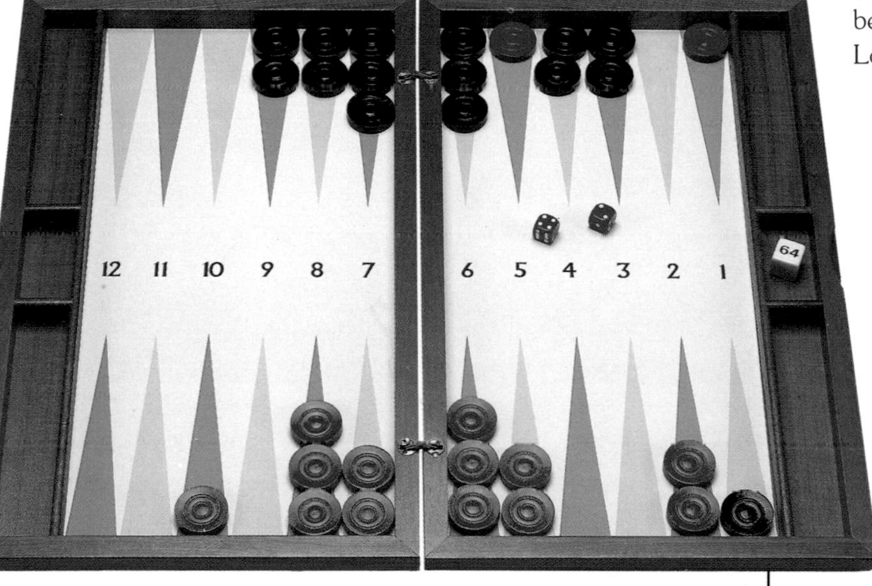

Look ahead. Try to spot an enemy prime before it descends upon you. Take this example (**7**) for instance. You roll 4-2. What is your best move? Do you make your own 4 point with R8 to R4 and R6 to R4? If you do, you could end up in serious trouble, and you will have missed a golden opportunity to sabotage Black's imminent prime. The proper play is B1 to B5 and R10 to R8. Your defence is now strong and Black's plans for a prime have come to nothing.

Obviously, the best way to defend against a prime is to prevent it from forming in the first place. That is the reason why respective "5" points are so important. They are at the very heart of the game, the vital organs. Do not hesitate to secure either or both if the opportunity arises.

If, however, it is too late and you are already in the grip of a prime – what then? Well, your efforts must be directed at breaking it down as quickly as possible. Look at the next example (**8**).

8

9

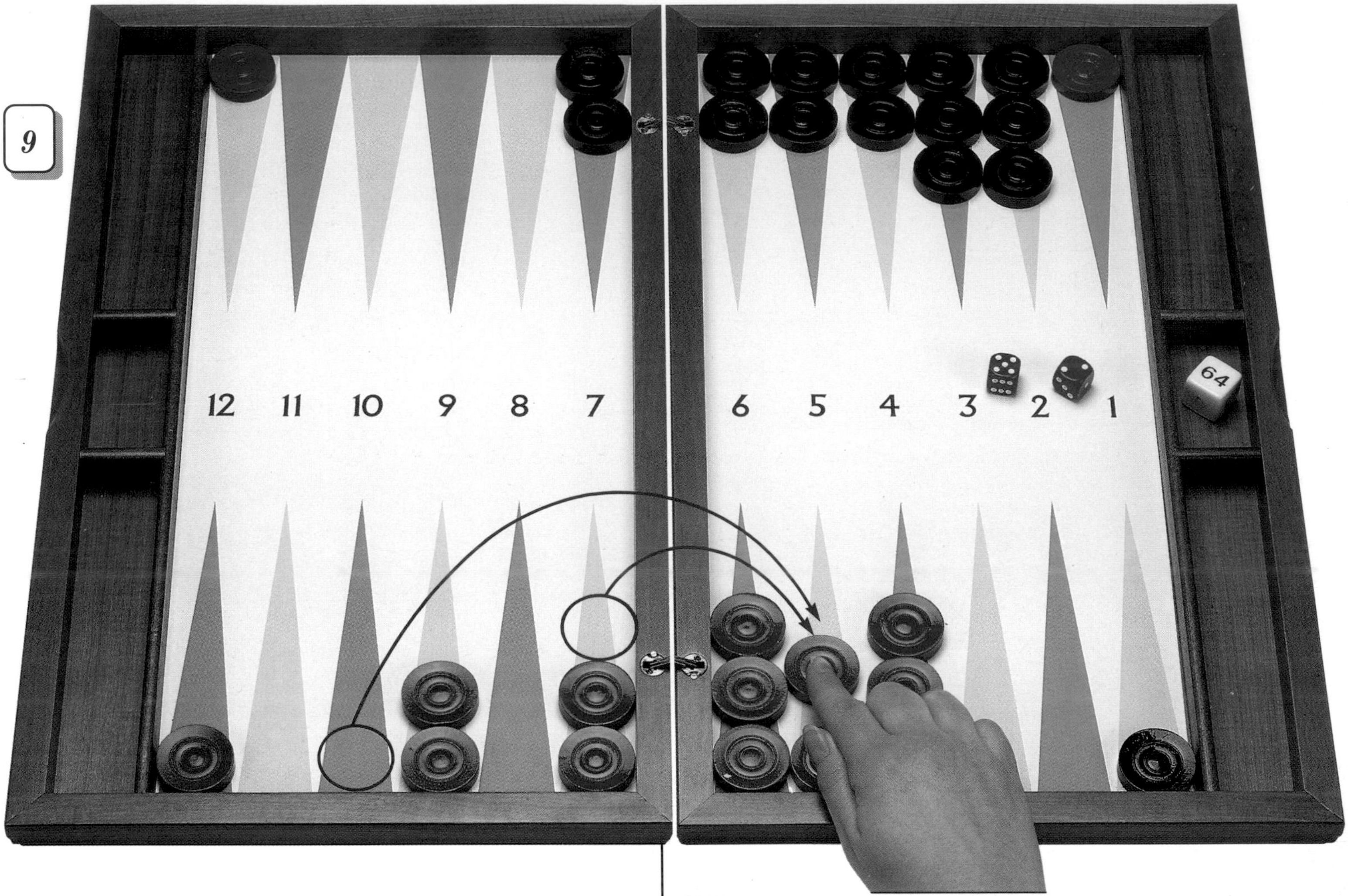

You roll 5-2. What is your best move? Should you play B12 to R8, R10 to R8 or R10 to R5, R7 to R5? The answer yet again is to make your "5" point with the latter play. You must get Black to break up his prime if you are to stand any chance of winning this game, so you must consolidate your own blocking points so that Black stands the *least* chance of escaping with his back men. Making your "5" point achieves this (**9**).

10

SIMULTANEOUS PRIMES

What happens if you both have a prime? Is it possible? It most certainly is. Here is a case in point (**10**). You (Red) are behind but this is one of the few occasions in backgammon when to be behind is to be ahead! If you control the doubling cube, this is a position in which you should offer it because you are most likely to win.

Why? Well, as Black is further advanced into his inner table than you are, it stands to reason that he will have to break his prime before you will have to break up yours. Just move carefully, and gradually ease your prime into your inner table by throwing one man up front into the pole position in the way that I have already shown you, and then close the point if you can. Above all – *do not hit his blot*.

Now let us see if you have grasped the important points outlined in this chapter. Three problems follow that you should now be able to solve. The answers are at the back of this book on page 120, but don't cheat! As if you would!

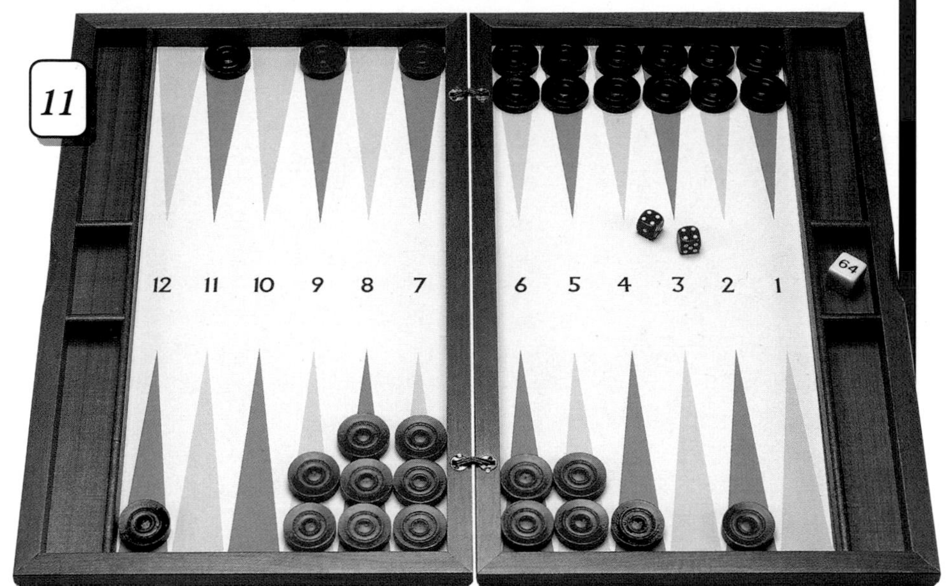

QUIZ QUESTIONS

In this position (**11**) you roll 4-4. How would you play it and why?
You now have to play this position (**12**). Your roll is 3-3. Once again – how and why?
Finally, how about this one (**13**)? How would you play 5-2? Be sure that you understand why.

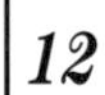

CHOOSE YOUR WEAPONS

Although you will never play two absolutely identical games of backgammon, you will play games that have a marked similarity to one another. There are four distinct types of game – each requiring its own individual strategy. It is important that you learn to recognize the type of game that you are engaged in as it develops, so that you can deploy the correct strategy. This chapter explains how you do this.

KEEPING YOUR OPTIONS OPEN

One type of game very often transforms itself into a different type of game as play goes on, because of the vagaries of the dice and the cut and thrust of this combative pastime. So you must keep your wits about you and, above all, *be adaptable*. The best players in the world are just that – adaptable. They never commit themselves completely to one type of strategy. To do this would be suicidal because in the event of your ploy failing, you would have no escape route to fall back on. Annihilation would follow.

Essentially there are three types of "forward" game:

- The Running Game
- The Blocking Game and
- The Shutout Game

There is also a "backward" game called, appropriately enough, the Back Game. I consider the back game of sufficient importance to warrant a section of its own – so the next chapter has been set aside for this purpose. This chapter deals with the three forward games and also teaches you **position counting** – an essential skill for the truly ambitious student.

THE RUNNING GAME

Almost all games end up as running games *eventually*. A running game position is where there is no longer any "contact" between the two armies. The infighting is over, the opposing men have passed one another and it is now a mad dash for home with both players praying for double sixes!

The players *can* find themselves in a running game after only two throws each (**1**). This position was arrived at by both players rolling 6-5 *twice* and choosing to run both of their back men to the "12" points. This, thankfully, is a rare occurence. It makes for a very boring game because in this situation the person who throws highest, wins. Skill does not come into it.

Although the accumulated men on R12 and B12 have not yet passed one another, it is, nevertheless, a running game position, because there will now be little or no conflict between the opposing men.

Normally it is quite a few rolls later before a running game position emerges. Here is a typical example. Red has two men on B12. She threw 5-2 and played B12 to R11, B12 to R8 (**2**), opting to go for a running game because she had worked out that she was already in a better position than Black and that by running she would put herself two complete rolls ahead.

The eye can see that Red is ahead, but by two complete rolls? How did Red work that out? Simple. She counted her position.

1

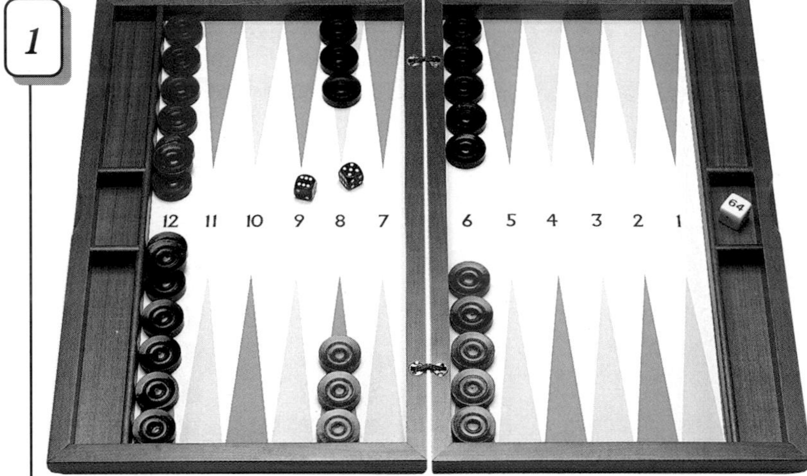

2

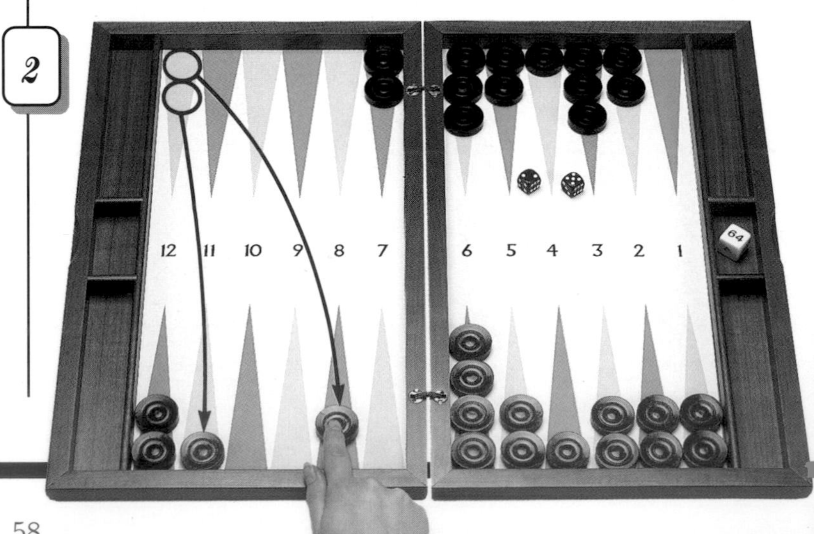

HOW TO COUNT YOUR POSITION

Here is a golden rule for you to remember: when you roll two dice *the average throw is 8*. Actually it is 8⅙, but, for our purposes, 8 will do fine. It makes our calculations so much simpler. Suppose you have a man on B1. You will have to throw a minimum of 24 pips on your dice to bear this man off (**3**). So, as you know that the average throw is 8, it is reasonable to assume that you will probably need three throws (24÷8=3) before you are able to bear off this man. This also applies to any man situated on these last eight points (B1 to B8) or on the bar.

Similarly any man situated on the middle eight points (R9 to B9) will need *two* throws to bear off and those on the first eight points (R1 to R8) only one throw (**4**).

Now look back at (**2**). If you now assess how many throws you need to bear off all your men, and then how many throws your opponent needs, and then subtract one total from another, you find out who is ahead and by how much. Red's tally is 16 – Black's tally is 17. Therefore, according to this simple system, Red is *one* throw ahead of Black.

But if we add up the number of *pips* that the respective opponents are away from bearing off we find that Red has a pip count of 69 (11 for the man on R11 + 8 for the man on R8 + 24 for the four men on R6 + 10 for the two men on R5 + 4 for the man on R4 + 6 for the two men on R3 + 4 for the two men on R2 = 2 for the two men on R1 = 69).

Assessing Black's position in the same way, we see that he ends up with a pip count of 85. The difference is 16 pips. Knowing that the average throw is 8, it becomes clear that Red is *two* throws ahead of Black (16÷8 = 2). This is the method of counting that most experts recommend and almost all first class players use.

I hate it and never use it!

I tried to use it in my early days but found that it was all too easy to make mistakes. It is difficult to add up two sets of large numbers, subtract one from the other, and finally divide by eight, quickly and accurately in your head under playing conditions.

There had to be another way. Well, necessity is the mother of invention they say. I needed an accurate but simple counting system, so I invented one. I pass it on to you in the hope you will use it well and often.

3

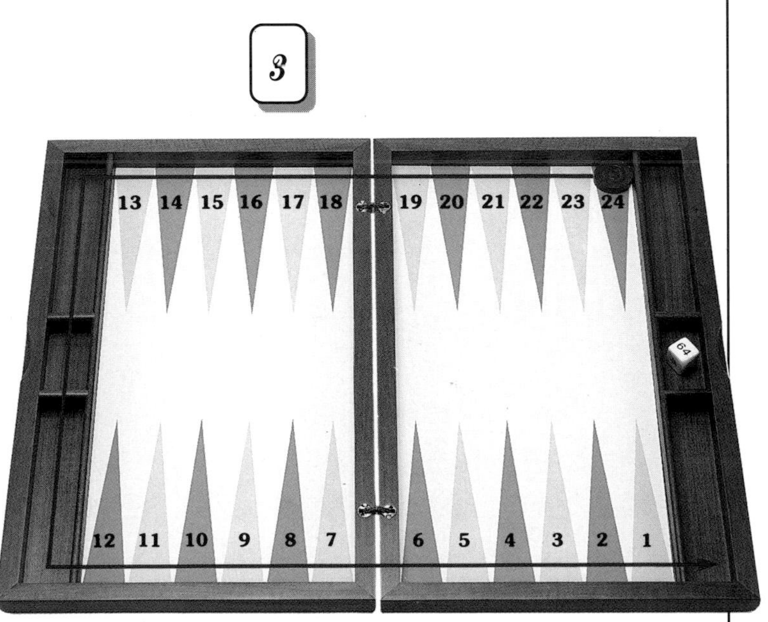

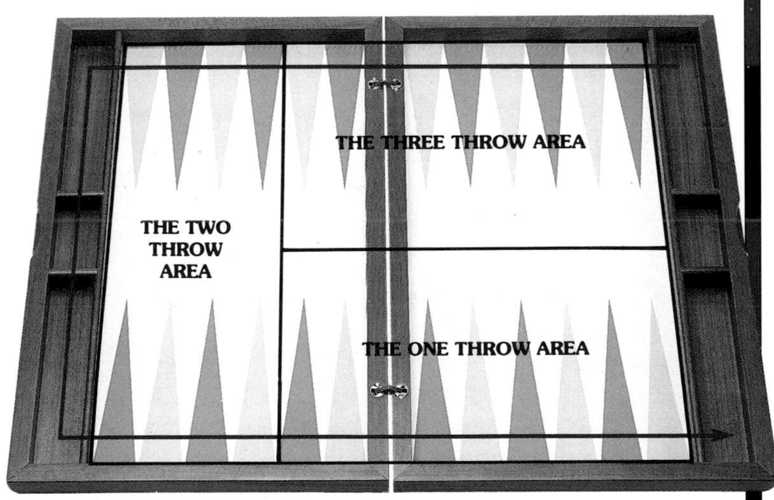

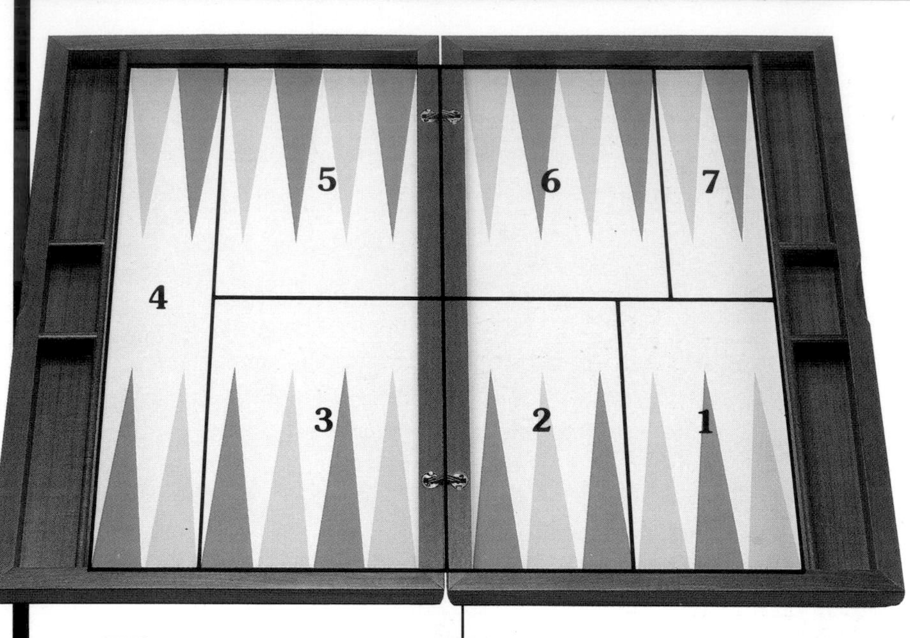

TREMAINE'S POSITION COUNT

This is what you do. Mentally divide the board into *seven* sections as illustrated (**5**). Now any of your men falling into these sections are designated the appropriate number. Men on the Bar also count seven. Look at illustration (**6**). It shows the red men only from (**2**) superimposed on our counting grid. Now our count is 27 (4+3+14+6).

Now take a look at Black (**7**). Black's count is 31 (8+6+12+5). The difference is 4. Four what? *Four dice*. Now, if you *divide by two* you will know how many rolls you are ahead. O.K.? Remember that the difference between the counts must be *divided by two* to discover how many rolls ahead the leader is.

5

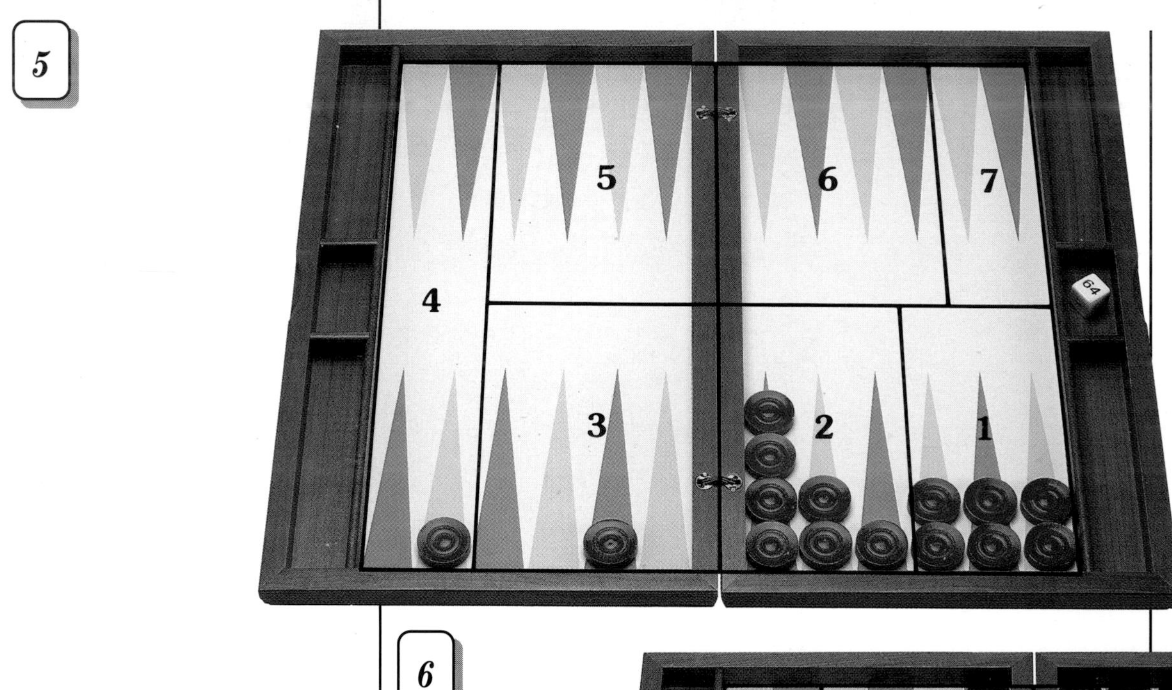

6

7

Here is another example (**8**). Red's count is 38, Black's is 41. The difference is 3, therefore Red is 1½ throws ahead of Black.

Using the old style traditional method of counting the pips, Red's count is 109, Black's is 118, for a difference of 9 pips. As the average throw is 8, Red can still be said to be one and a half throws ahead of Black. Our much simpler system has arrived at the same conclusion but in a fraction of the time and with a lot less chance of miscalculating.

TO RUN OR NOT TO RUN

If you have established an advantage over your opponent early in the game by rolling a couple of favourable rolls and getting your back men free of his inner table, you should opt for a running game.

You should not hit his blots unnecessarily. Bring your men round and into your own inner table as quickly and as safely as possible. Do not take risks. Always play the "percentage" move – the one that leaves any blot that you have left, or may have to leave, least vulnerable.

Then, once any contact between the opposing men has ceased, you should be in good shape to win. Look at (**9**) and do a position count. Red scores 41 and Black scores 48. Difference = 7. Therefore Red is already 3½ rolls (7 dice) ahead of Black, plus the fact that it is Red's roll.

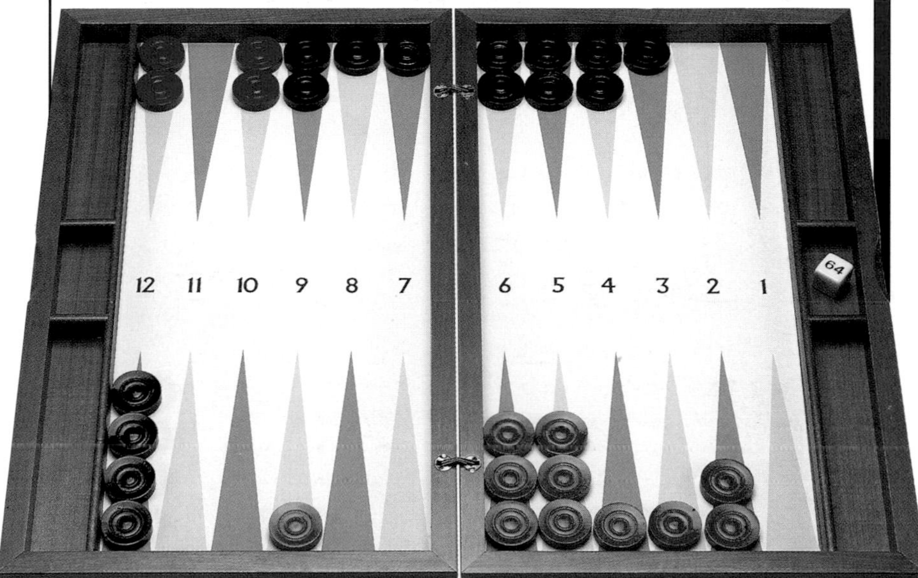

8

9

Red rolls 2-2. Here is an example of not hitting Black's blots unnecessarily. Red could play both men from B12 to R9 making the point and sending Black to the bar. Do you see how foolish this play would be? Black would still be a thorn in Red's side because he has to re-enter in Red's inner table. No, the proper move is B12 to R11 (two men) and R10 to R6 (**10**). Contact is virtually over and in a running game you are streets ahead and should offer the doubling cube.

Keep ever watchful for the right moment to run. It is not always obvious. If you *sense* that a running game is imminent, quickly do a position count. Do not let your opponent rush you into a miscalculation. Take it easy. It takes but a few seconds anyway.

If your calculations tell you that you are ahead and that you should run, then – get going! Do not hang around on the offchance of winning a gammon or backgammon.

Be watchful, also, of your opponent's intention to run – or of any favourable roll that he *may* throw that would enable him to make a run for it, thus upsetting your apple cart. Look at (**11**). Red rolls 2-1 and plays B9 to B12 (**12**)!

Can you see why Red moved in this manner? Can you see why it is the only correct move for her to make on the whole board? Why is it *essential* that she plays B9 to B12?

10

The answer is that if, on his next roll, Black were to roll 6-6 then Red could kiss the game goodbye. Red guards against the possibility of Black making this golden roll by moving to B12, placing herself in the direct line of fire.

Black would *have* to hit this man – sending it to the bar – from where Red would get a shot at Black's blots on B4 and B5, thus turning the tables once more if she should hit one of them.

This then, is the running game.

11

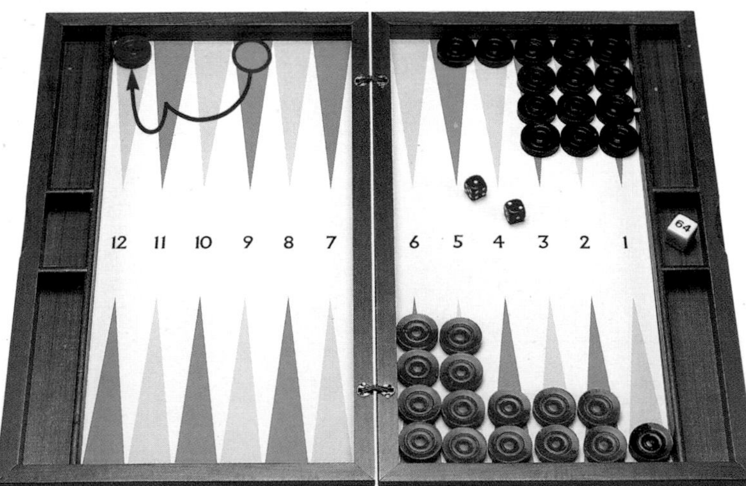

12

THE BLOCKING GAME

The blocking game, as its name implies, is played by blocking the escape of your opponent's back men by establishing a side prime – six blocking points in a row.

If your opening two or three rolls successfully establish your "5" and bar points, then a blocking game is probably for you. In establishing your side prime you should take care that your own back men are not too hemmed in. This may cause you to break your prime, ruining your blocking points – so be warned.

Chapter Six dealt at some length with primes and how to play them, so little more need be said here. Just refer back to that chapter and make sure that you fully understand every point.

THE SHUTOUT GAME

The shutout game is very lethal and, if you are on the wrong end of it, can be most painful!

Look at illustration (**13**). Red rolls 6-3 and plays R9 to R3 and R6 to R3, sending one of Black's blots to the bar (**14**).

13

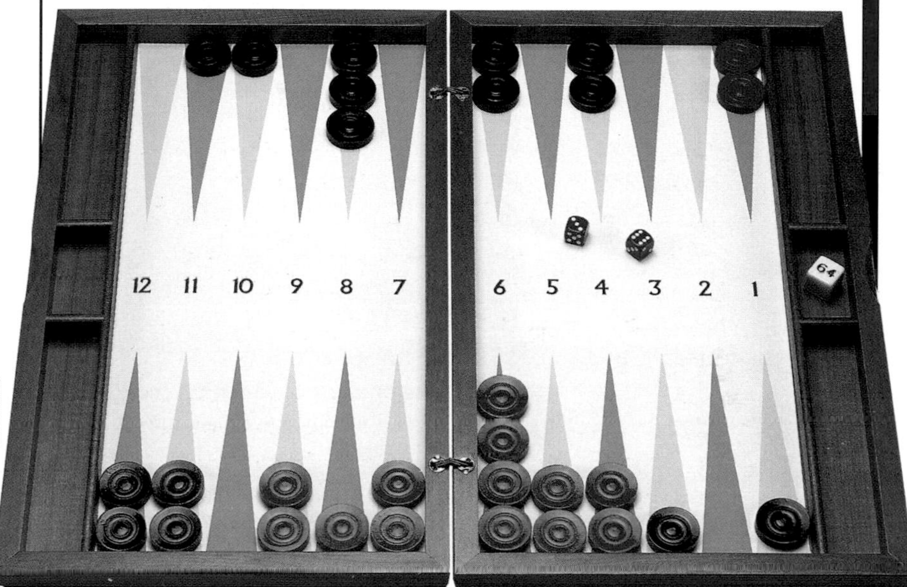

14

Black rolls 6-4 and fails to enter. Red now rolls 6-5 and hits the other Black blot. She plays R7 to R1 and R6 to R1 (**15**). She has closed off *five points* in her inner table.

Black rolls 5-1 and again fails to enter. Red rolls 6-5 again. R8 to R2 and R7 to R2 (**16**). The shutout is complete. Black has got real problems now. He cannot re-enter his men from the bar so it is pointless for him to even roll the dice!

Now, barring atrocious luck, Red will be able to get her back men moving and safely home without having to open up the shutout. At the same time Red *should* be able to pick up at least one more of Black's men (he still has blots at B10 and B11). This would give Black three men shutout on the bar and Red could confidently expect to win a gammon, while a backgammon is more than possible.

Red's odd man at R9 is important and should be played correctly. This is your safety valve in case either of your back men becomes bogged down and immobile. Therefore your R9 man must not be moved until all contact between Black's pieces and your two back men is over.

Once all your men are safely home, your bearing off begins. Make sure that you start opening up the shutout from your six point. When Black re-enters, you want him past you if possible. To this end, use small numbers to advance your men from the higher to the lower points in your inner table. This ensures that he will have to re-enter behind you. You are so far ahead that you can afford to take your time!

IN CONCLUSION

So, to sum up the shutout game, consider these points:

- If your opponent splits his back men and you have three or four points already made into a semi-prime, plus maybe a few extra builders, you could well be in a position to attempt a shutout.
- Always leave a safety valve man to facilitate the escape of your back men.
- Always advance your men as far as possible onto your lower points as you bear off.
- Remember that the greater the number of blots Black has on the bar, the longer he is likely to remain there and, therefore, the greater the chance of him hitting a blot should you have to leave him one during the course of bearing off. So do not be greedy – three is ample. If you get the chance to hit a fourth, it is generally good policy to avoid the temptation.

Winning with a shutout is a fantastic feeling! Your opponent is helpless and cannot move. You just have to twist the knife! I told you that this was a sadistic game. Kicking a man when he is down is quite legitimate when you play backgammon.

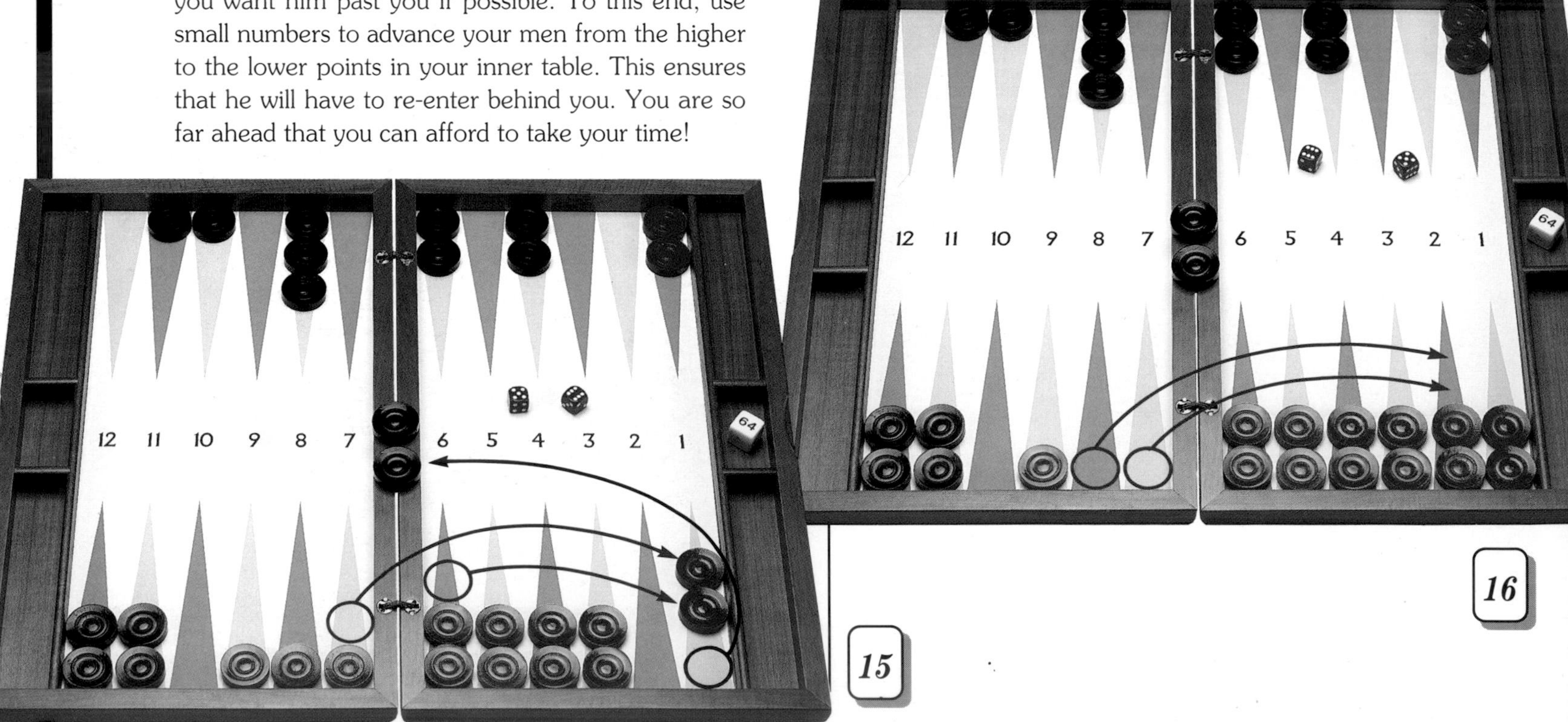

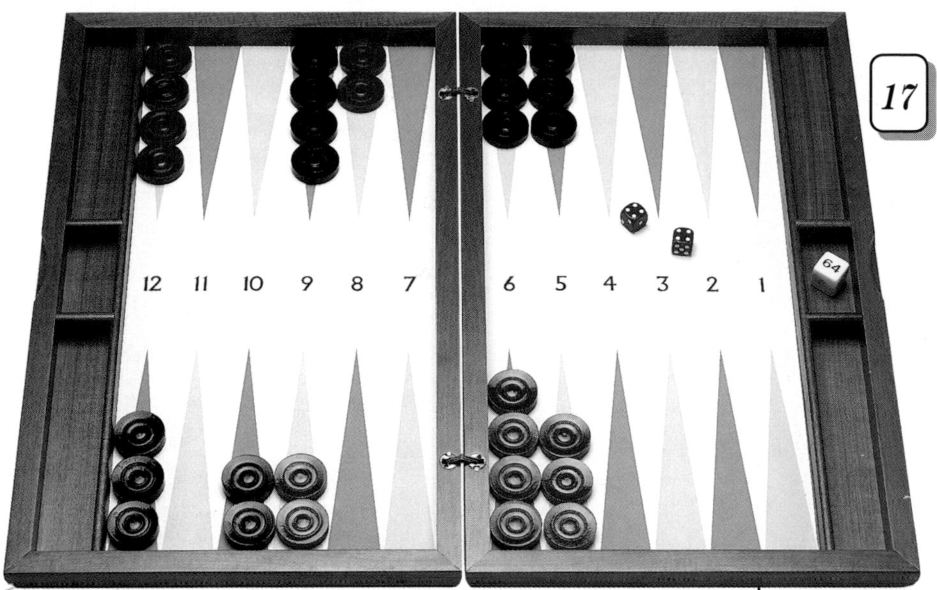

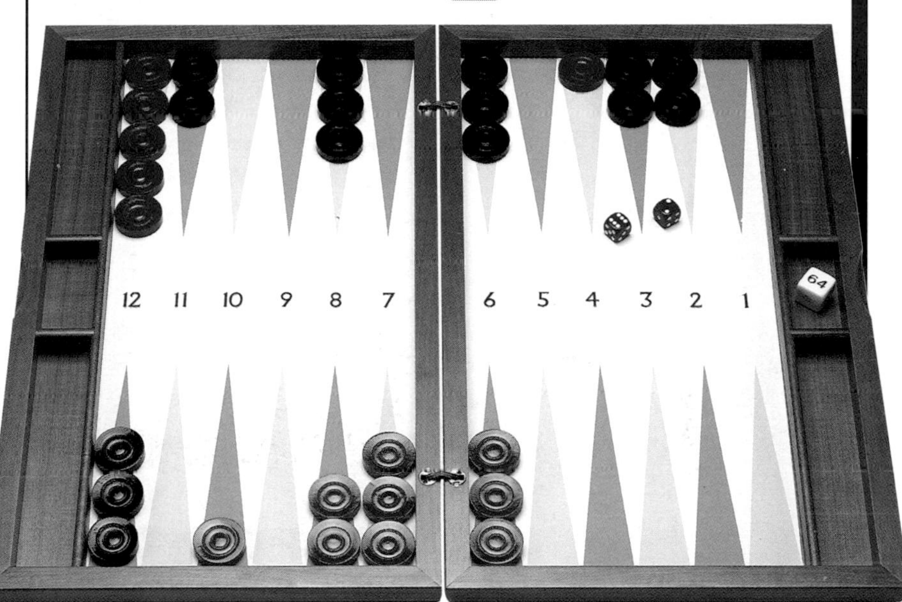

QUIZ QUESTIONS

It is problem time again. Please try them. They *will* improve your game. As before, answers are found on page 121. In this position (**17**) you roll 4-4. What play is best and why?

Now consider picture (**18**). The roll is 6-2. How should you play it and why?

It is Red's roll (**19**). Make a position count. Who is ahead and by how many throws?

WHAT IS A BACK GAME?

Picture a player attempting to get his men around the board and borne off *before* his opponent, yet making moves that are guaranteed to slow himself down; leaving intentional blots and praying that they will be hit. It is a bit like playing backgammon in reverse – backwards backgammon. That is the back game! Show me a man who plays a back game through *choice* and I will show you a masochist! No – today's golden rule is to avoid becoming involved in a back game. Avoid it like the plague. Your chances of pulling it off successfully are less than even – most unattractive odds. The only time to play a back game is when you have no choice – no other course of action being left open to you.

WHEN YOU HAVE NO CHOICE

Because it is harder to play than the three forward style games and because its timing is so critical, the back game is very often overlooked by students of backgammon who neglect their studies in this direction. I must state, quite categorically, that mastering the techniques of the back game is a prerequisite if you are to become a good backgammon player.

You only find yourself having to play one when your back is against the wall and it is essential therefore that you learn the commando tactics, the street-fighting, the sniping, that makes the back game such a fascinating branch of the game.

You begin to play a back game when, during the early stages of the game, a couple of your blots are hit and you suddenly find that you have *four* back men in Black's inner table instead of your original two. At the same time Black manages to get his own back men to safety.

You are now so far behind in a forward style game that the only way for you to win is to wait for Black to bring his men round and hope that in so doing he will leave a blot for you to hit. While you are waiting for this to happen, slowly, steadily you build up blocking points in your inner table. First a semi-prime . . . then a prime . . . even a shutout . . . waiting for a chance to hit a blot. Of course there is no guarantee that your chance will come. Neither is it certain that you will be able to hit the blot even if it is offered to you.

Let us run through a game together. I am sure that this will be the quickest way for you to grasp the essentials of a back game. I shall discuss each move as we go and at the end of the game I shall try to answer any unanswered questions that you may have. Get your board out . . . let's go!

ANOTHER DEMONSTRATION GAME

Black wins the opening roll and leads off with 6-1. She plays R12 to B7, B8 to B7. Red rolls 3-2 and plays B12 to R11, B12 to R10. Black 6-4. She hits one of Red's blots with R1 to R11. Red 3-1. Time to re-enter from the bar. Bar to B3, R6 to R5. Black again rolls 6-4 and plays R1 to R5 (hitting the blot), and then moves R5 to R11. Red rolls 3-1 and plays, bar to B3 and R6 to R5.

The board now looks like this (**1**). A position count shows Red *six* throws behind already! However, those two points that Red has in Black's inner table will prove invaluable if she can possibly hold on to them. Black rolls 5-5 and plays R11 to B9 (two men), R12 to B8 (two men) (**2**).

Now Red throws 6-1. She plays B12 to R7, R6 to R5 (**3**). Note that she chooses to make her five point before her bar point. She figures that this play is fractionally slower and, of course, the "5" point is more valuable anyway.

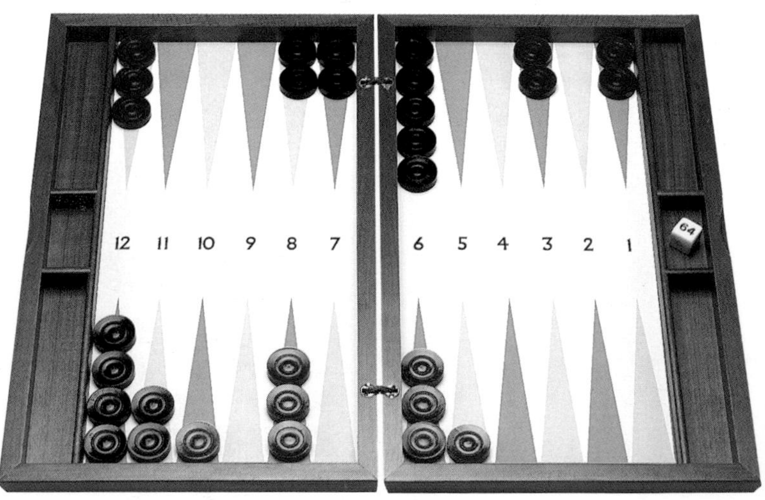

1

BLACK 5-5

RED 6-1

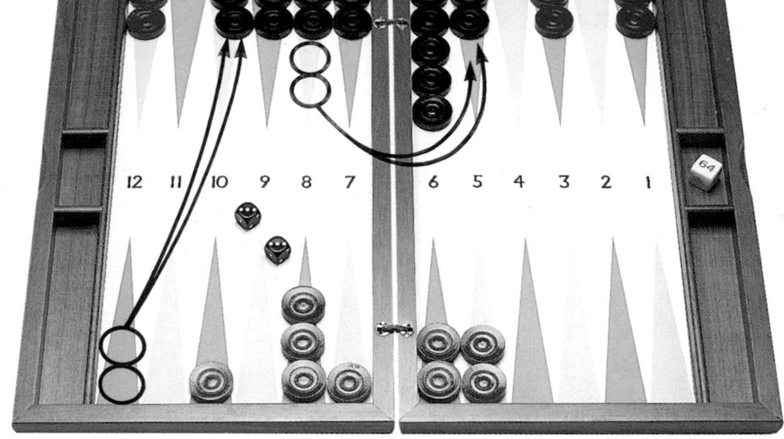

4

BLACK 3-3

Black rolls 3-3. She cannot miss today can she! The play is R12 to B10 (two men) and B8 to B5 (two men) (**4**). She makes a very tidy prime but must be anticipating trouble as she moves her men in. She will have to break up that prime very soon, maybe even next roll. Red's four back men are just waiting to pick up any stragglers.

Red's "timing" is excellent. Her prime is beginning to take shape, yet she is not too far advanced so she can leave her back men intact for a few throws yet. Red rolls 4-3. She plays R7 to R4, R8 to R4 (**5**) and makes her "4" point.

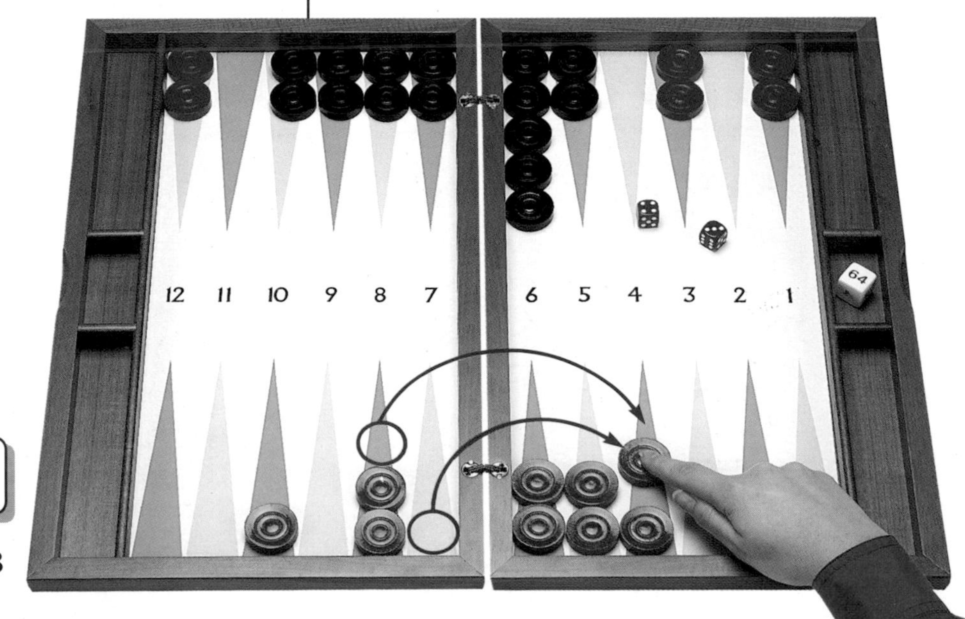

5

RED 4-3

Black rolls 6-2. A safe throw. She plays B10 to B4, B6 to B4 moving her prime further in (**6**).

Red rolls now. 3-1. The move is R10 to R7, R8 to R7 (**7**). This creates a semi-prime – four blocking points in a row. The only thing missing at the moment is something to block!

Black rolls 6-6 and plays B8 to B2 (two men) and B10 to B4 (**8**). She has no option. The moves are the only ones available to her and she can only use three of the "sixes". Note how Red's men on B1 and B3 are beginning to make things uncomfortable for Black.

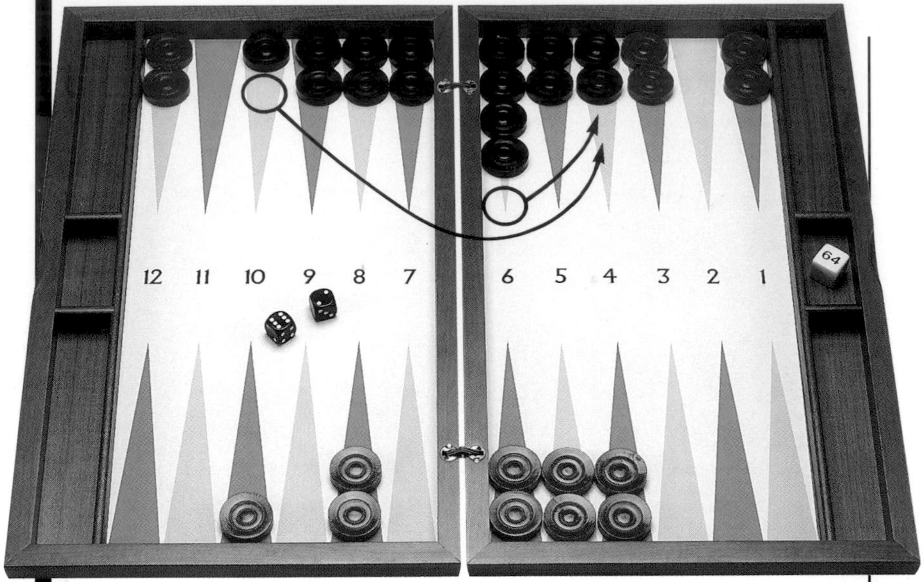

6 **BLACK 6-2**

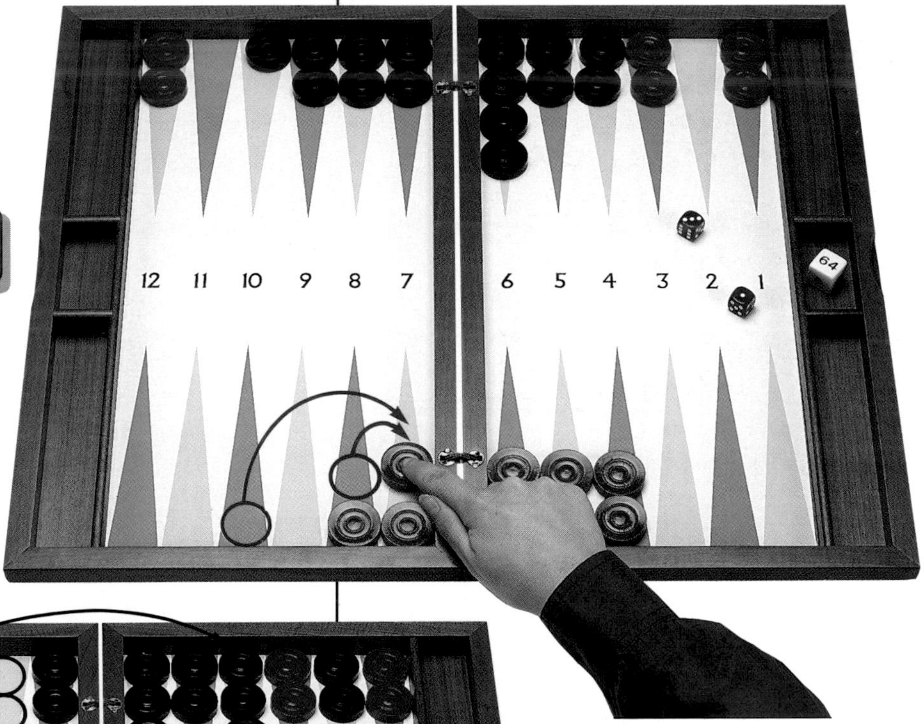

7 **RED 3-1**

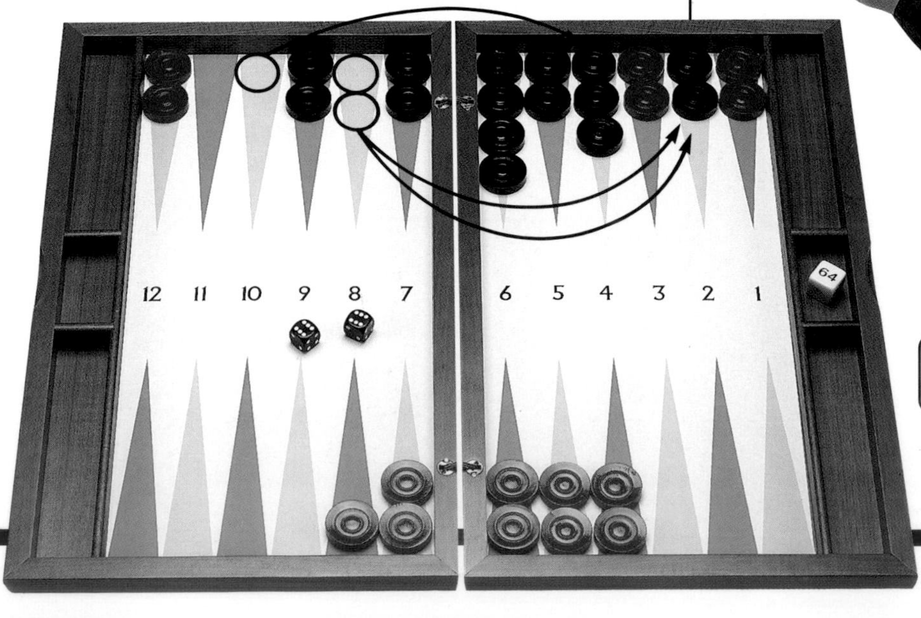

8 **BLACK 6-6**

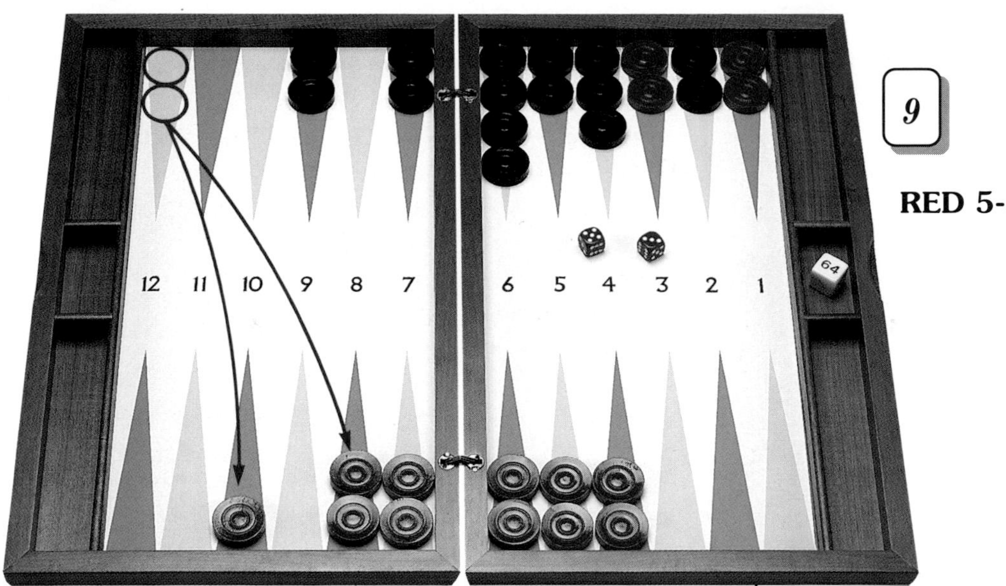

9

RED 5-3

10

BLACK 6-5

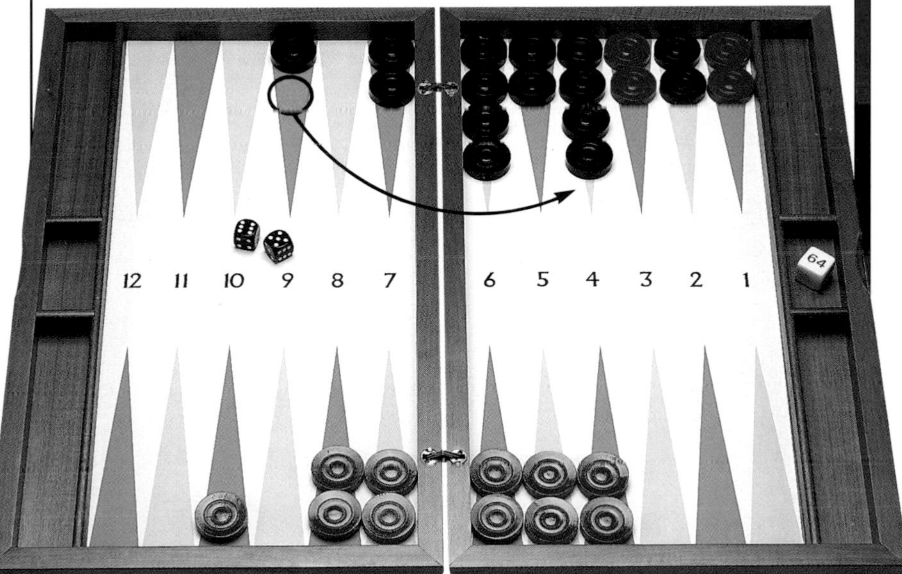

Red rolls 5-3 and continues to build her fortress B12 to R8, B12 to R10 (**9**). That makes five points in a row now. A blot, a blot, my Kingdom for a blot!

Black rolls 6-5. Now she has got problems. She has no legal "6" move and she *must* make a five move. She cannot make it from B6, so it must come from B7 or B9. Which would you choose? Both leave blots. Black chose B9 to B4 (**10**) leaving the blot at B9 because Red can only hit it in 13 ways, whereas if she had left the blot at B7 it would be vulnerable in 20 ways. Quite a difference.

Red misses! She rolls 5-2 and plays R10 to R3 (**11**).

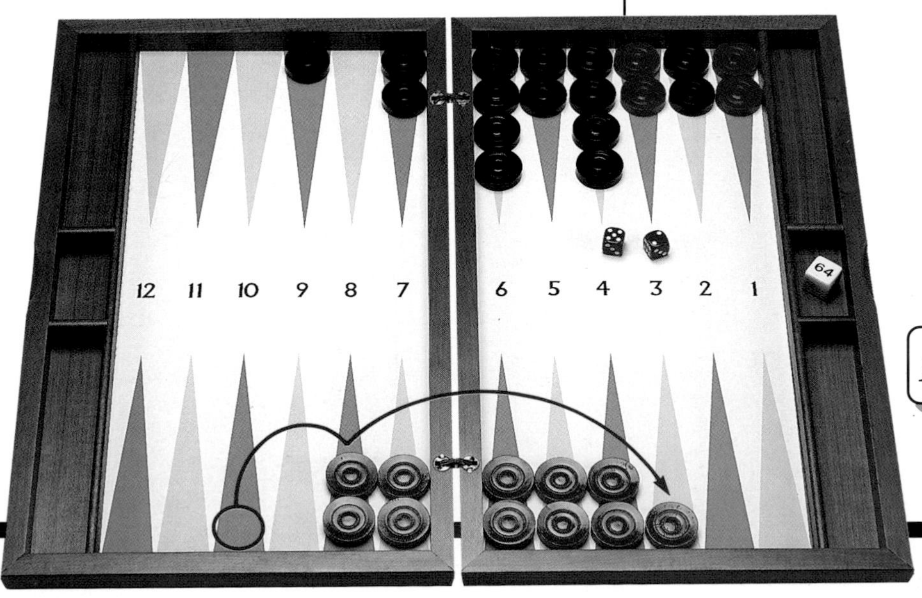

11

RED 5-2

Black now rolls 5-2, bringing her vulnerable blot to safety with B9 to B2. All is tidy once again (**12**).

Red's timing is still good. With four men still in her outer table she will not have to shift her back men on B1 and B3 for a little while yet. Or will she? Red rolls 5-5. She plays R8 to R3 (two men) and R7 to R2 (two men) (**13**). Although Red has secured her own "2" and "3" points she would really have preferred not to have advanced so many men so quickly.

Black rolls 5-4. The moves again are the only ones possible. B7 to B2, B6 to B2 (**14**). It should now be clearer to you how important those two points in Black's inner table are to Red. Black has no option but to leave a blot on R7.

12 **BLACK 5-2**

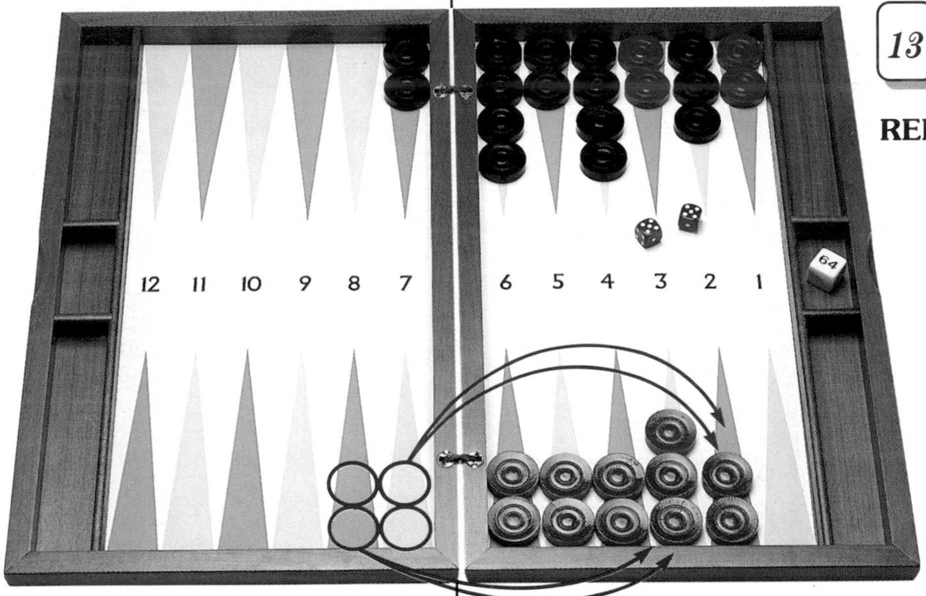

13 **RED 5-5**

14 **BLACK 5-4**

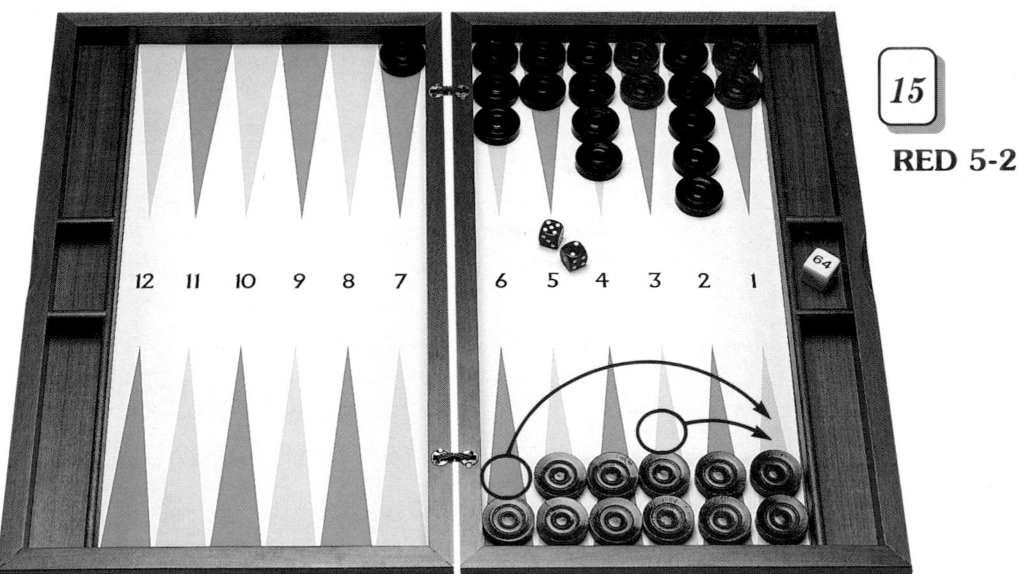

15

RED 5-2

16

BLACK 4-2

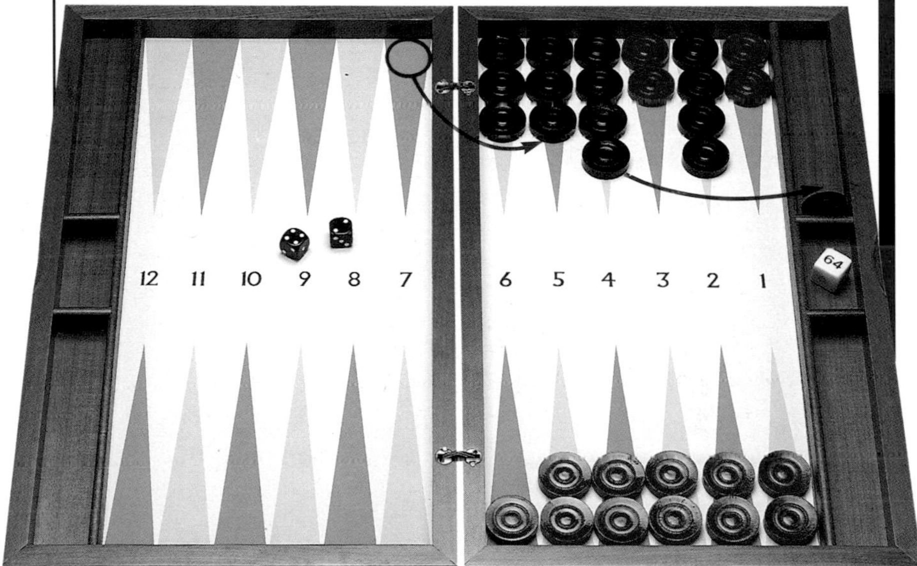

Red misses. She rolls 5-2 and plays R6 to R1, R3 to R1 (**15**). She chooses to break her R6 point rather than split her back men.

Black rolls 4-2. She plays B7 to B5 and bears off one man from B4 (**16**). She tidies up some loose ends and bears off her first man.

Red has now got what we call a timing problem – the downfall of most back games. It is imperative that Black leaves her another blot at once. Failing this she must roll *low* numbers, so that she can move in her inner table while keeping her back men in position. One of her prayers is answered. Red rolls 3-2 so plays R6 to R1 (**17**). A good roll for Red as it enables her to hold her position.

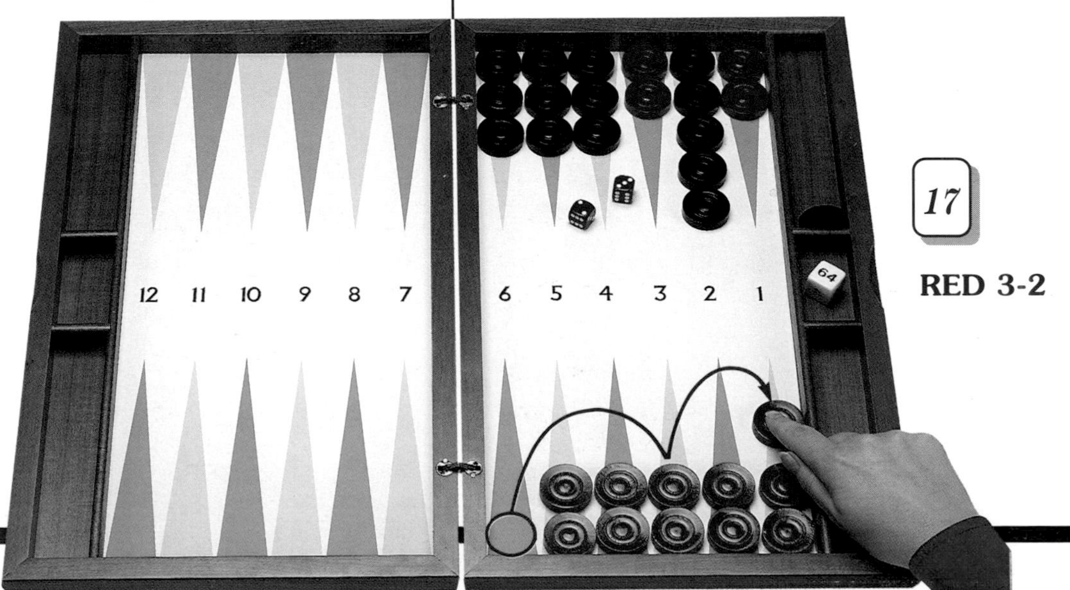

17

RED 3-2

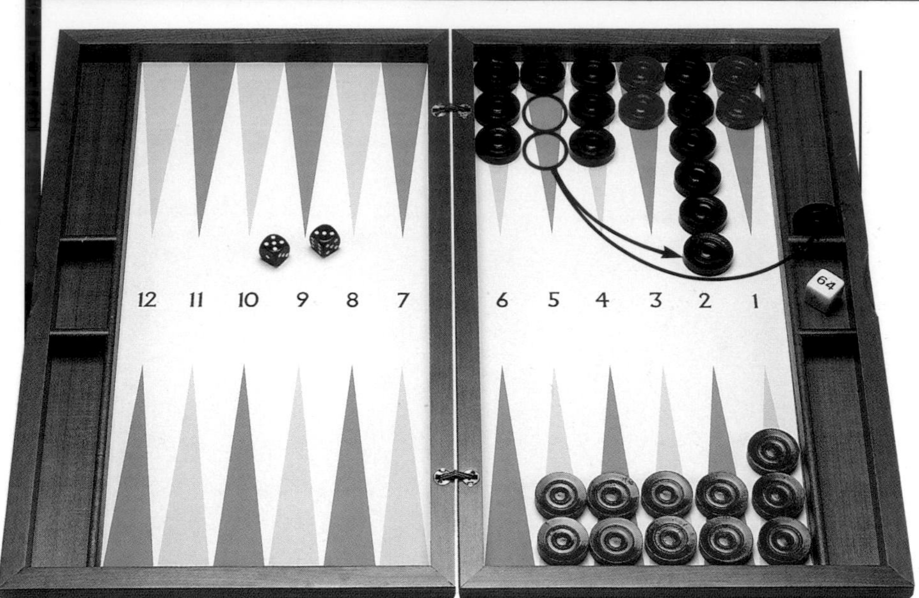

18 **BLACK 5-3**

Black rolls 5-3 and Red's second prayer is answered! Black has to bear off at B5 and has to move B5 to B2 because she does not control her B3 point (**18**).

This means leaving a blot at B5 giving Red another chance, which she takes. She rolls 6-2. B3 to B5 and B3 to B9 (**19**). She hits the blot, sending Black to the bar. Red's policy has been rewarded.

Black throws 6-2. Bar to R6 and R6 to R8 (**20**). The odds were 25/11 against Black re-entering first time. However, she beats the odds this time, duly enters at the R6 point and continues on to R8.

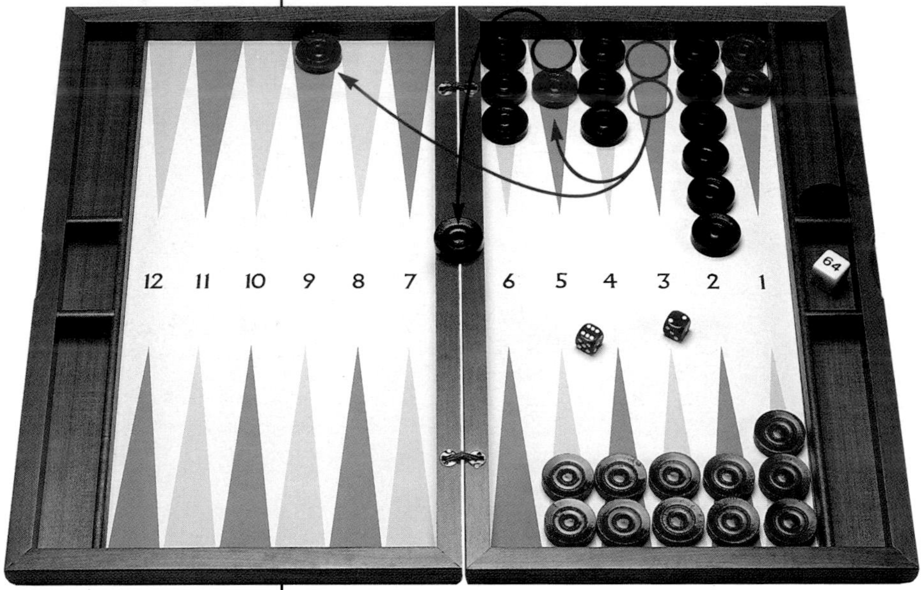

19 **RED 6-2**

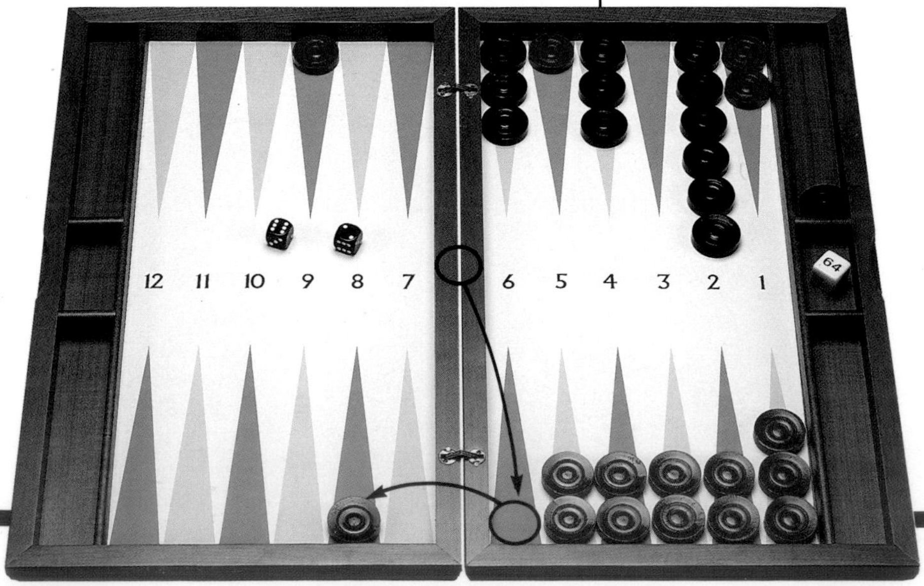

20 **BLACK 6-2**

Now watch Red spread out her remaining pieces like a net. It is essential that she hits Black again if she is to stand any chance of winning. Red rolls 6-4. B1 to B7, B1 to B5 (**21**). With this move Red blocks many rolls that Black might throw. 6-6, for example, brings Black to a halt at B11! 5-5 gives Black a multitude of problems. 4-4 is blocked and cannot be used to full advantage . . . and so on. Red knows that the *average* roll is 8 and that after Black's next roll her blot, now on R8, will in all probability be moved to B9 or B10. If Black throws any 6 she will have to move it to B11 whether she wants to or not. So Red, on B5, B7 and B9 is nicely poised for attack. Red is not concerned about being hit herself. Black has already borne off two men and a position count shows her seven throws ahead – so without a doubt Red has lost this game *unless she can hit Black again*. She therefore throws herself into the attack.

Black rolls 6-2 and moves R8 to B9 (**22**). She throws the "average" roll and hits Red's blot. Back to the bar for Red. Red rolls 6-2 and fails to enter. Black rolls 6-3 and plays B9 to B6 and B6 off (**23**).

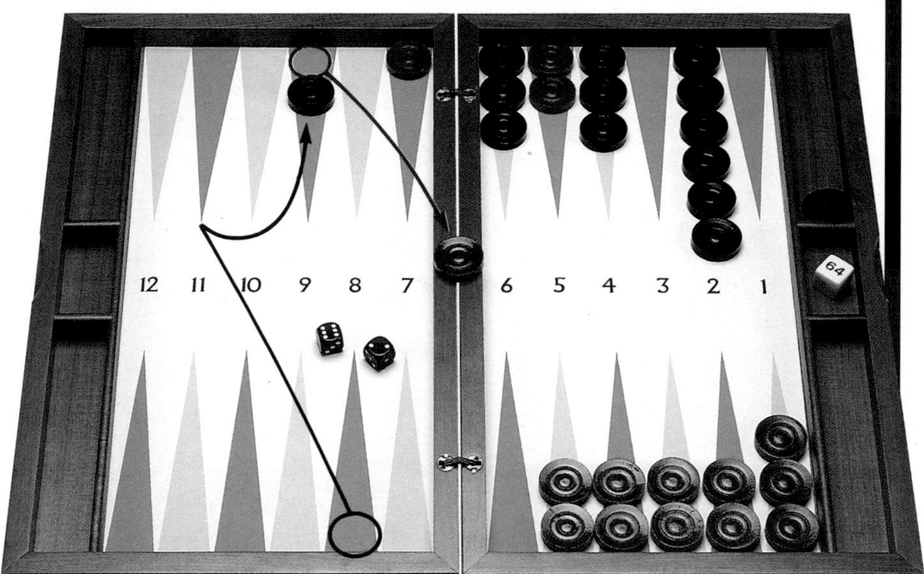

22 **BLACK 6-2**

21 **RED 6-4**

23 **BLACK 6-3**

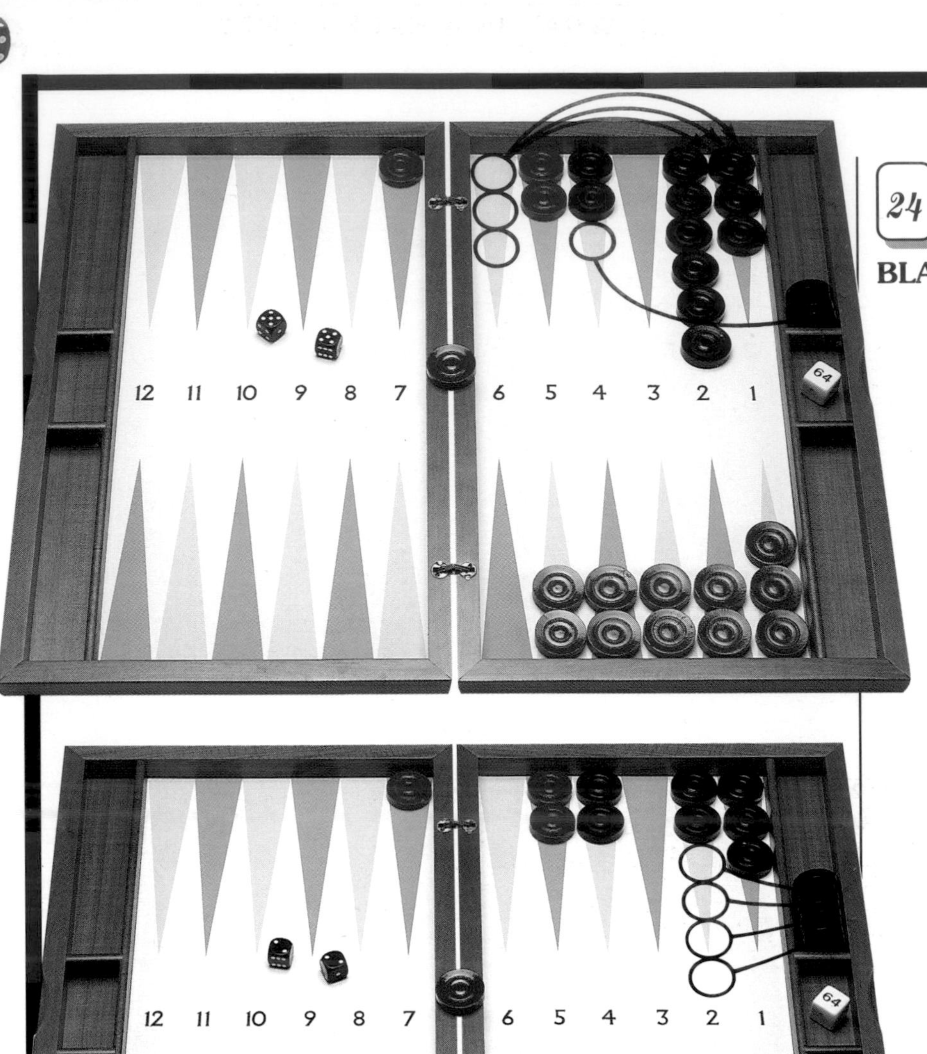

24

BLACK 5-5

Black can breathe again! Red rolls 4-2 and again fails to re-enter. Black rolls 5-5. The move is compulsory. Three men B6-B1 and bear off one man at B4 (**24**). Red rolls 2-1. Still she cannot enter but this time she does not mind. She *must* hit a blot from the bar. A seemingly impossible task.

Black's throw again. This time it is 2-2. Her move is to bear off four men from her two point (**25**). She seems to smell a backgammon here and goes all out for it. However, several rolls could now get her into trouble should Red once again fail to re-enter or enter on B3. She could and, maybe she should, have played safe and moved B4-B2 (two men), two men off at B2, for a virtually certain gammon.

True to form Red again fails to enter by rolling 4-1. Black now rolls 6-1. Horror of horrors! One man is borne off at B4 for the six (compulsory) and she moves B4-B3 to shorten Red's odds of hitting her. The board now looks like this (**26**). Black has had to leave a blot at the eleventh hour.

25

BLACK 2-2

26

BLACK 6-1

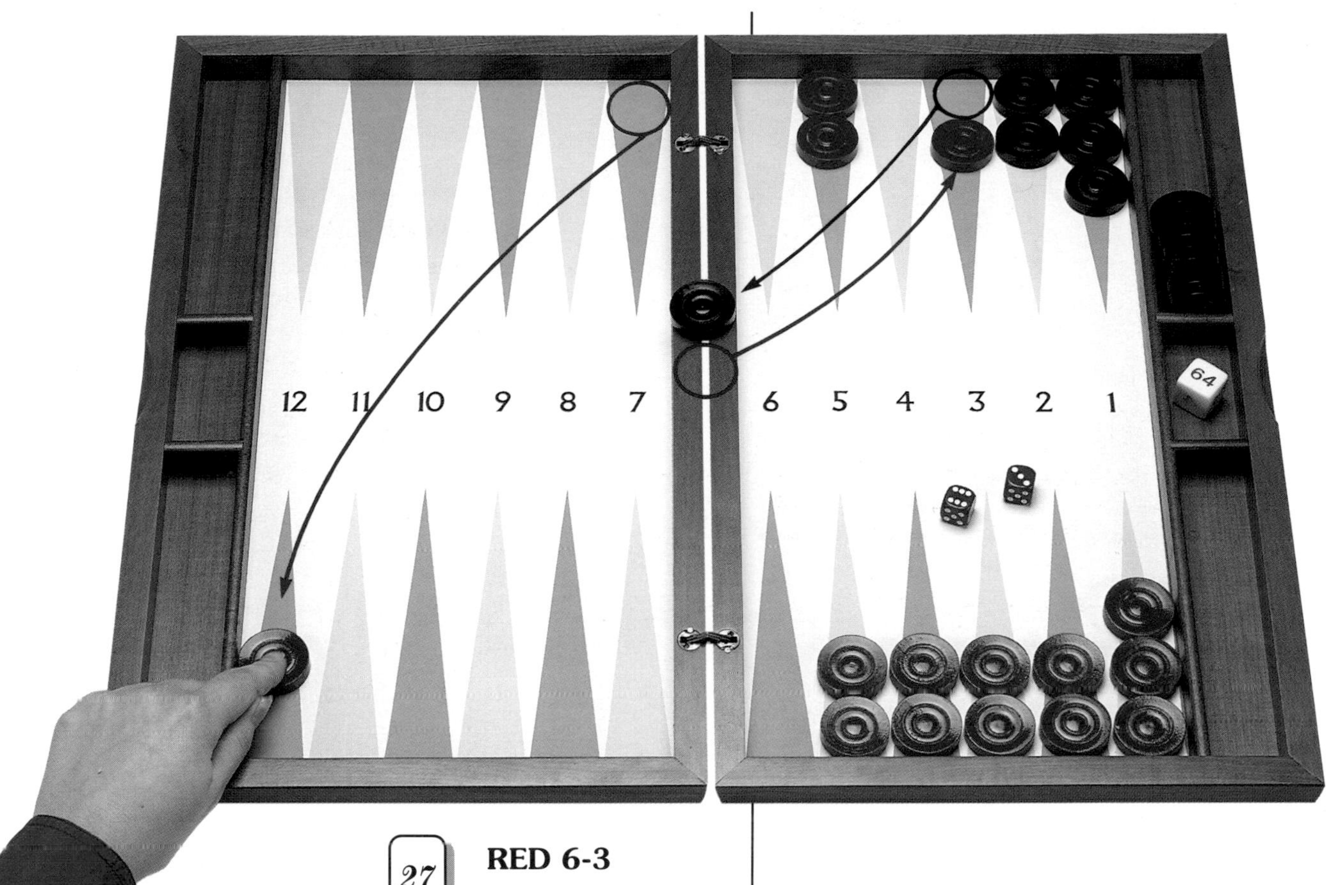

27 **RED 6-3**

28 **RED 6-6**

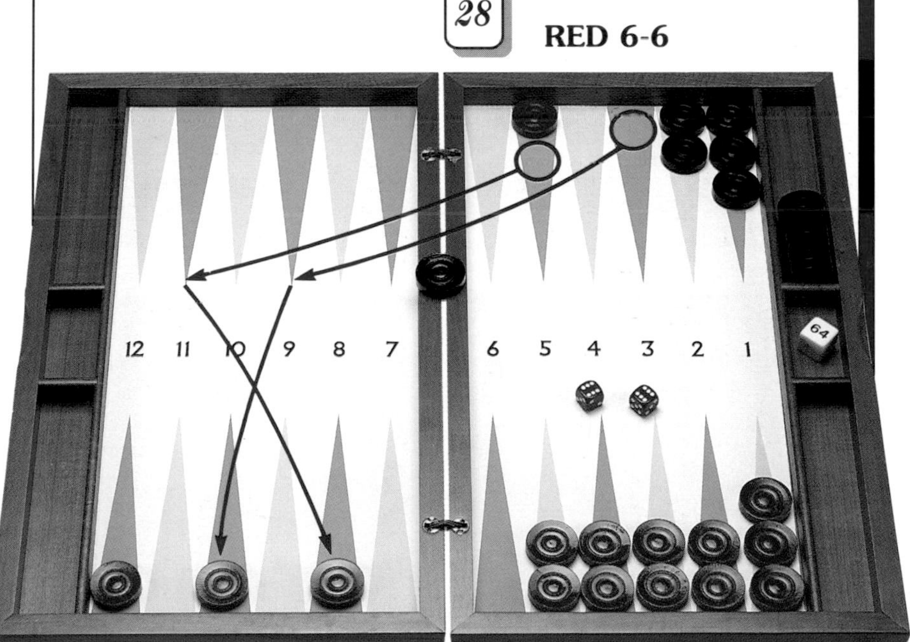

Red rolls 6-3. Bar to B3, B7-R12 (**27**). Red hits the blot (of course!) and moves B7-R12. On B7 or R12 the blot can only be hit with a 6-6 so Red chooses to advance the piece to a position where it is directly in range of her R6 point which she would dearly love to close.

Black, now on the bar, rolls 5-1 and cannot re-enter. Red rolls 6-6. She plays B3-R10, and one man B5-R8 (**28**). Very well played. Red has now given herself many combinations that will immediately close off the R6 point. By spreading her men in this way Red forces Black to hit her, should she re-enter next roll, with rolls of 6-2, 6-4 and 6-6, thus giving Red another back man to hit with as Black comes round again.

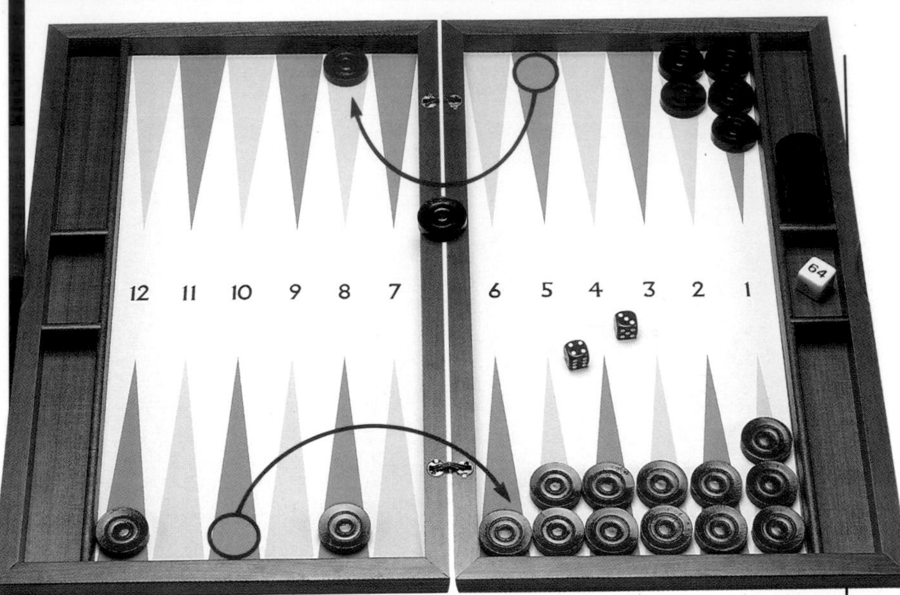

29 **RED 4-3**

Black fails to re-enter with a throw of 4-1. Red rolls 4-3. The play is R10-R6, B5-B8 (**29**). She uses the four to start establishing her six point, gambling that Black will not throw a six next time. Now, any six or any two will close the point next roll: that is 24 rolls for, to 12 rolls against, making Red a 2/1 favourite to close the point if Black does not roll that six. And, if Black *does* roll the six and send her to the bar, what then? Well, Red just re-enters in Black's naked inner table and awaits a chance to hit Black again as she comes round.

Black rolls 2-1 and stays on the bar. Red rolls 6-2! She promptly plays R12-R6, R8-R6 (**30**). Red has now completed a shutout but will still need to throw some great dice to win. Black has already borne off *nine* men. In closing her six point Red also brought her other man to R6 as well. Her one remaining back man, now on B8, will be brought round and an attempt will be made by Red to bring it to R6 or R5 so that it may be borne off directly from that point.

30 **RED 6-2**

This is no time for fancy calculations. Red must now bear off as many pieces as she can, as quickly as she can, in order to make up the deficit.

Red rolls 3-2. She moves B8-R12 (**31**).

31 **RED 3-2**

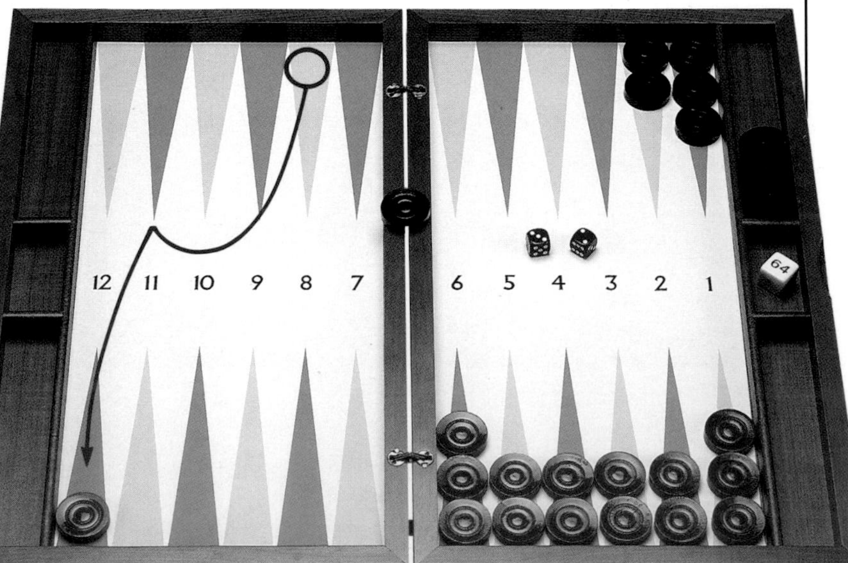

No comment needed. Next roll for Red is 6-1. Nice! She plays R12-R6, R1 off (**32**).

Black just has to sit on her hands for the time being. There is no way in for her man on the bar.

Red's next roll is truly fortuitous. 6-6. She just bears off four men from R6 (**33**). Red feels a lot better because Black is now only *certain* to win if she rolls 6-6 also. The odds are 35/1 that she will not. And she does not! It is 5-4 for Black. No move.

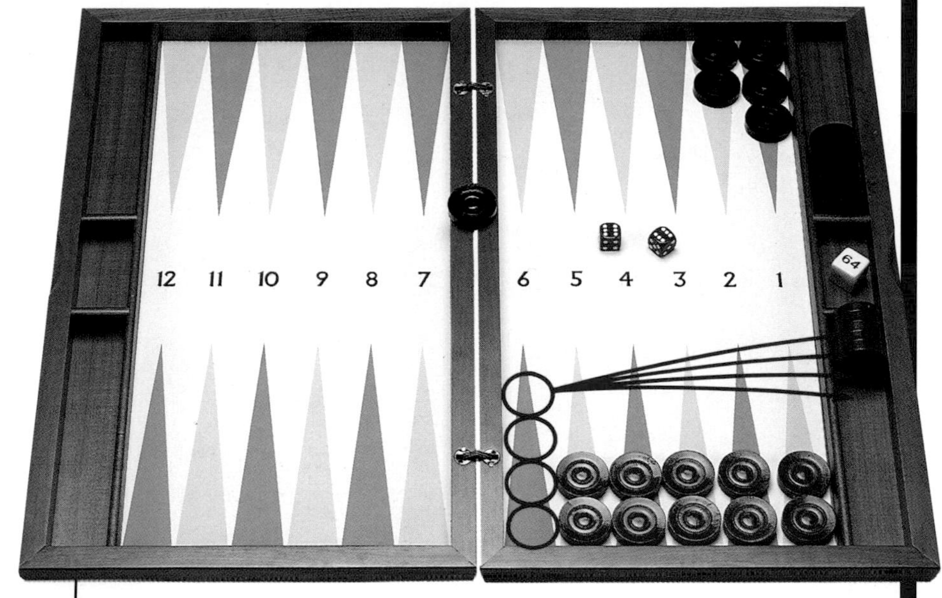

33 **RED 6-6**

32 **RED 6-1**

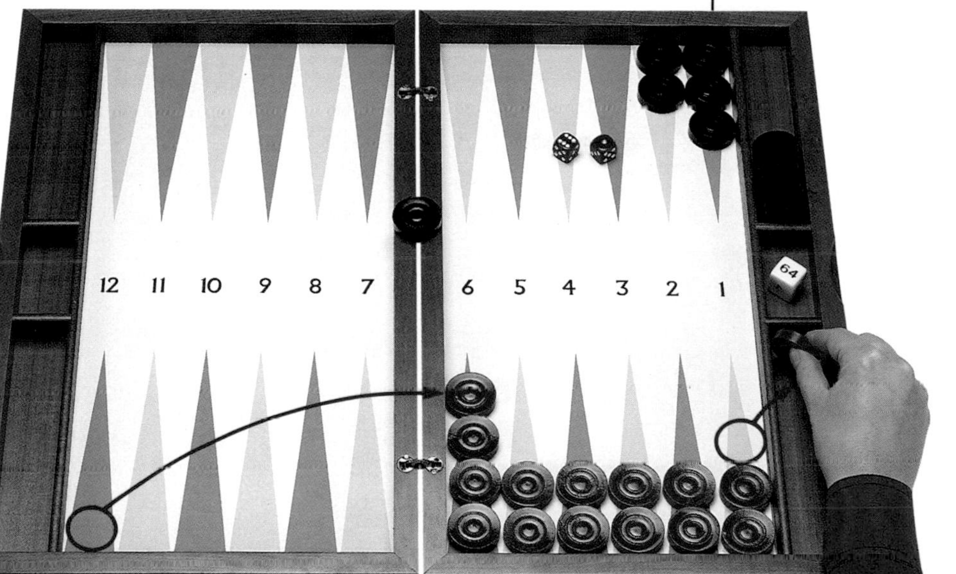

Red rolls 5-4 also. She bears off at R5, and moves R5 to R1 for the four (**34**). Black now has two points open to her and can still most probably win with a 6-6 or 5-5 roll, but the odds are against her. She proves the odds to be correct. She rolls 4-4 and, once again has entry failure. She must hit Red or get back into the game soon or her goose will be well and truly cooked! You can almost hear her praying that Red does not roll a double this time!

34 **RED 5-4**

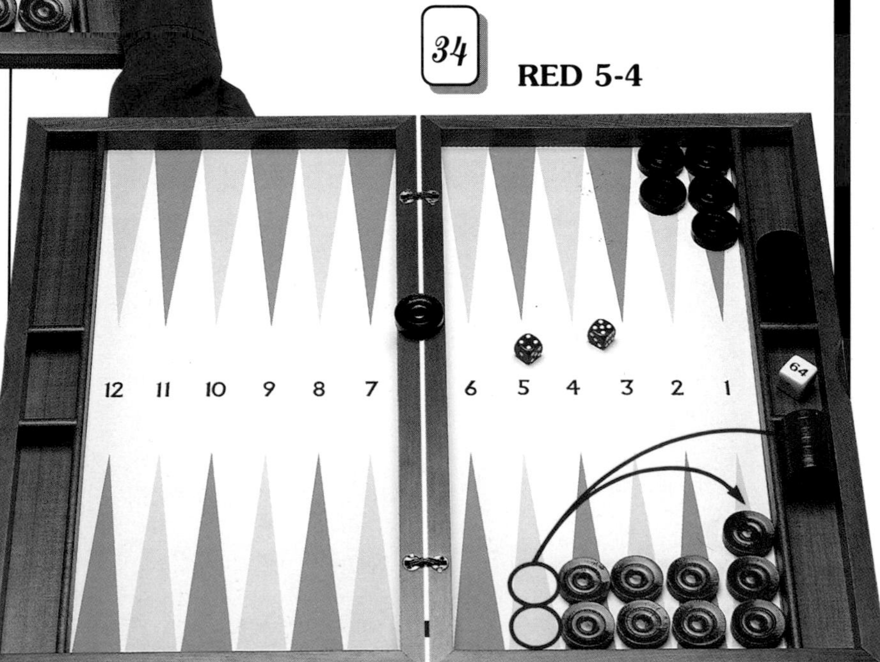

But Red does. She rolls 3-3. Her move is R4 to R1 (two men) and R3 off (two men) (**35**) . . . an automatic choice. Black rolls 6-6. The compulsory move is Bar to R6 and R6 to B1 (**36**).

Fantastic! What a time to roll double six! It puts Black right back in the race again. Red's face has gone quite pale and she needs to steady her nerves for her next roll! Red rolls 3-2 and bears off two men from R2 (**37**).

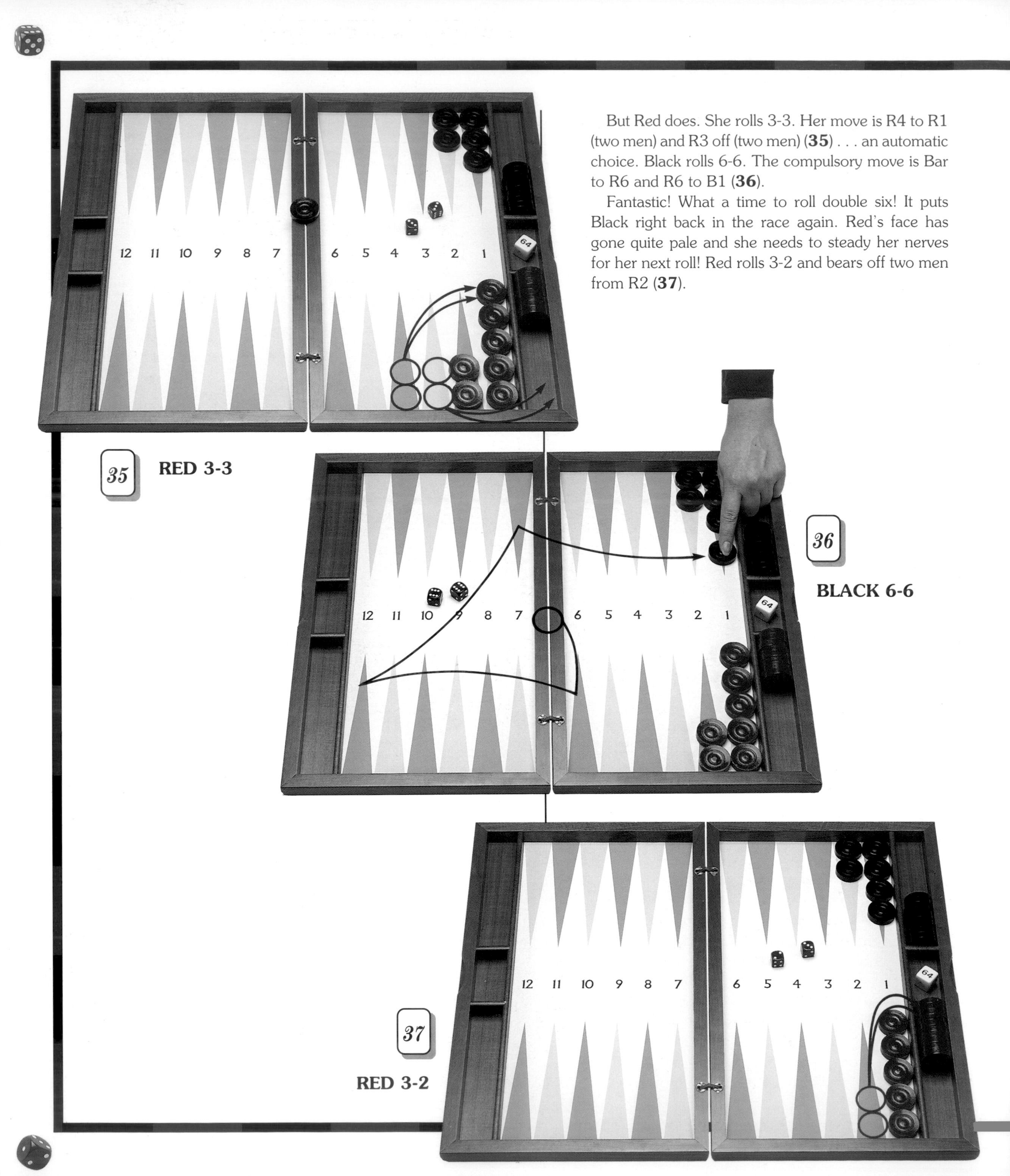

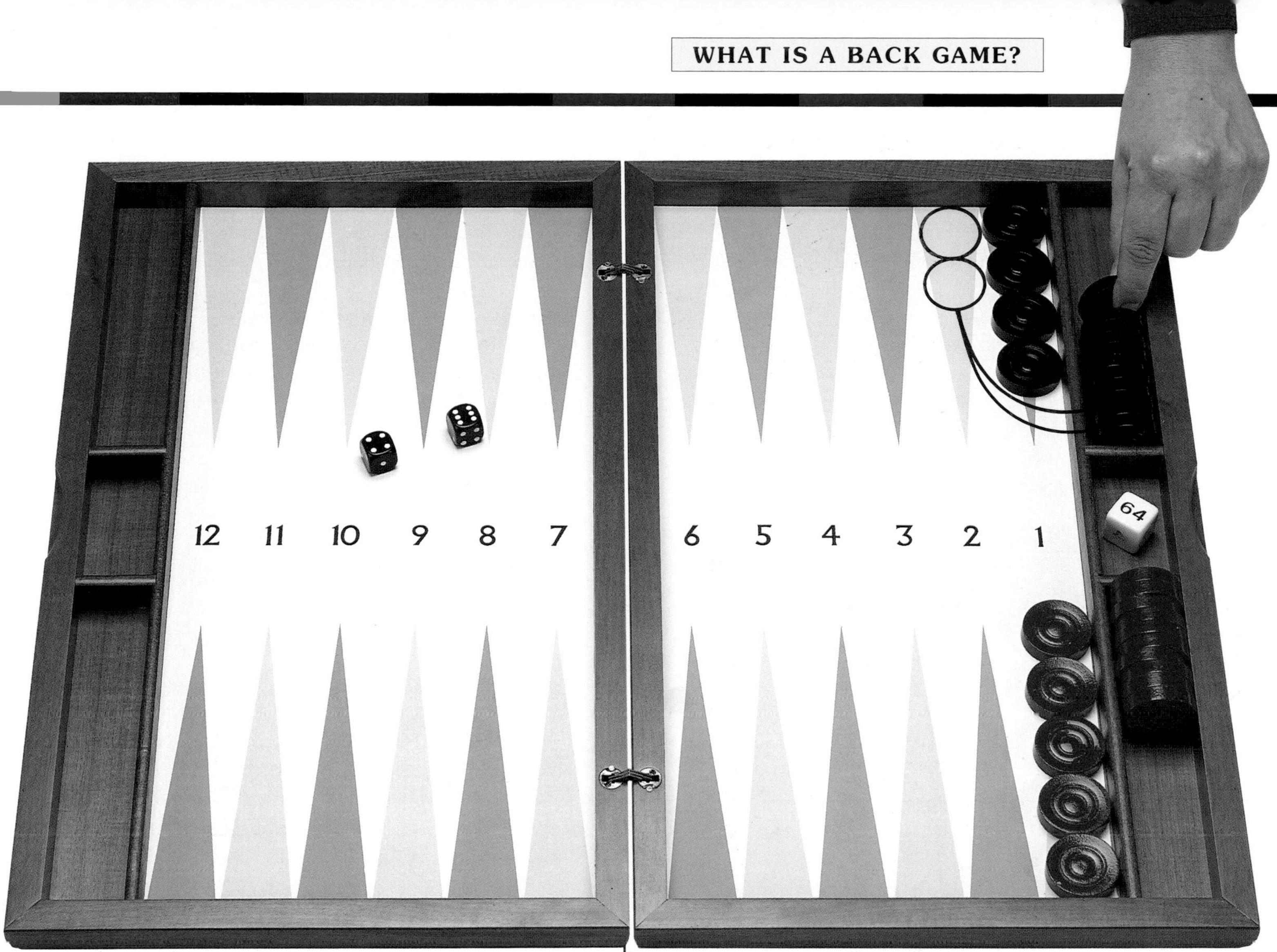

38 **BLACK 6-4**

Black – shaking the dice furiously – rolls 6-4. She bears two off from B2 (**38**).

Red is now wishing that she did not have that extra man because she sees that Black can now bear off her remaining four men with a maximum of two rolls. Red, however, with five men, may need three rolls to bear them all off. Red rolls 3-2. She takes two men off (**39**).

39 **RED 3-2**

Black can end the game here and now if she rolls a double. She does not. She rolls 6-5 and bears off two more men (**40**).

It is all down to the final roll now. If Red rolls a double, she wins. If she does not, she loses. It is as simple (and as lethal) as that! The odds are 5/1 against, just to add to her problems. She takes a deep breath . . . you could hear a pin drop. The two players eyes meet. Red forces a smile, then rolls. It's a double! Double three! Red pulls it off after all (**41**). Red gives a victorious chuckle and starts setting the pieces out for the next game.

40 **BLACK 6-5**

LOOKING BACK

Who would have thought, going back to (**5**) that the game would end like this? It just goes to show that the back game is very rewarding – when it works! The trouble is that it does not come off often enough.

In this demonstration game Red had more than her fair share of luck, but to my mind Black made one very bad move (her 2-2 at **25**) and deserved to lose the game because of it. *Greed has no part in the make-up of a successful gambler.*

The biggest problem in playing a back game successfully is correct *timing*. All too often you throw high dice and have to advance so quickly that you are unable to maintain your blocking points or your back position. Result: chaos.

WHAT POINTS TO CONTROL

Remember that for a successful back game you need to control at least *two* points in your opponent's inner table. Which two? All top players agree that the "1" and "3" points offer you the best chances to disrupt your opponent's end game. Here is a list of the two back game points to aim to control in my order of preference: 1 and 3, 1 and 2, 2 and 3, 2 and 4, 3 and 4, 1 and 4, 3 and 5, 4 and 5. Any other combination is really not worth considering when trying to mount a back game.

RED 3-3

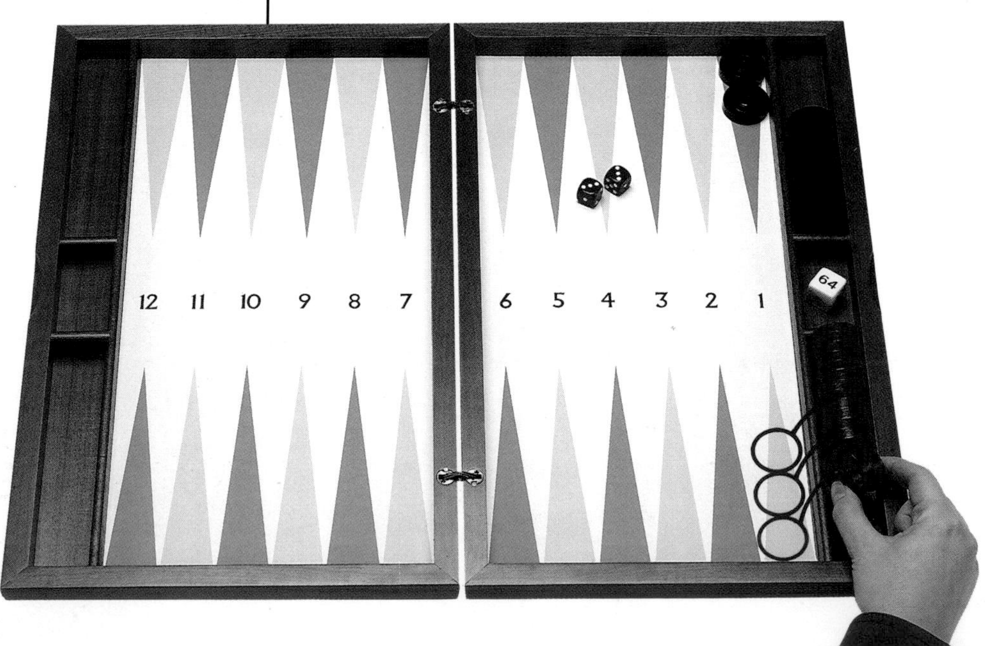

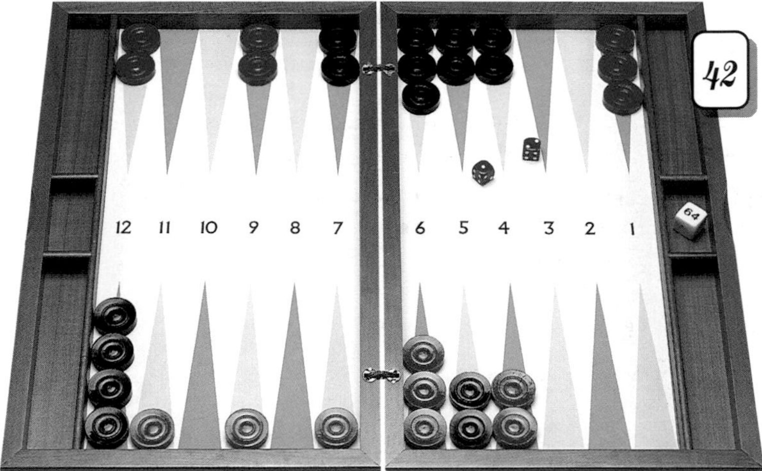

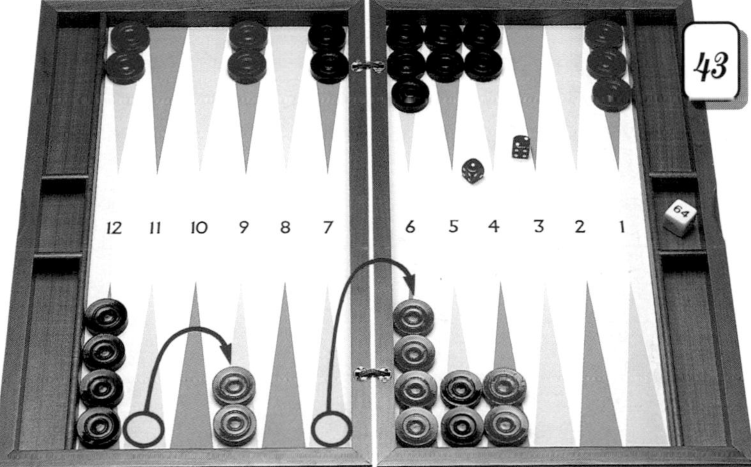

If you have a very retarded game and *three* men back you should *open up* and try to force Black to hit a fourth. Look at illustration (**42**). Red rolls 2-1. Now you *could* tidy everything up by playing R11 to R9, R7 to R6 (**43**). Not a blot in sight, *but* what are the chances of you winning now? Pretty slim I assure you. Black controls your "5" point and has a four-point semi-prime against you. What have you got? Zilch! No, in this position you must opt for a back game. The best play is B1 to B3, B9 to B10 (**44**). By playing it this way, you start to build on the B3 point with the 2 and split your pair on B9 with B9 to B10 for the 1. *You want to be hit* and with so many blots scattered about, Black will be hard put not to hit you!

The object of the exercise is that you want another man back. You pray that you will be able to re-enter this man on B3 thus securing this point and setting you up for a healthy looking back game.

You need a great deal of courage to play a successful back game. Once you have decided to play one, stand by your decision. Remember that one solitary high roll is not sufficient reason for you to change your policy. You should only abandon your back game if the dice consistently show you that a forward game is now your best bet.

Our demonstration back game has illustrated most back game techniques to you, so I sincerely hope that you have played through the moves on your own board and fully digested the comments I have made after each move. Once again I must emphasize the importance of learning to play a good back game. This ability (together with a thorough knowledge of the doubling cube) separates good players from ordinary players in backgammon. You become like a footballer who can score goals equally well with his left foot as he can with his right. Once you have mastered the cube, you can knock them in with your head as well!

GETTING YOUR TIMING RIGHT

Let us go back to timing problems again. We have established that, once two points in your opponent's inner table have been made, you must slow everything down, open up, get hit as often as you can, and at the same time slowly build a blocking point prime.

There is a right and wrong time to hit your opponent. For example, look at illustration (**45**). You roll 6-3. Under no circumstances should you hit Black's blot on B8. The timing is wrong. It is too early. You have no defence to speak of and Black will have no problem re-entering his man and coming round again. While he is doing this you will inevitably have to advance. Without a doubt, your best move in this example is to make your "5" point with R11 to R5 (*not* R8 to R5), and B12 to R10 (**46**). You have advanced your semi-prime to R5 and still have useful builders at R7, R8 and R10. You are slowly building up your defences.

COUNTERING A BACK GAME

The best way to learn to *counter* a back game is thoroughly to understand how to *play* a successful back game. Remember, also to keep the following rules in mind.

- Do not hit your opponent. If he has got three men back already, under no circumstances give him a fourth.
- Do everything you can to make him advance quickly.
- Do not take unnecessary chances.
- Play steadily and slowly. Go for the "percentage" roll every time.
- Take extreme care moving your men into your inner table. Do not make any "hunch" moves. Calculate every one.
- Take the same degree of care over bearing your men off. A frightening fact to remember is that you can have fourteen men borne off before your opponent has borne off his first man and yet *still lose* the game. I know – it has happened to me!

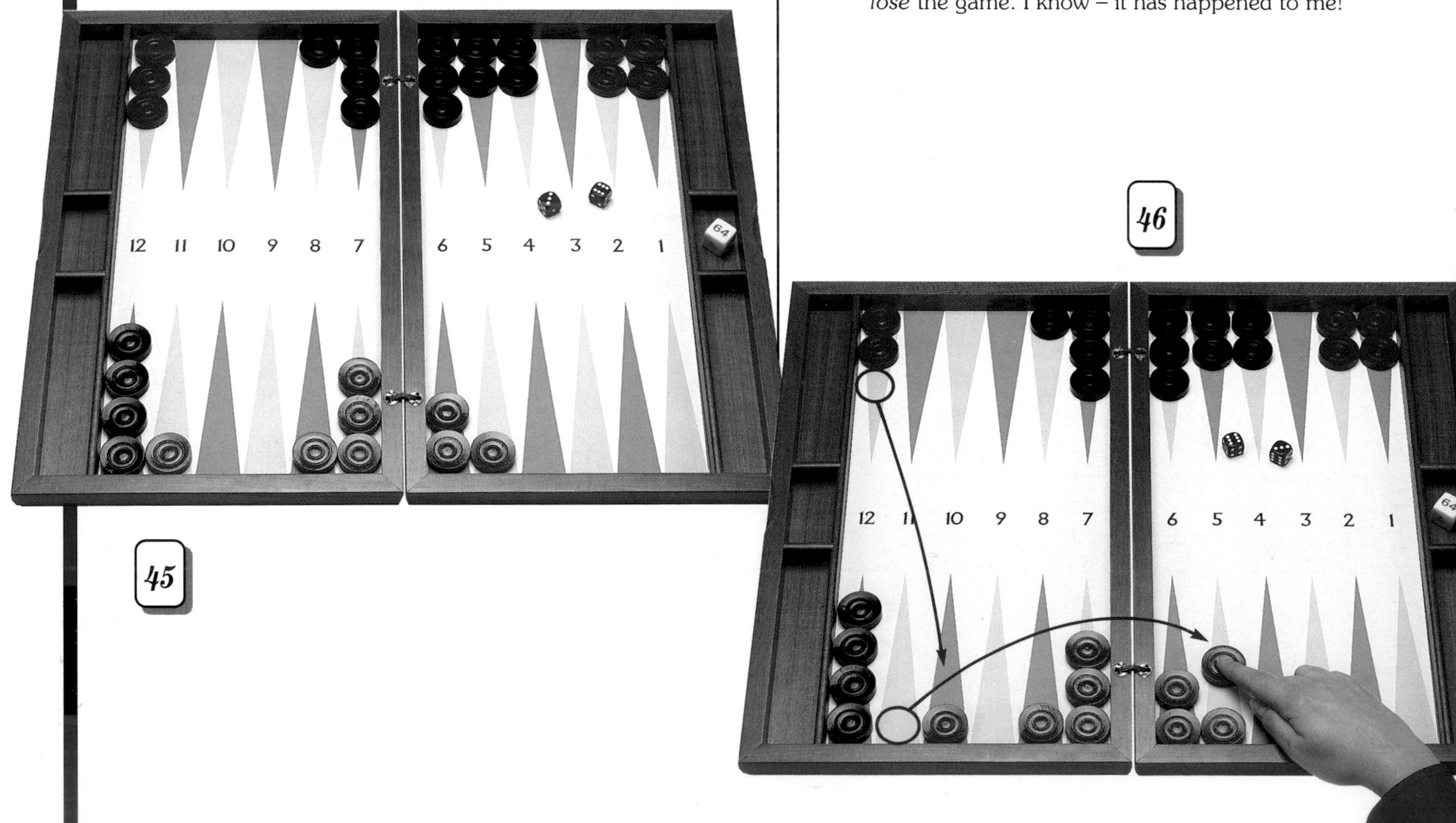

45

46

47

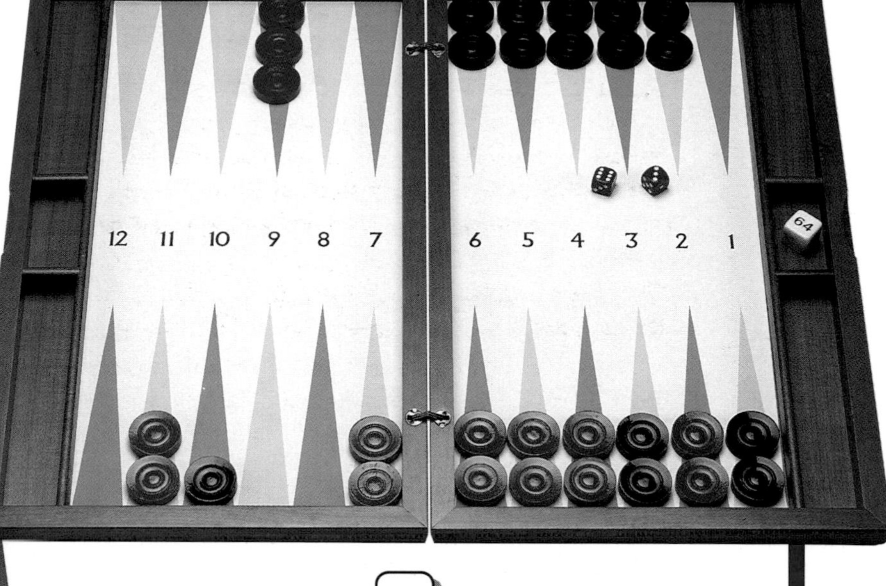

49

QUIZ QUESTIONS

Try your hand at a few problems now. First look at illustration (**47**). You roll 6-1. What is your best move and why?

What would you do with 6-5 in this position (**48**)?

Your roll is 6-3 in the position shown in (**49**). How would you play it? Why?

Now look at position (**50**). You have rolled 6-3. What is your best move? Be sure that you understand why.

The answers can be found on pages 122-123.

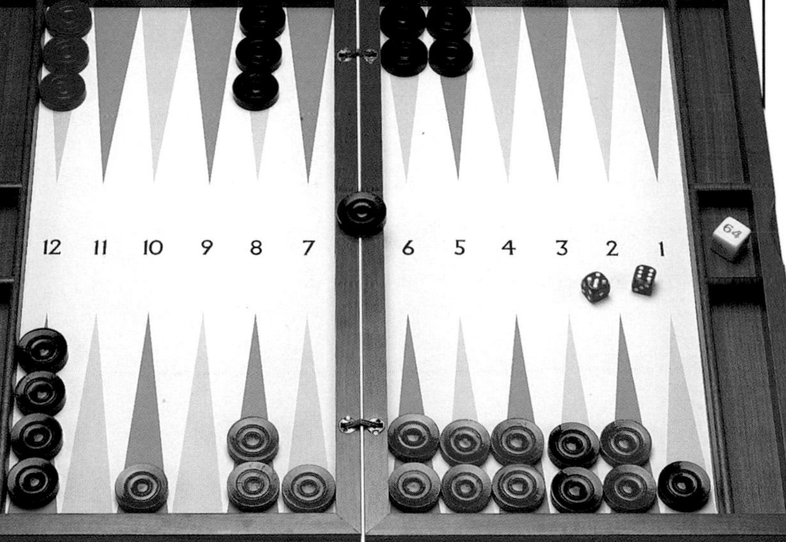

48

50

12 11 10 9 8 7 6 5 4 3 2 1

64

RETURN PLAY

The style of play known as "Return Play" is very subtle and a most useful addition to your repertoire of backgammon skills. It might even be called *"Beware of Greeks who come bearing gifts!"* For this you must keep an eagle eye on your opponent's inner table, because the opportunities for return play happen a lot more often than the average player realizes. Frankly the "average" player has never heard of return play anyway! So what is Return Play? Look at illustration (**1**).

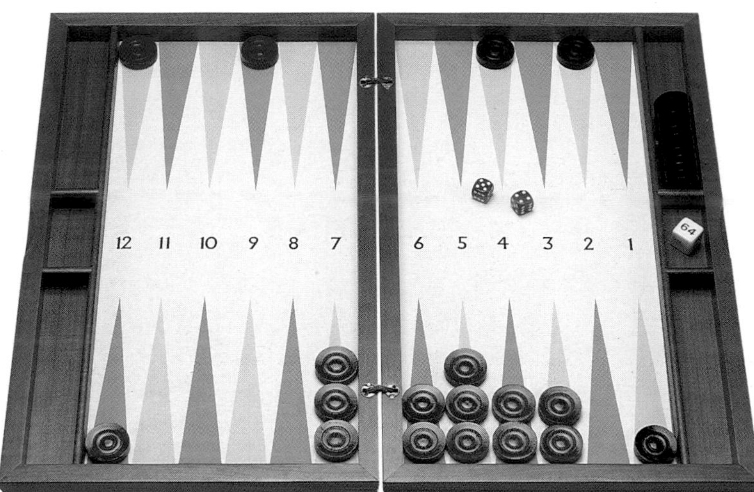

A TIMELY RETURN

Red rolls 5-4. How would you play it? Would you make your prime with B12 to R8 and R12 to R8? If that is your choice, you would be wrong! The correct move is R7 to R2 and R5 to R1 (**2**).

You see, Black with twelve men already borne off, is a strong favourite to win the game even though he has still got one back man in your inner table. So, to stand a chance of winning, you must try to capture one of Black's blots on B4 and B2, ideally both if you can! You would then be in a very strong position indeed.

To this end, you hit Black's blot on R1 and *deliberately* leave blots on *both* the open points in your inner table. Black has to hit you in order to re-enter. If Black fails to re-enter at his first attempt, leave the two blots undisturbed and make your next move elsewhere. You must get Black to hit you.

Once you have been hit you are able to *return* for an onslaught on the blots at B2 and B4. A roll of 2-2 or 1-1 would hit both of them! It is possible! Only 17/1 against!

If you hit the blot at B2 with any of the other "2" rolls, i.e. 6-2, 5-2, 4-2, 3-2, or 2-1, you should leave your man on B2 and make the second half of your roll elsewhere. By so doing you get a second chance to hit the blot on B4 as well.

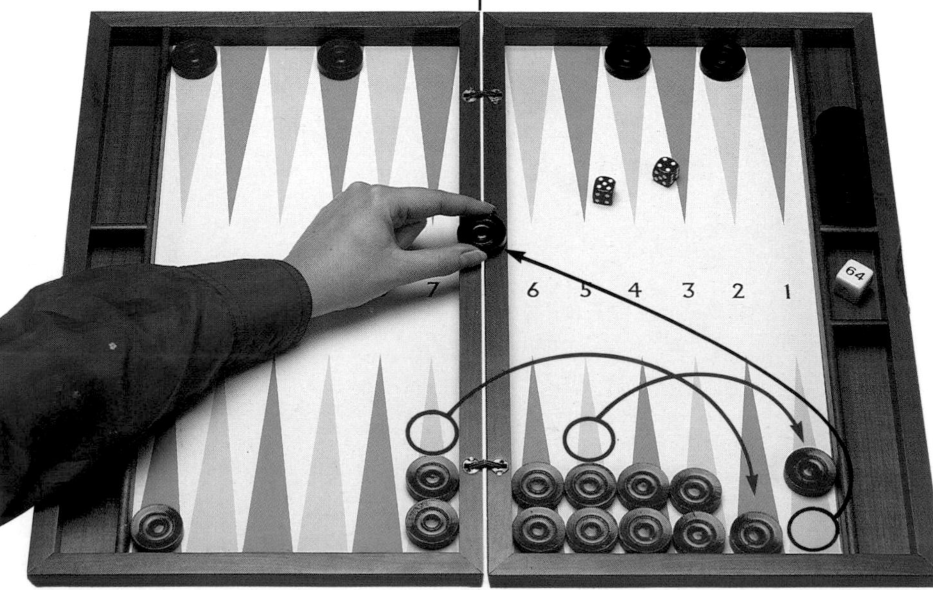

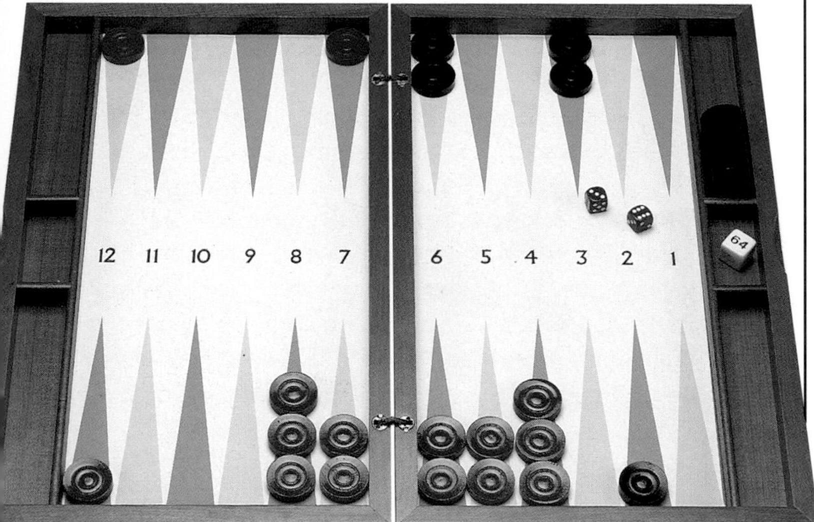

3

Return play is not always obvious. For example, take the next illustration (**3**). You roll 6-3. Using return play strategy, you hit with the "6" (R8 to R2) and play the "3" R4 to R1 (**4**). You now have two exposed blots in your inner table and Black will *probably* have to hit one of them, sending you to the bar. Now just suppose that in hitting you he rolls 4-1, 4-2, 5-1, 5-2 or 2-2. In each instance he hits you and is *compelled* to break the pair on his B6 point leaving you *two* blots to aim at. That makes nine possible rolls that can get him into trouble. It is a 3/1 chance but still the best strategy for you in this late stage of the game. The return play may yet save your bacon!

4

QUIZ QUESTIONS

I hope that you have grasped the technique now. Try the following problems to see if the lesson has sunk in. The answers are found on page 123. In this position (**5**) you roll 6-1. Should you play R8 to R1 for a return play? Explain your answer.

Now take a look at position (**6**). You roll 6-1. Should you play R8 to R1 for a return play? Explain your answer.

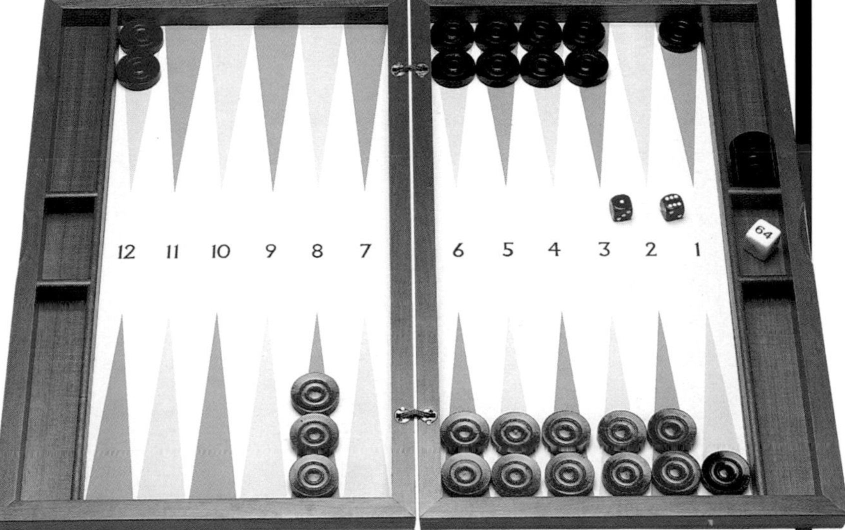

5

6

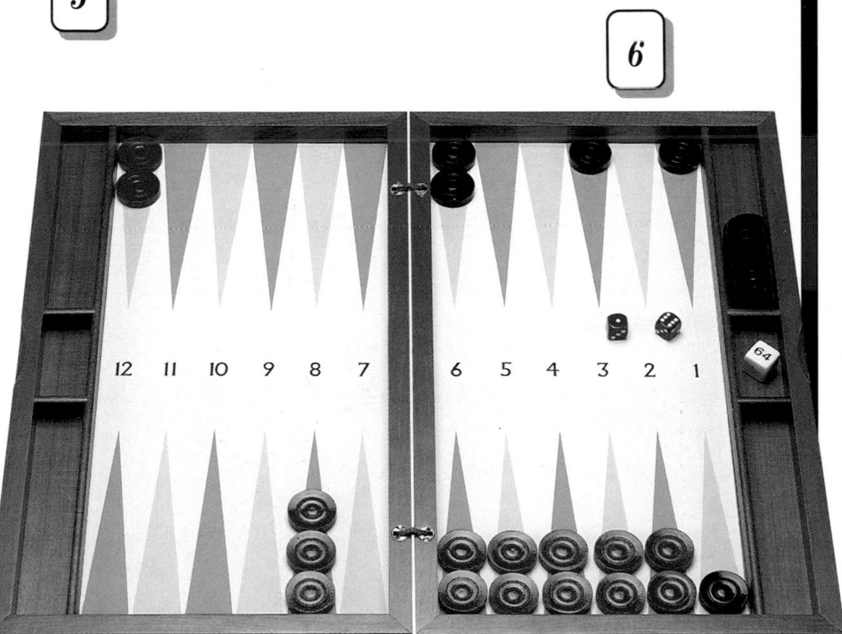

BEARING OFF

More games are lost by thoughtlessness in bearing off your men from your inner table than for any other single reason. Bearing off is almost a science in its own right, a strange combination of mathematics and logic. There are certain mathematical principles to abide by but, paradoxically, all these principles may be broken on occasions. Logic tells you when. The whole object of bearing off is to remove your men as quickly as possible without exposing yourself to unnecessary risk. You must look ahead. When contemplating a move always say to yourself, ". . . but if I make this move, what is likely to happen to me on my next throw? How many rolls would then create problems for me?"

WEIGHING UP YOUR OPTIONS

At the end of Chapter One I set you a bearing-off problem. Let us take another look at it. In the following position (**1**) you roll 5-3. How would you play it and why? This position is typical of many similar bearing off situations. There are three possible ways to play it. One is right, the other two are dreadfully, horribly wrong. Yet time and time again I have seen people misplay this type of roll. Not all of them were beginners either!

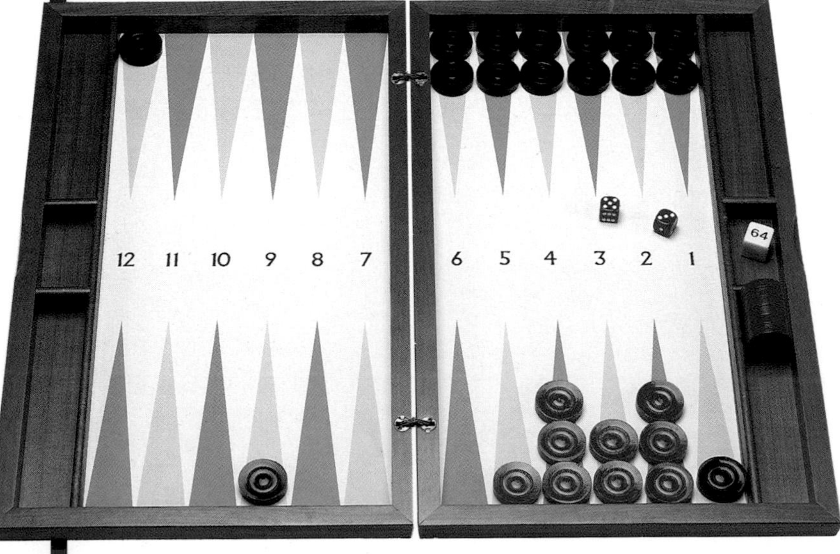

1

The roll should be played by moving the blot on R5 to R2 for the "3", and bearing off one man from R4 for the "5" (**2**). You play *the "3" first*, then the "5"!

The rules of backgammon state that as long as you play both halves of your roll (wherever possible), it is immaterial which half you play first. Some players fall into the habit of always playing the higher half of the roll first. To them, this is a 5-3 roll; they cannot see it any other way. The fact that it is also a 3-5 roll escapes them.

With a rigid attitude like that it is so easy to play this roll by bearing off one man at R5 and another off at R3 (**3**). Alternatively, you might even bear off at R5

2

3

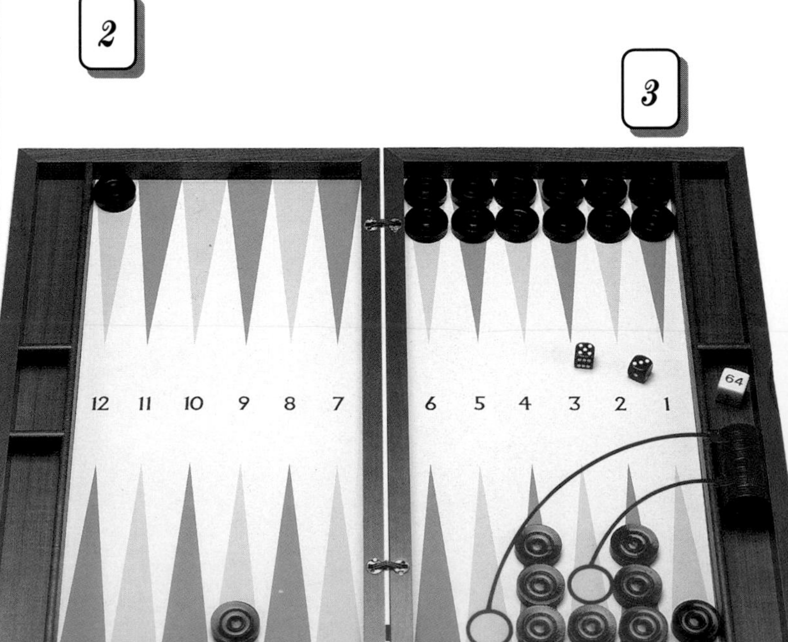

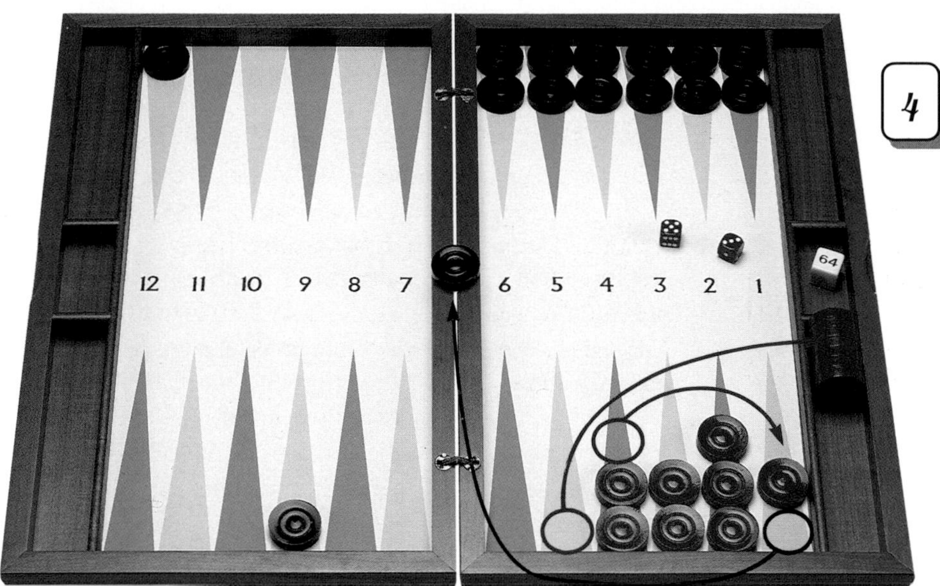

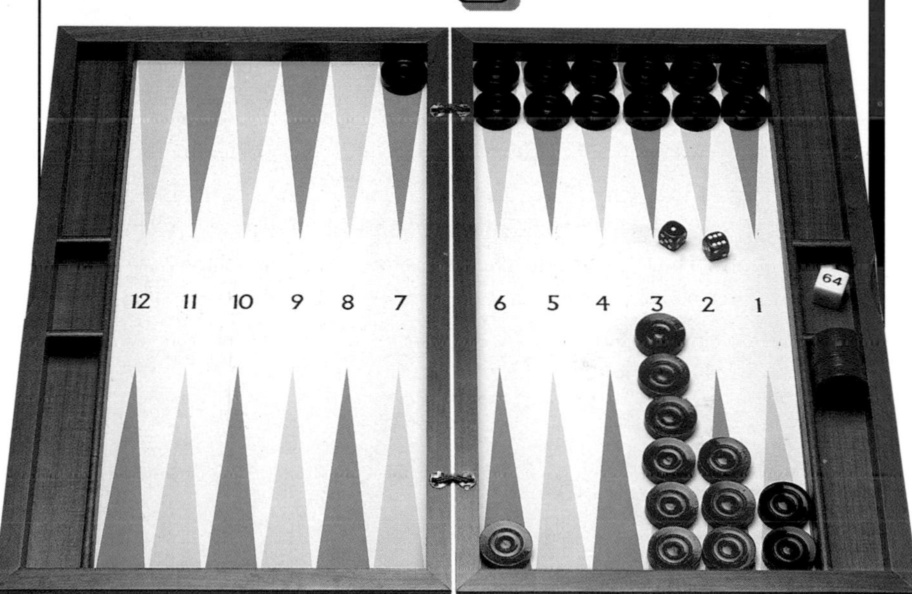

and then play R4 to R1 for the "3" (**4**). Both these alternatives are suicidal. You would not make such a silly mistake would you? You would be surprised how many people would. I wish they would all play against me . . . for money!

Here is another example (**5**). The roll is 6-1. The correct play is R6 to R5 for the "1" and then bear off at R5 for the "6" (**6**). You do not use the "6" to bear off at R6 and play the "1" R3 to R2 because then you leave *five* men on R3. A subsequent throw of 4-4, 5-5 or 6-6 would leave you in trouble, forced to leave a blot on R3.

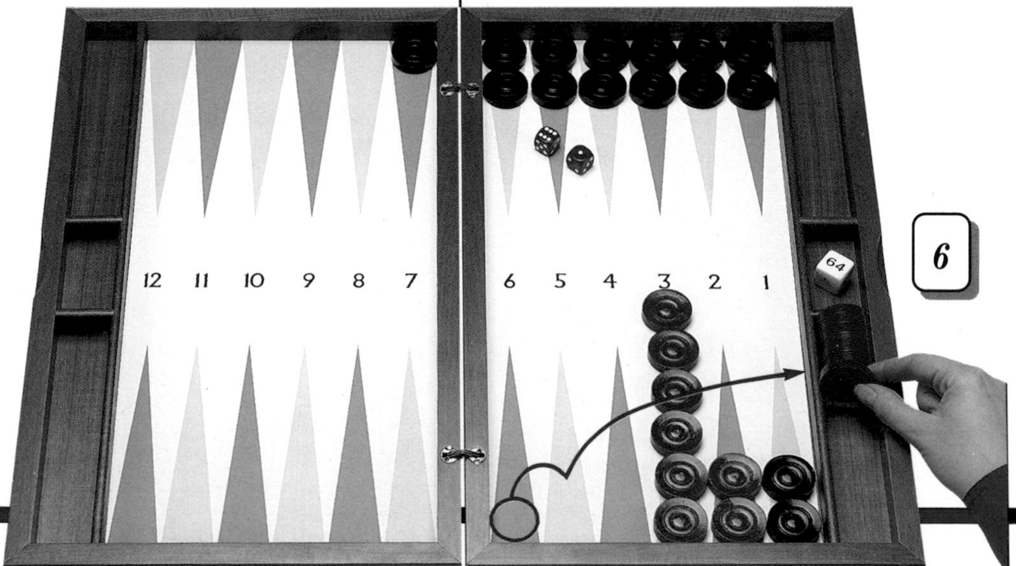

Now look at the next example (**7**). The roll is 6-1 again. To all intents and purposes the situation appears to be the same. *Beware!* It is quite different. Here the correct play is to bear off at R6 for the "6" and move one man from R3 to R2 for the "1" (**8**). On your *next* roll you will leave a blot if you roll 6-6, 5-5, 4-4 or 3-3 – that is a total of four bad potential rolls.

If you were to play the "1" first, as is the normal procedure in positions similar to this, with R6 to R5 and then bear off at R5 for the "6", you would expose yourself to *twice the danger* of leaving a blot on your next roll. The nightmare rolls are 6-2, 2-6, 5-2, 2-5, 4-2, 2-4, 3-2 and 2-3. Eight bad rolls compared to only four bad rolls if you play the way that I recommend. The exception that proves the rule!

Basically there are five different bearing-off situations that you are likely to find yourself in. They are:

- Bearing off with no enemy pieces behind you – all contact between the opposing men by this stage having ceased.
- Bearing off with an enemy piece or pieces sitting on the bar.
- Bearing off with one enemy piece in your inner table.
- Bearing off with two enemy pieces in your inner table.
- Bearing off when your opponent is playing a back game and controls two or more of the points in your inner table.

The following general rules, if observed, will assist you in bearing off correctly and help you win more games.

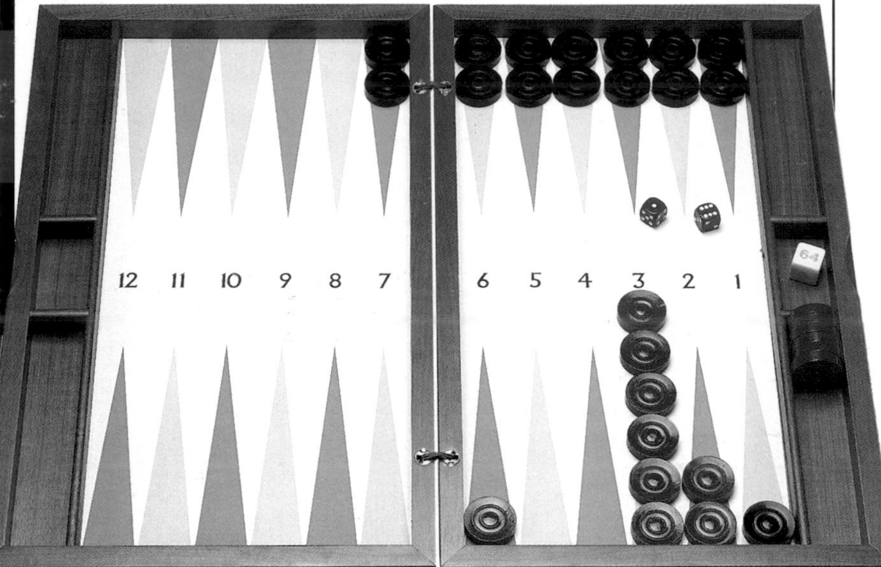

7

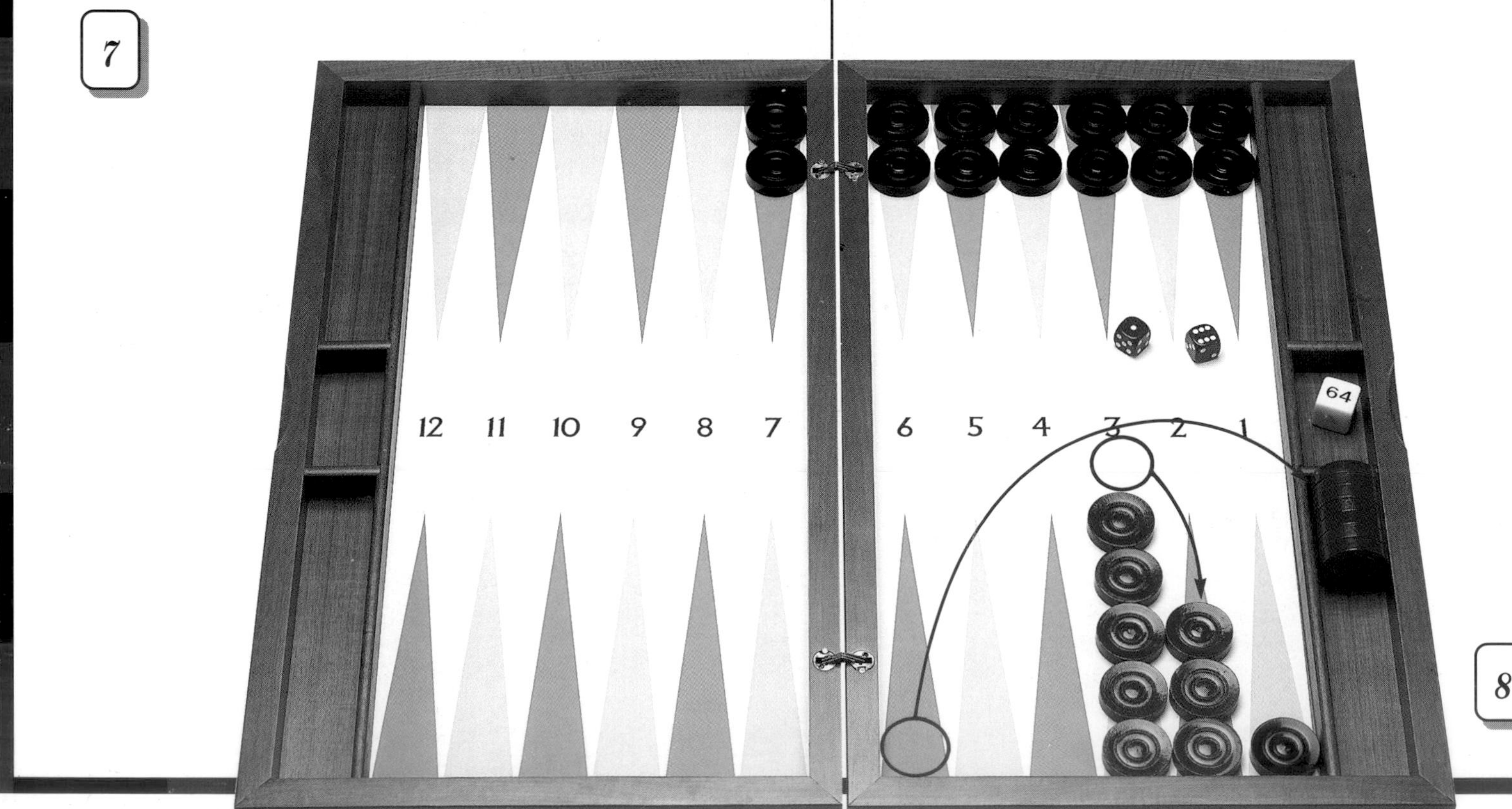

8

BALANCING YOUR BOARD

When bringing your men into your inner table prior to bearing off, an even distribution of your pieces is preferable. Look at example (**9**).

Both sides are ready to bear off and it is Black's roll. However, given equal luck, Red is more likely to bear all her men off first because of the more even distribution of her men. Black is quite likely to have a "miss" or two and be forced to make moves within his inner table because of an inability to bear pieces off. Even a position count at this moment shows Red one throw ahead.

When coming around and into your inner table, "ones" can be deployed usefully in offloading overloaded points and distributing your men more evenly throughout your inner table.

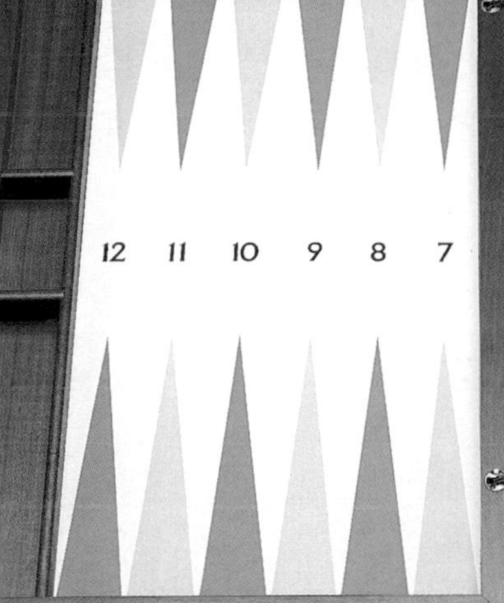

9

OVERLOADING POINTS

Try not to "overload" your points anywhere on the board and especially not within your inner table. More than three men on a point is a waste. The extra men can normally be deployed more usefully elsewhere.

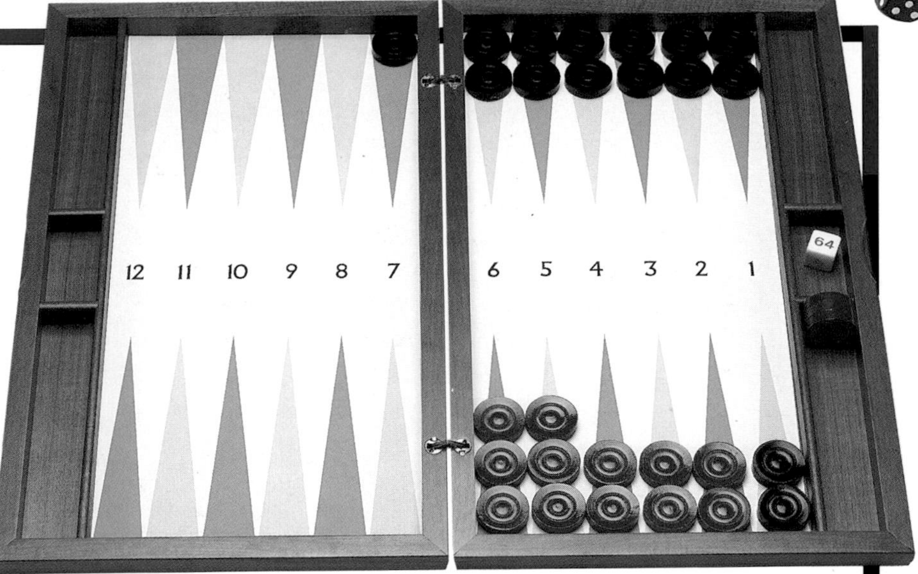

10

"ODDS AND EVENS"

When humanly possible you should leave yourself with an even number of pieces on your *two highest* points. This needs some explanation and as pictures speak louder than words, look at position (**10**). Red has six men, an even number, on her R6 and R5 points (her two highest). Now her only bad rolls are 6-4, 4-6 and 4-4. That is a total of *three* bad rolls.

Let us re-arrange just one piece (**11**). Now Red has an uneven number of men on her highest two points (five). On the next roll she leaves herself open to leave a blot with rolls of 6-6, 4-4, 6-5, 5-6, 5-3 and 3-5. That makes *six* bad rolls – twice as many as in our previous example.

11

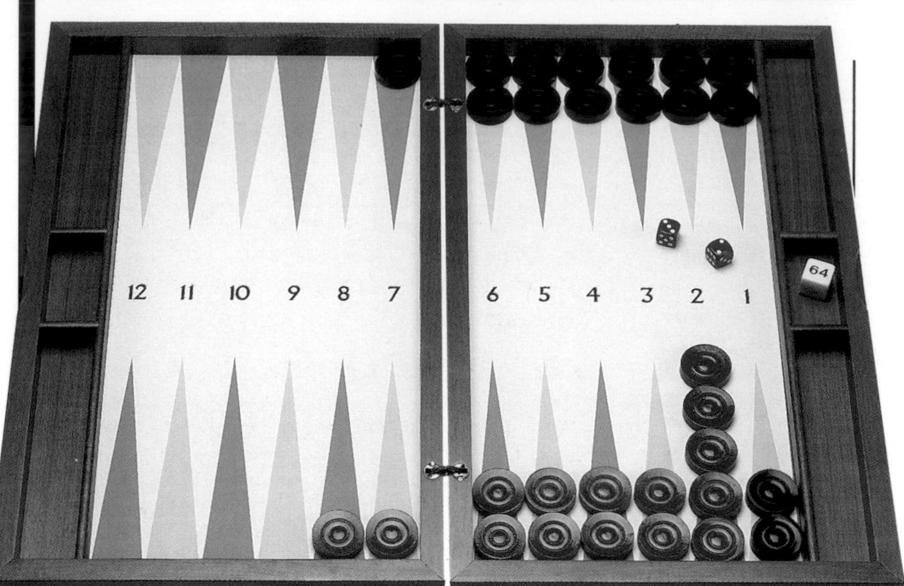

12

So care must be taken in bringing your men into your inner table prior to bearing off, so that this "odds and evens" rule is observed. For instance, look at example (**12**). Red rolls 3-2. She should *not* move R8 to R6, R7 to R4 (**13**). This leaves an odd number of men on the two highest points and is asking for trouble. She should move R8 to R5, R7 to R5 (**14**), leaving six men on the highest two points. As a result, she will be less vulnerable on future throws.

COMING IN

When a running game situation emerges you must use your rolls with the greatest economy. It is a race and you must *aim your remaining stragglers at your "6" point*. Let me show you what I mean with the following example (**15**).

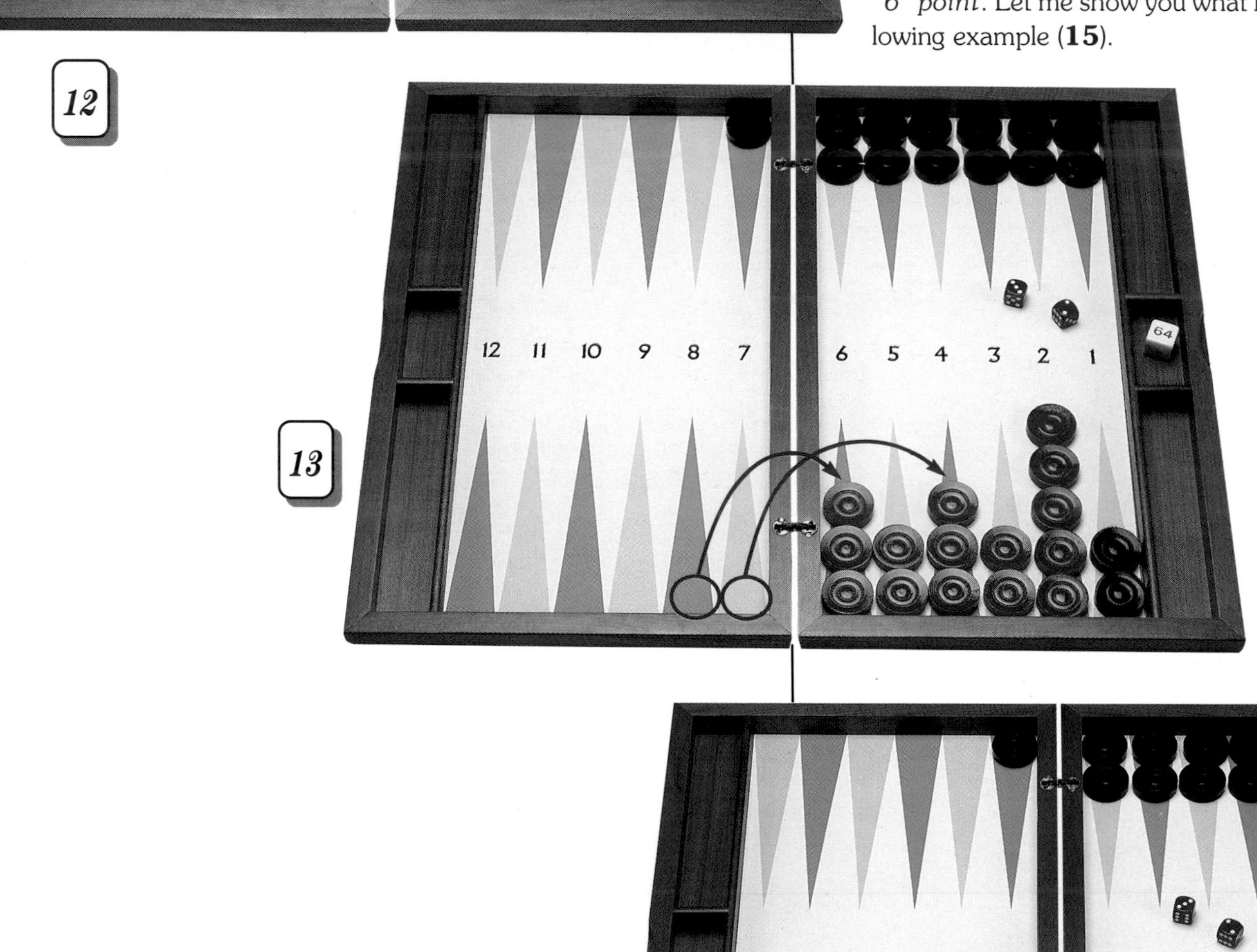

13

14

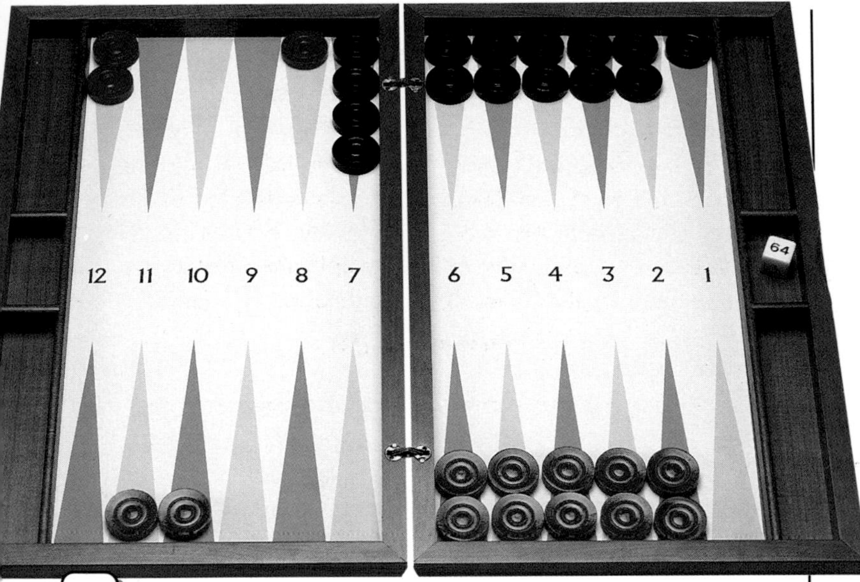

15

A position count shows Black 29 and Red 36. As it is your roll you are *two and a half* throws behind and the disposition of your men is definitely inferior. You must, therefore, play your rolls with the greatest care if you are to have any hope of making up the lee-way and winning the game.

Now assume that I have just set up this position on my board. I shall throw the dice and move into my inner table explaining my actions as I do so. I shall dis-regard Black's moves completely for the benefit of this demonstration.

1st roll: 6-1 B12 to R6. One man home without wasting a single pip.

2nd roll: 5-4 R11 to R6, R10 to R6. Two men home. I am overloading the "6" point but when involved in a race like this, you cannot always place your men as you would prefer.

3rd roll: 4-1 B12 to R9, R2 to R1. Here the odd "1" was utilized to most effect by filling the empty R1 point.

4th roll: 6-5 B8 to R11, R11 to R5. The back man is brought all the way home leaving only a "3" to bring in my last man. I could have played the last roll B8 to R11, R9 to R4 but this would have been a mistake. Every pip counts now. My recommendation leaves you only a "3" to play next time. The other way leaves you a "5". In those circumstances five rolls would not even get you home, eight more only get you in – not off. That is not good enough when you are two and a half rolls behind, is it?

THE "CLOSEST-CLOSER" RULE

Another general principle that you should learn is the "closest-closer" rule. Like most backgammon rules, there are exceptions to it, but in the majority of cases the rule holds good. In example (**16**) the roll is 4-1. The correct play is to bear off at R4 (of course) and R3 to R2 (**17**).

16

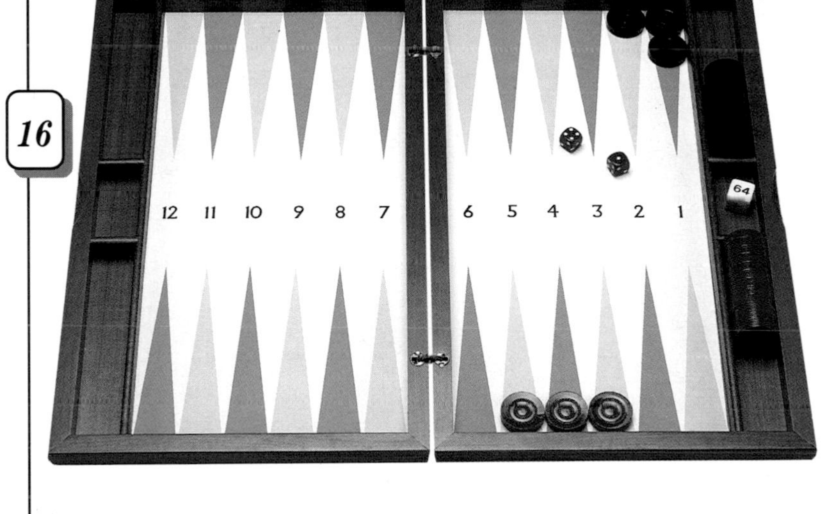

17

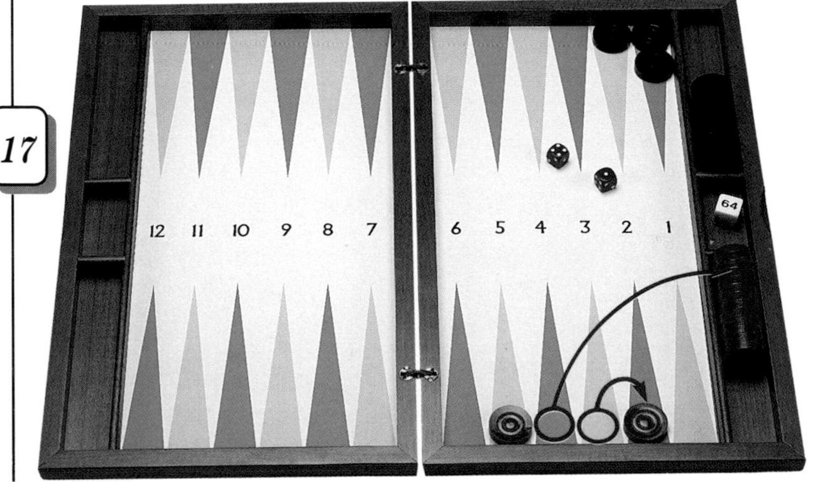

It is the move from R3 to R2 that is significant. As a general rule, whenever you have a small number to be played (rather than borne off) in a similar situation, move the man *closest* to your "1" point. The closest man gets closer still!

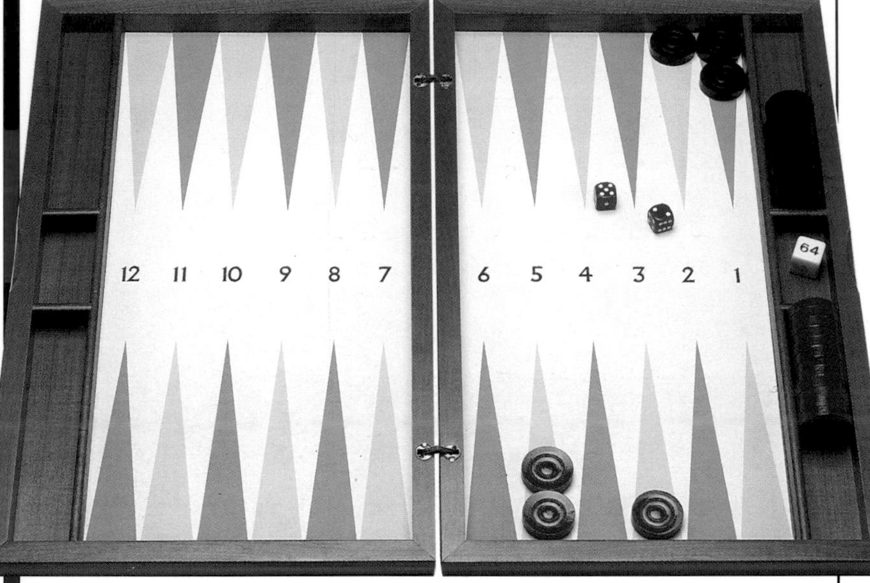

18

Black, even assuming he does not roll a double, will still definitely be off in two rolls, therefore you must bear off both your remaining men on your next roll if you are to win. Moving this man gives you a greater number of winning rolls on your next throw than if you had used the "1" to play R5 to R4 (as some unthinking players would). You are now a slight favourite to bear them both off. Nineteen throws achieve this. Only seventeen out of thirty-six possible rolls would bear both men off if you had played R5 to R4.

These fractional differences really matter. Do not give an inch! If you do, your opponent (if he or she is worthy of the name) will take a mile!

Here is another example (**18**). The roll is 5-2. The "5", of course is no problem. It is borne off. But what about the "2", should you play R5 to R3 or R3 to R1? If you play R5 to R3, the following nineteen rolls will *not* get you off on your next roll: 6-1, 1-6, 6-2, 2-6, 5-1, 1-5, 5-2, 2-5, 4-1, 1-4, 4-2, 2-4, 3-1, 1-3, 3-2, 2-3, 2-1, 1-2 and 1-1.

The "closest-closer" play of R3 to R1 fails to get you off next roll with only thirteen bad rolls: 4-3, 3-4, 4-2, 2-4, 4-1, 1-4, 3-2, 2-3, 3-1, 1-3, 2-1, 1-2 and 1-1. So the "closest-closer" rule is obviously best (**19**). Most of the time!

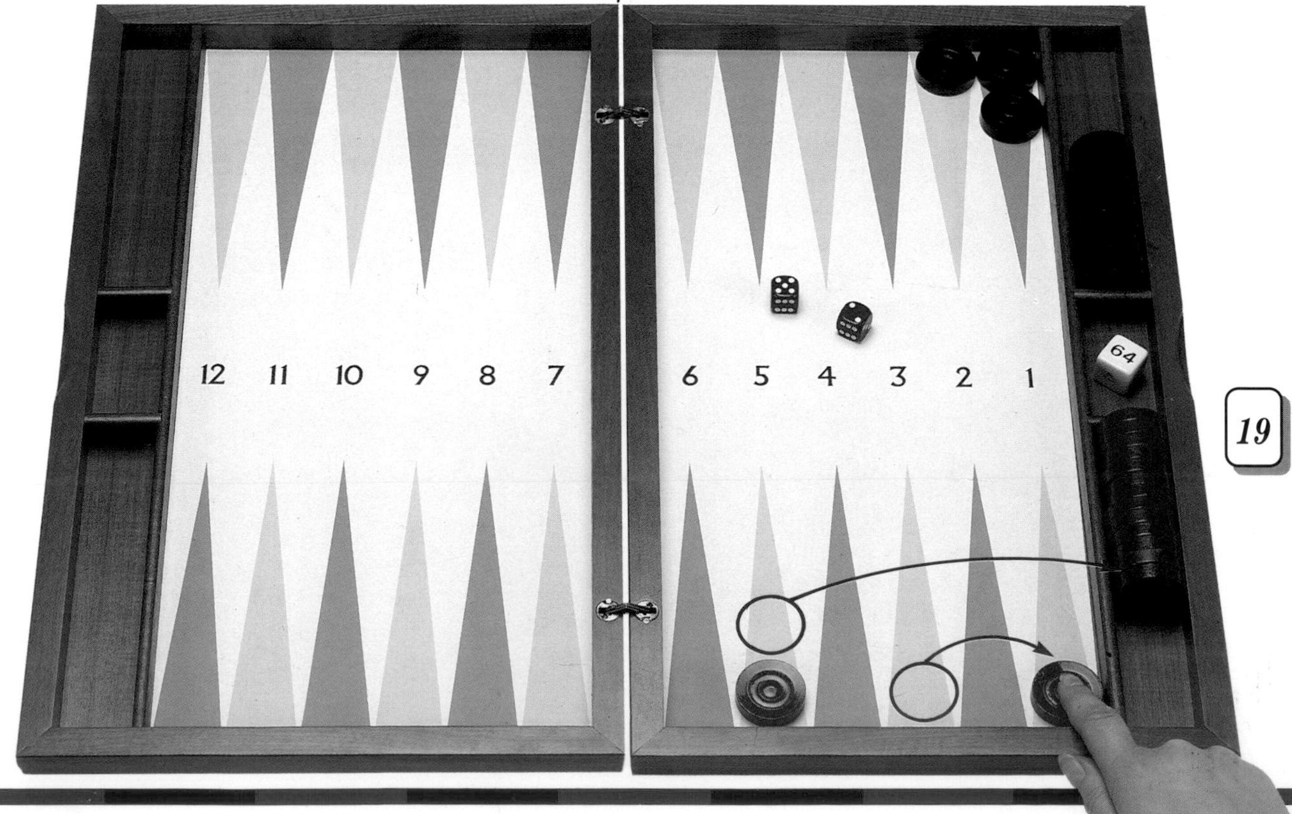

19

In the next illustration (**20**) the throw is 6-1. If you were to play the "closest-closer" rule in this instance, you would be wrong. The correct move is to play the odd "1" R6 to R5 (**21**) and not R3 to R2. There are fourteen different ways of bearing both men off on your next roll with the move that I recommend. There are only thirteen if you apply the "closest-closer" rule of R3 to R2.

To save you the trouble and tedium of working out when or when not to play the "closest-closer" rule, I have done the donkey work for you. There are *four* positions when the rule does not apply. All other positions should be played according to the rule.

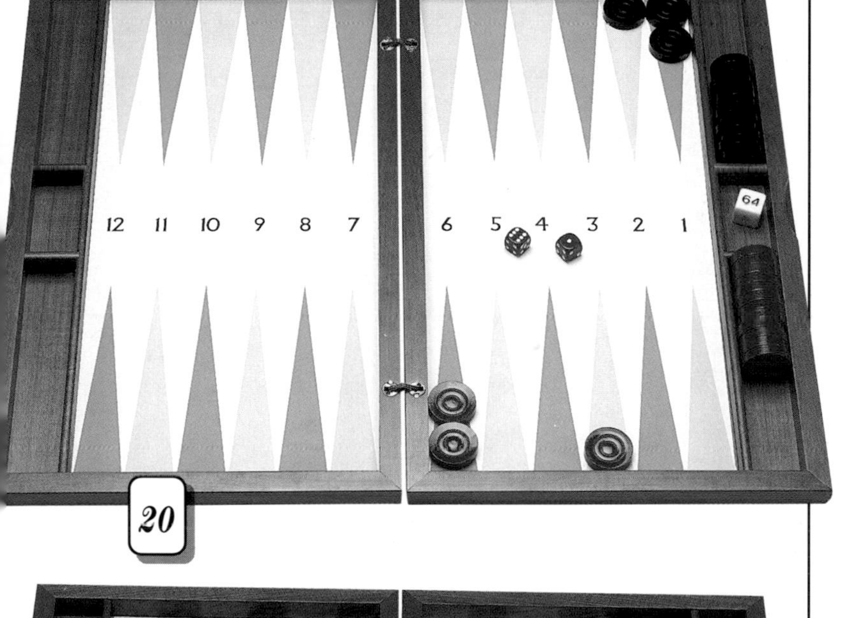

20

21

So, when you have three men left in your inner table and your throw enables you to remove only one of them, you should play the "closest-closer" rule in all cases except the following, which you play off the "6" point:

- When you must play a "2" with the pieces on R3 and R6.
- When you must play a "3" with the pieces on R5 and R6.
- When you must play a "3" with the pieces on R4 and R6.
- When you must play a "4" with the pieces on R5 and R6.

It is worthwhile remembering this list. It could mean the difference between success and failure for you.

THE "5-2" RULE

The break-even position for you to remember in this type of situation is 5-2. If your two remaining pieces are positioned at R5 and R2 (or better) you stand *more* than a 50-50 chance of bearing them both off next roll. With 5-3 (or worse) you stand *less* than a 50-50 chance.

THE "OLD ONE-TWO" RULE

Another useful point to remember is that a solitary man on a high point is of more use to you than two men on lower points, even if the pips required to bear off are the same in both cases. Look at example (**22**). The roll is 3-1. Should you take off the man at R4 for the 3-1, or should you play R6 to R3 and R4 to R3 bringing both men to your "3" point?

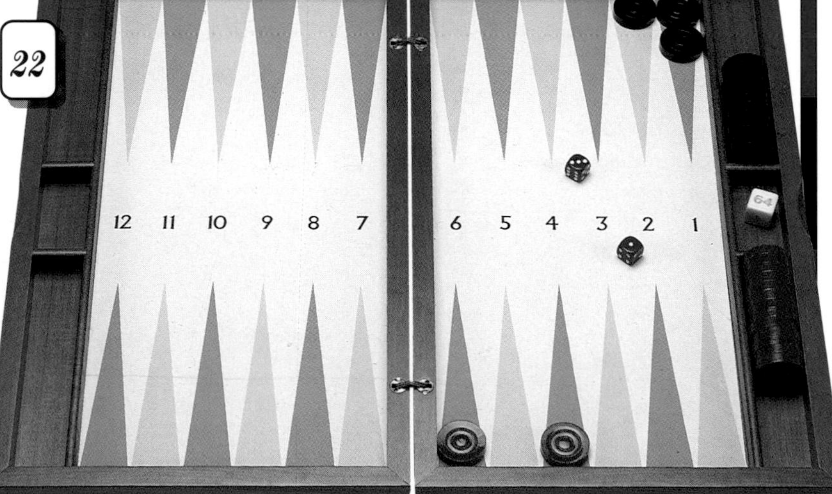

22

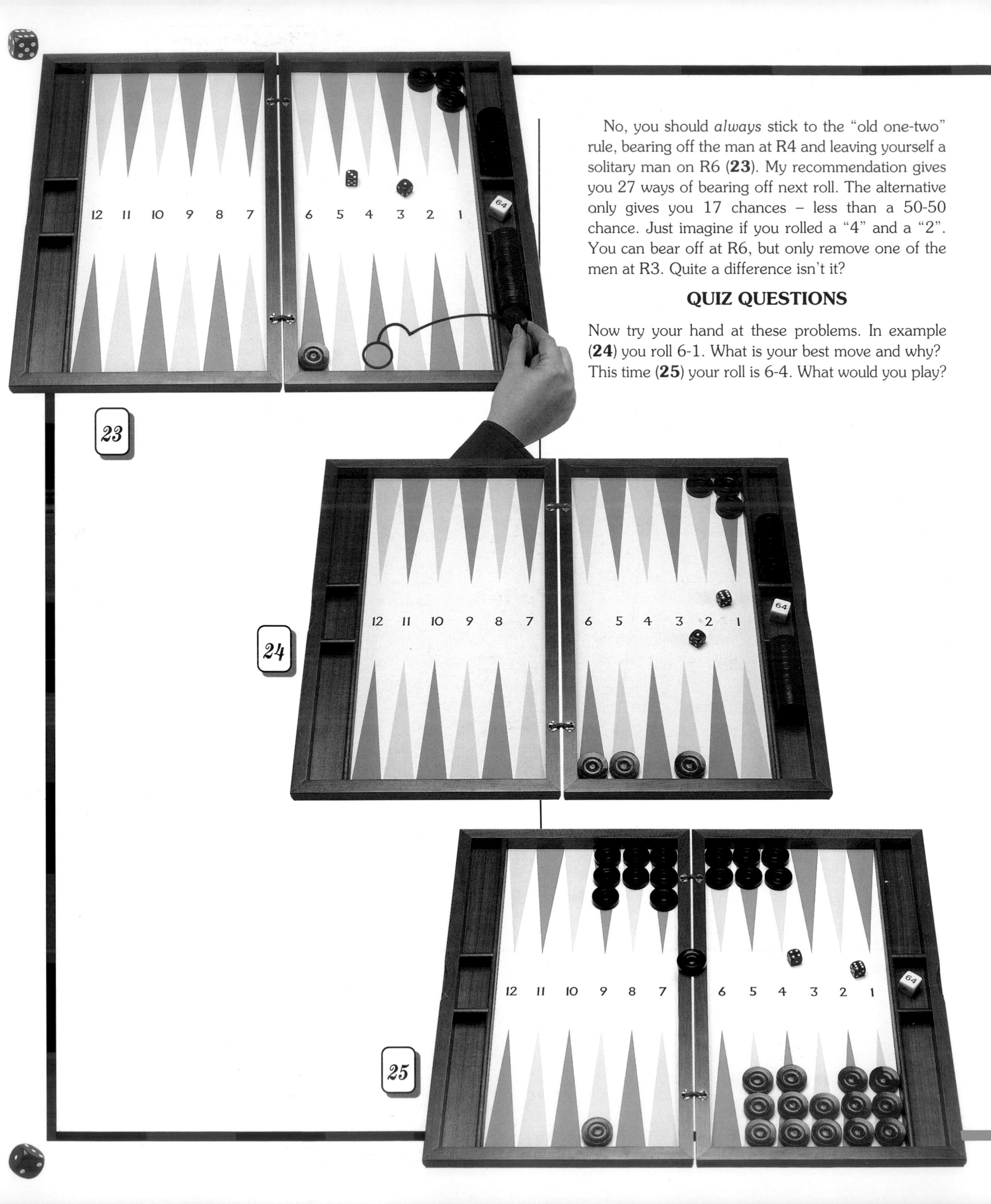

No, you should *always* stick to the "old one-two" rule, bearing off the man at R4 and leaving yourself a solitary man on R6 (**23**). My recommendation gives you 27 ways of bearing off next roll. The alternative only gives you 17 chances – less than a 50-50 chance. Just imagine if you rolled a "4" and a "2". You can bear off at R6, but only remove one of the men at R3. Quite a difference isn't it?

QUIZ QUESTIONS

Now try your hand at these problems. In example (**24**) you roll 6-1. What is your best move and why? This time (**25**) your roll is 6-4. What would you play?

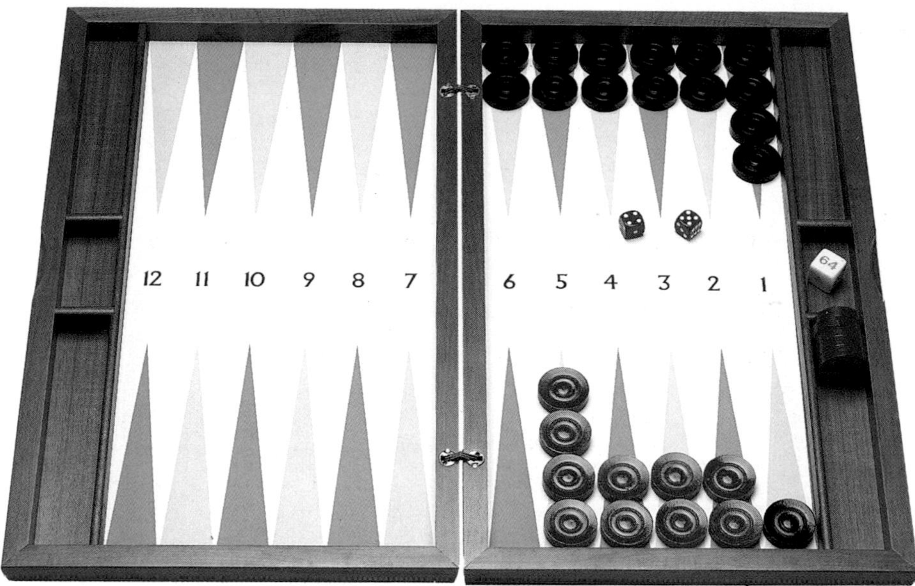

26

27

If you roll 5-4 in this position (**26**), how would you move?
What about 6-3 in *this* position (**27**)?
In this position (**28**) you have rolled 4-1. What is your best move and why? All the answers will be found on pages 124-125.

ODDS AND ENDS

Learning to calculate odds quickly and accurately is a most useful accomplishment for the student of backgammon. Contrary to general opinion, it is a very easy thing to do! Backgammon odds are very simple. Everything revolves around the magic number 36. Why 36? Well, if you refer back to Chapter Two, you will remember that there are 36 possible rolls of the dice. So every roll in backgammon must be a fraction of 36.

WORKING OUT THE ODDS

For example, we know that double six can only be thrown one way. Therefore there are 35 ways that it *cannot* be thrown. Therefore the odds that you will throw 6-6 on any given occasion are 35/1 against.

However, 6-5 can be thrown in *two* different ways (6-5 or 5-6). Therefore there are 34 ways that it cannot be thrown. So, the odds that you will throw 6-5 are 34/2 or 17/1 against.

The 36 possible rolls and their appropriate odds are show in the table on pages 18-19 of Chapter Two. I shall sum up here by simply stating that:

- The odds are 35/1 against you throwing any *specific* double.
- The odds are 17/1 against you throwing any *specific* combination shot (all rolls other than doubles).

The operative word here is specific.

In a *non-specific* situation we can now say that as there are six different doubles, each of which can only be rolled one way, there are six ways in which we can roll a double and *thirty* ways that will not produce a double for us. Therefore the odds are 30/6 or 5/1 against throwing a non-specific double. You can work out, therefore, that if you need a double in order to win a game, and any double will do, the odds are 5/1 against you succeeding.

A direct shot at a blot (i.e. one where all the intervening points are closed and the blot is no further than six points away from you) is a 25/11 against shot. The second table in Chapter Two shows very clearly the odds against hitting a blot supposing that the intervening points are open. I advise you to go over this table, and indeed the whole of Chapter Two, and make sure that the information that it contains has really "sunk in".

How do you calculate the odds of being hit if some of the intervening points are not open? Look at example (**1**). It is Black's roll. What are the odds against him hitting your blot at R8?

First you work out which rolls *will* hit it. There are six – 6-1, 1-6, 5-2, 2-5, 4-3 and 3-4. Therefore there

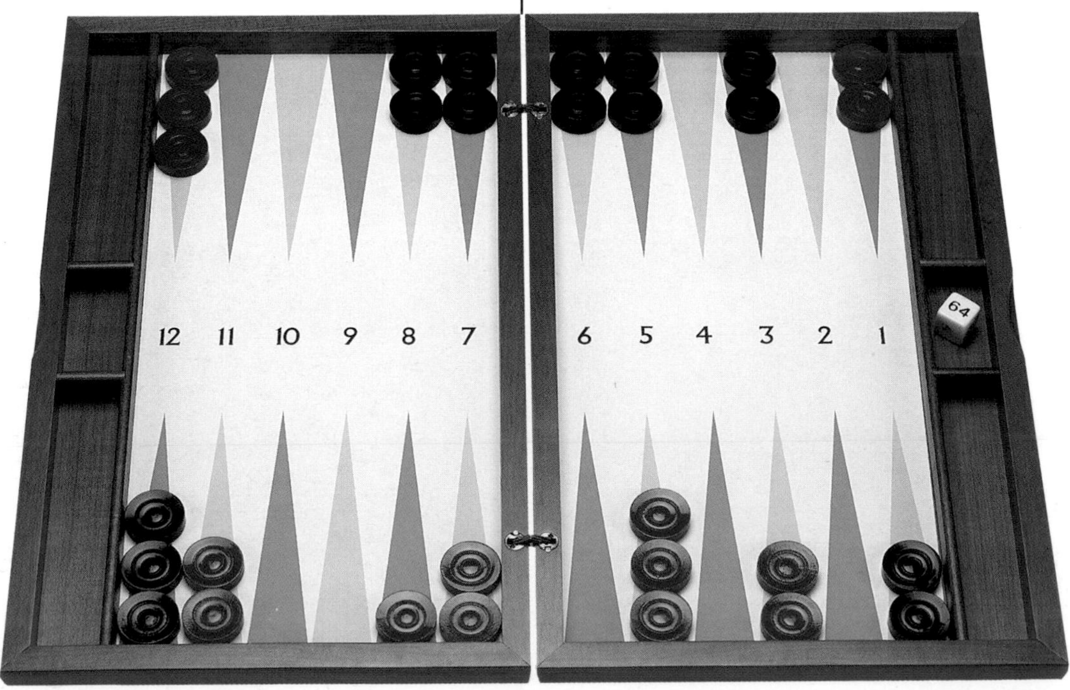

1

are thirty ways of *not* hitting it. The resulting odds are 30/6 or, in other words, 5/1 against. So the rule is work out how many rolls *will* hit, then subtract that number from 36 and there's your answer expressed as a fraction.

In example (**2**) your blot on R8 can be hit in *18 different ways*: 6-5, 6-4, 6-3, 6-2, 6-1, 1-6, 2-6, 3-6, 4-6, 5-6, 4-2, 2-4, 6-6, 2-2, 3-4, 4-3, 5-2 and 2-5. 36 less 18 = 18 ways it cannot be hit. Therefore the odds are exactly 1/1 or even money that you will be hit. If Black played this identical position thirty-six times he would *probably* hit your blot eighteen times and miss it on the other eighteen occasions.

Now let us break some new ground. Look at example (**3**). What are your chances of re-entering your man from the bar? Well, let us take a look. Half of Black's inner table points are open, half are closed. So half the time we will re-enter, half the time we will not. It is 50-50, an even (1/1) chance. That's right isn't it? Is it? No it isn't!

Only nine rolls prevent you from re-entering: 6-6, 4-4, 2-2, 2-4, 4-2, 2-6, 6-2, 4-6 and 6-4. Therefore 27 rolls will enable you to re-enter. It is correct therefore to say that you are 9/27 (odds-on) favourite to re-enter on your first roll. 9/27! That is a far cry from 1/1!

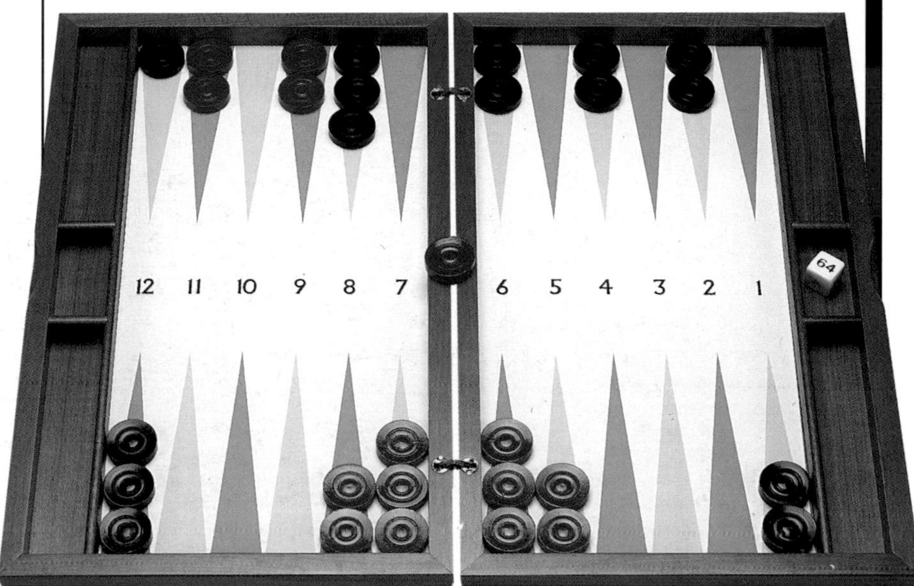

3

2

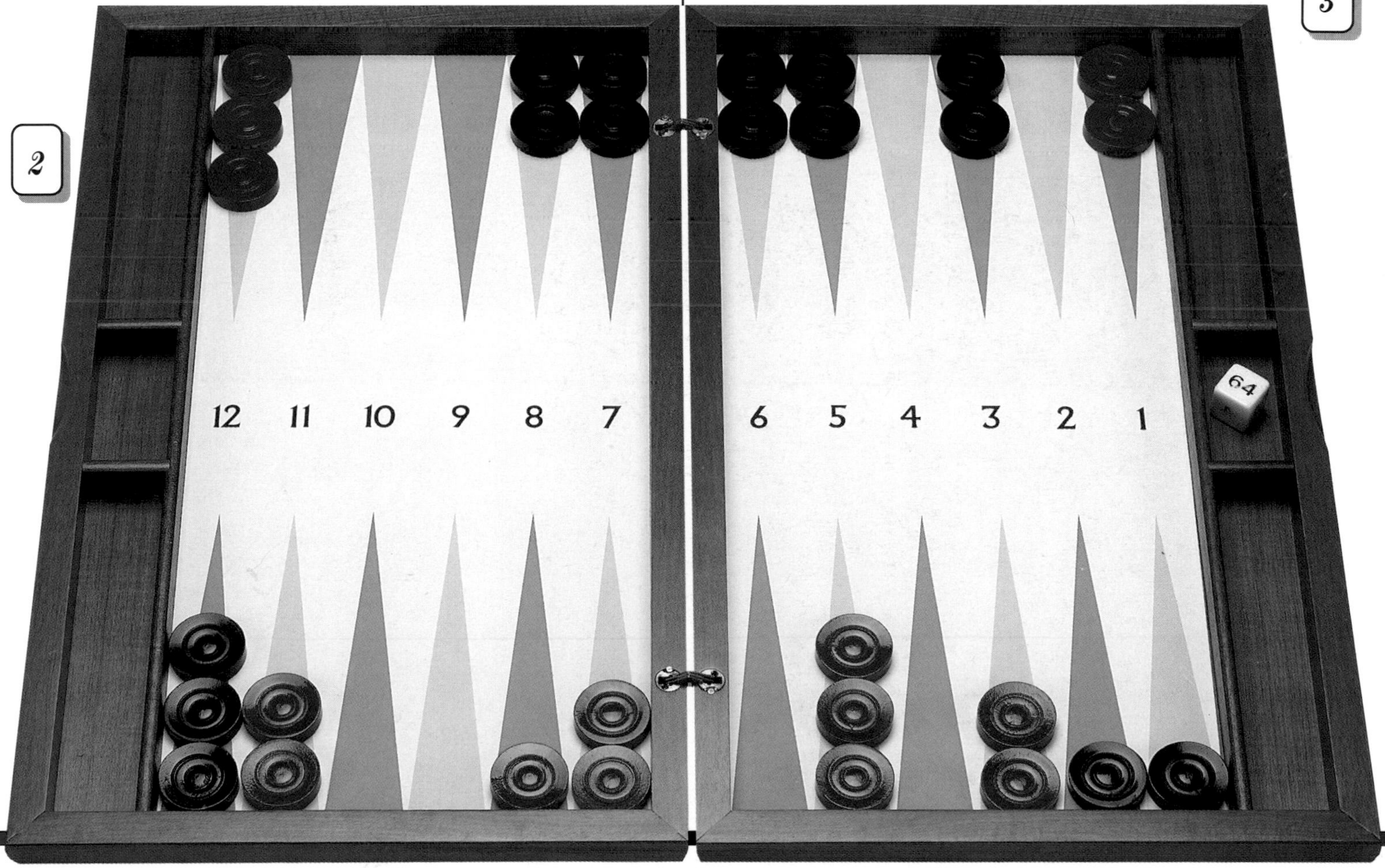

12 11 10 9 8 7 6 5 4 3 2 1

64

The table which follows, gives you the odds for and against you re-entering one man from the bar.

NUMBER OF OPEN POINTS	WAYS TO COME IN	% CHANCE OF RE-ENTERING	ODDS FOR OR AGAINST
5	35	97%	35/1 in favour
4	32	89%	8/1 in favour
3	27	75%	3/1 in favour
2	20	56%	5/4 in favour
1	11	31%	25/11 against

ODDS FOR AND AGAINST RE-ENTERING ONE MAN FROM THE BAR

My next table of odds shows you what happens when you have *two* men on the bar and have to re-enter. Are your chances of re-entering halved? Let us see:

NUMBER OF OPEN POINTS	WAYS TO COME IN	% CHANCE OF RE-ENTERING	ODDS FOR OR AGAINST
5	25	69%	25/11 in favour
4	16	44%	5/4 against
3	9	25%	3/1 against
2	4	11%	8/1 against
1	1	2·7%	35/1 against

ODDS FOR AND AGAINST RE-ENTERING <u>TWO</u> MEN FROM THE BAR

POINTS ON WHICH MAN OR MEN ARE LOCATED	NUMBER OF WAYS TO BEAR ALL OFF FIRST TIME	ODDS IN FAVOUR OR AGAINST	YOUR % PROBABILITY OF BEARING ALL OFF IN TWO ROLLS
6 and 6	4	8/1 against	78%
6 and 5	6	5/1 against	88%
5 and 5	6	5/1 against	92%
6 and 4	8	7/2 against	93%
5 and 4	10	13/5 against	96%
6 and 3	10	13/5 against	97%
4 and 4	11	25/11 against	98%
6 and 2	13	23/13 against	99%
5 and 3	14	11/7 against	99%
6 and 1	15	7/5 against	99+%
4 and 3	17	19/17 against	99+%
3 and 3	17	19/17 against	99+%
5 and 2	19	19/17 in favour	100% certain
5 and 1	23	23/13 in favour	100% certain
4 and 2	23	23/13 in favour	100% certain
3 and 2	25	25/11 in favour	100% certain
2 and 2	26	13/5 in favour	100% certain
6	27	3/1 in favour	100% certain
4 and1	29	29/7 in favour	100% certain
5	31	31/5 in favour	100% certain
3 and 1	34	17/1 in favour	100% certain
4	34	17/1 in favour	100% certain
2 and 1	36	Certain to bear off	100% certain
3	36	Certain to bear off	100% certain
1 and 1	36	Certain to bear off	100% certain
2	36	Certain to bear off	100% certain

ODDS FOR AND AGAINST BEARING YOUR LAST MAN OR LAST TWO MEN OFF IN ONE OR TWO ROLLS

To help you remember this last table of odds it will be useful to notice that the odds column is exactly the *reverse* of the odds column in the previous table. So you need only commit *one* of the lists to memory.

In the previous chapter I explained the "closest-closer", the "5-2", and the "old one-two" rules. The next, rather forbidding-looking table sets out the proof of these rules by showing every conceivable two and one man endgame situation that you can encounter and your odds of bearing off first throw. With the use of the doubling cube being so much a part of the modern game of backgammon, the information contained in this table will prove to be very useful. If you take the trouble to absorb it, it could save you much money. What better reason could you have for studying anything?

The thick dividing line about midway down the table indicates the break-even point. If your man or men are located in a position *below* the line, you are a favourite to bear off on your next roll and win. If, however, your position is *above* the line, the odds are against you bearing off next time. Just how much against you will depend upon your exact position. The table tells all.

The chapter on the doubling cube that follows will show you how to use this table to great advantage. But first I have another problem for you.

QUIZ QUESTION

What are your chances here (**4**) of hitting Black's blot at B12 on your next roll? Work out how many rolls will hit it and the exact odds of this eventuality happening. The answer is on page 125.

4

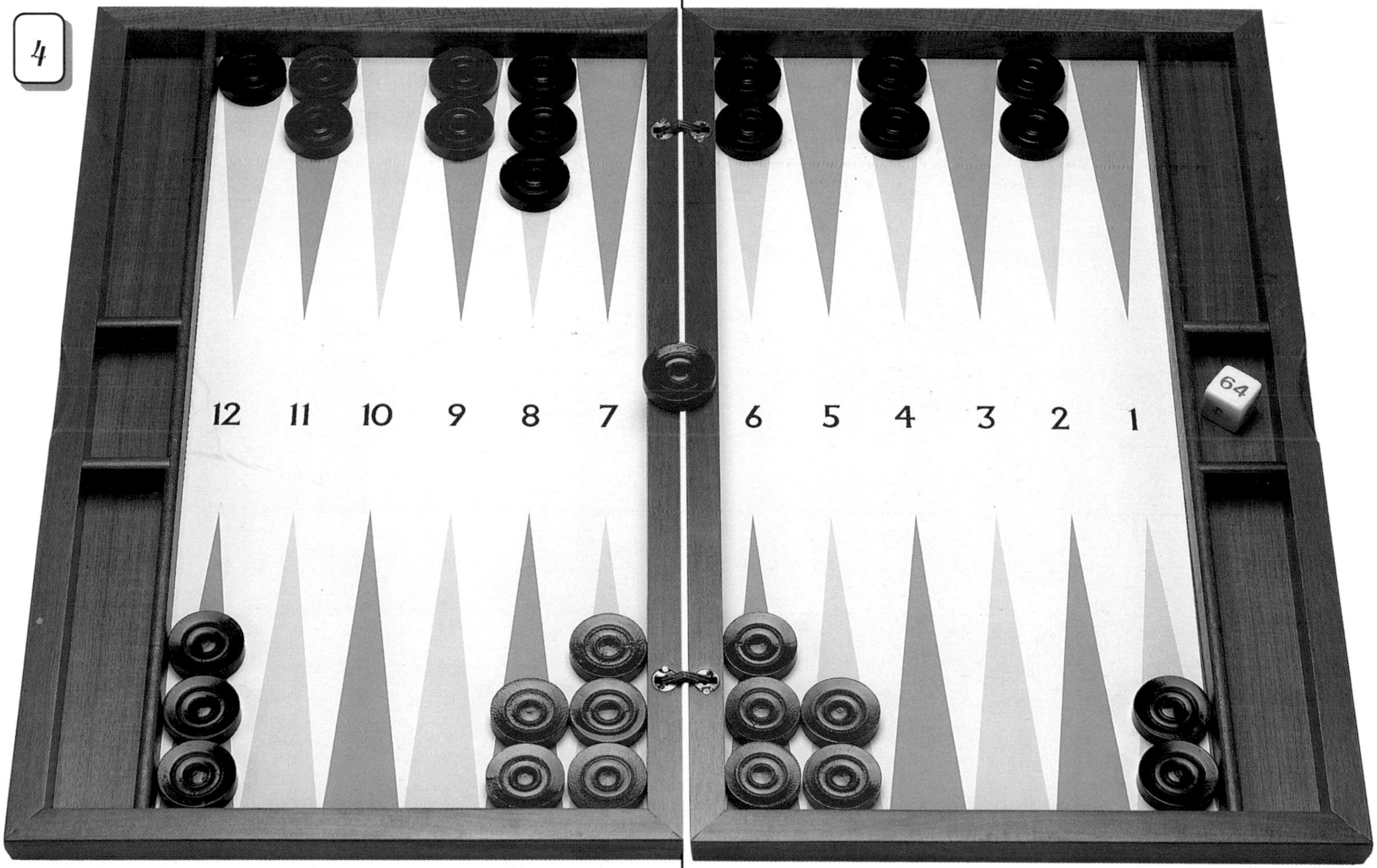

12 11 10 9 8 7 6 5 4 3 2 1

THE DYNAMIC DOUBLER

This is the most important chapter in the whole book. In the first chapter I gave you a description of a doubling cube and its use. In case you have not already digested this information, I repeat the salient points below. I must stress, *The player who masters the use of the doubling cube also masters backgammon!* This may be a slight exaggeration but I cannot emphasize too strongly how important the principles surrounding its use are.

AT THE DOUBLE!

Although the history of backgammon can be traced back thousands of years, it is only in the last seventy or so years that we have seen the doubling cube introduced into the game. The transformation has been miraculous! What was just an enjoyable game of strategy has, in modern times, emerged as a game of consummate skill and fascination. All thanks to the "Dynamic Doubler". It has added an extra element to the game – **excitement**!

A doubling cube is shaped like a die, and is usually larger than the other dice. Instead of dots the six sides are numbered: 2, 4, 8, 16, 32 and 64 (**1**). The doubling cube is used to increase the points value (stakes) of the game and must, therefore, be treated with great respect.

At the beginning of the game the doubling cube is placed on the centre of the bar with the number 64 showing. Any player may start to double after the first roll – and may double or re-double at any stage of the game, even on the last roll. To double your opponent, you pick up the cube and place it in front of him on the board with the 2 uppermost (**2**). This must be done *before* you throw the dice.

1

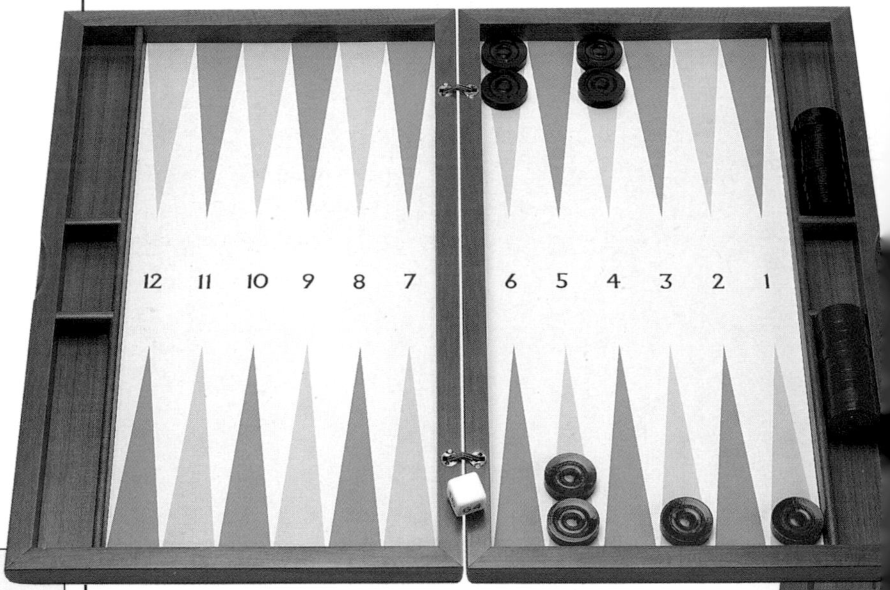

2

He now has two options. He can accept or refuse the double. If he accepts your double it means that he is willing to play on for double the original stake money. He merely picks up the cube and places it in front of himself off the playing surface. He is now said to "control" the cube and he, and only he, may re-double it to 4 (**3**).

If you now win this game he has to pay you twice the original stake. If you win by a gammon he will have to pay you *four* times the original stake (two points the game x two points on the cube = four), while a backgammon will relieve him of six times the original stake (three points the game x two points on the cube - six).

If he refuses the double, he forfeits the game. It is over immediately, regardless of the stage you have reached in the game. He then pays you only the original stake agreed upon.

These then are the "mechanics" of the doubling cube. We will now look at each point in greater detail, and I will pass on to you some very useful advice. Remember that if, through sheer bad luck, you are losing a game, a thorough knowledge of when to offer, accept or refuse a double will prove invaluable to you. You will minimize your losses and may even turn the tables on Lady Luck. Obviously, if you are winning, shrewd doubling judgement will reap even richer rewards for you.

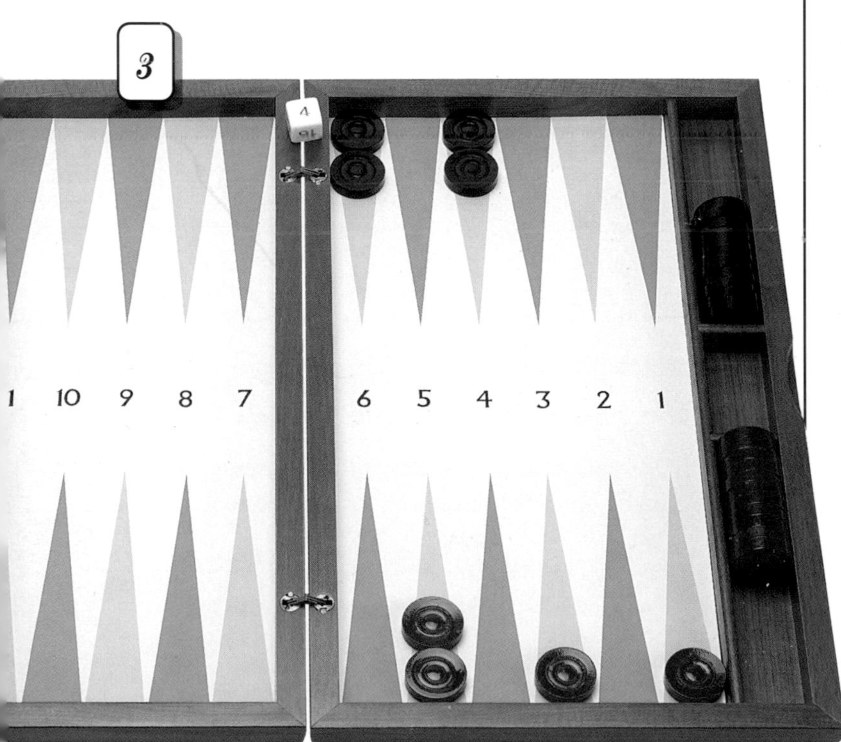

Too many so-called backgammon players play the game in a very half-hearted way and never use the cube at all. Time and time again I meet players of quite a good standard who say, "Oh! I don't want to be bothered with that thing!" or "I don't want to use the cube because I always like to see how the game ends – I like to play it out." What they are really saying is that they are frightened of the cube, as they are of anything that they do not understand.

So your first golden rule for successful play is *always use the doubling cube*.

If you have accepted a double, keep the cube where you can see it at all times. I place it on the bar at my side of the board. It gets in my way at times but at least I can never forget that I have it. With my favourite backgammon set I have an enormous doubling cube. It is 2 inches (51mm) square. As the doubling cube is the most important weapon in your armoury, it deserves to be noticed. Get yourself a large one. If you cannot find a decent sized one in your local shops, it should not be too hard for you to make one.

Although it is vital that you learn to handle the cube well, I am unable to offer you any magical formula for its successful use. I can almost hear you saying, "If you are smart enough to write a book, why cannot you give me a simple thing like that?" Well there is no simple answer. Doubling is a very complex art. So many things have to be taken into consideration. Your relative positions have to be assessed. Is your opponent easily bluffed? Does he readily accept doubles regardless of his position? So many questions. You are the only person who can answer them all.

A FEW SIMPLE RULES

I can, however, offer some general rules that should help you. The first is: *Never give premature doubles.*

You may find yourself storming ahead in the early stages and feel like doubling your opponent. Resist the temptation. Fortunes in backgammon tend to fluctuate and, obviously, there is more chance of a double turning sour on you if you have doubled early on in the game. You will also have lost "control" of the cube and your opponent can pick his moment to throw it back in your face.

Before you offer a first double make sure that all the following pointers have been observed:

- Your opponent must have two or three (but not four) men bottled up in your inner table.
- You have at least four strong blocking points in a semi-prime.
- You must be further advanced than him by at least two or three throws.
- Your opponent must be sufficiently advanced so as to make a satisfactory back game unattractive to him.

We can generally sum up these points by stating another golden rule: *When further advanced than your opponent, if he has no chance for a good back game – double*. If he has any sense he will *not* accept.

Whenever you believe that your opponent will not accept the cube, you should double. If you think that he will accept the cube, do not offer it unless you are quite confident that you will win the game.

WHEN TO ACCEPT A DOUBLE

What about accepting doubles? Well, your decision to accept a double or re-double should be based only on your chances of winning *not* on the number currently showing on the doubling cube. If it would be correct for you to accept a double with the cube on 2, it must be equally correct for you to accept a similar situation with the cube on 32! Similarly if it would be wrong to accept on 2, it would be equally (not more) wrong on 32. So you must always have the courage of your convictions and refuse if you see that you have an inferior game.

The only time that these points *may* not apply is during Tournament Play when the object is to reach a pre-arranged points total before your opponent. This need not concern us here.

The next golden rule to observe is: *You should accept any double if you are not more than a 3/1 underdog*. Why? Well it is a simple matter of mathematics. Let us do some sums and see what happens. Odds of 3/1 against you means simply that, by the law of probability, you will lose three out of every four times that you encounter the same situation. Why then should you accept?

Well, if you *do not* accept you will lose all four games for a total loss of four points (or pounds, or dollars, or whatever). If you accept all four doubles, you are likely to lose three of them (-6 points), and win one (+2 points) for a net loss of four points.

Exactly the same situation as if you had refused all four – so you lose no more. By playing the doubles you are inviting the tide of fortune to turn in your favour and you *could* defy the odds and win a couple of games thus breaking even and losing nothing.

If you are only a 2/1 underdog and you refuse, say, three doubles, you will be minus three points. If you accept all three and the odds remain true, you will lose two (-4 point) and win one (+2 points) for a net loss of only two points. That is one point better off than if you had refused all of the doubles. Remember that the break-even rule of acceptance is 3/1 against. If the odds are worse – drop out.

If you have a slight doubt about a double that is being offered to you – accept it! If you have a slight doubt about offering a double – do not. In backgammon, as in real life, it is usually more profitable to receive than to give!

When you offer a double, what you are actually saying is . . . "My position is so much better than yours, I cannot lose. You would be a fool to accept this double. You must retire at once." You must, therefore, only offer a double to your opponent when you feel sure that he will refuse. If he accepts the double, it is *he* who has made a mistake and you should profit by it.

It will be obvious, therefore, that if you are in a position to win a gammon or even a backgammon, it would be foolish to offer him the cube even though you are ahead. It would give him the chance of refusing the double, thus immediately bringing the game to an end and allowing him to get away with only paying you the original stake or the amount of the previous double. So this must be the only exception that proves the rule.

THE 5-2 ENIGMA

There is one instance when one player doubles, his opponent accepts – and yet both are perfectly correct. Study the following position (**4**).

It is Red's roll. Black will definitely bear off on his next roll. Should Red double? The answer is yes. He is 17/19 favourite to bear off on his next roll. From Black's point of view it is also a "take" because there are 19 winning rolls for Red and 17 winning rolls for Black. 19/17 against. That is a far cry from our

4

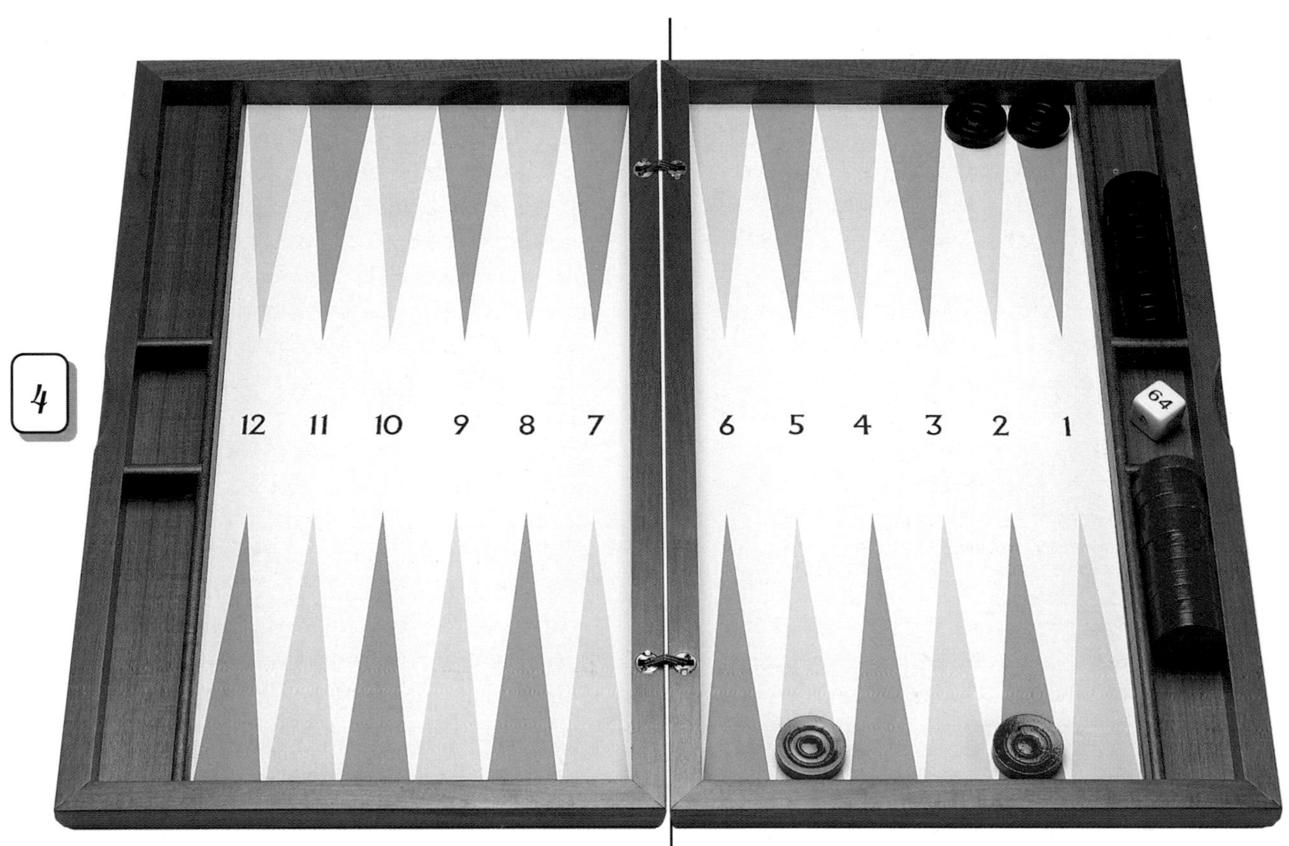

5

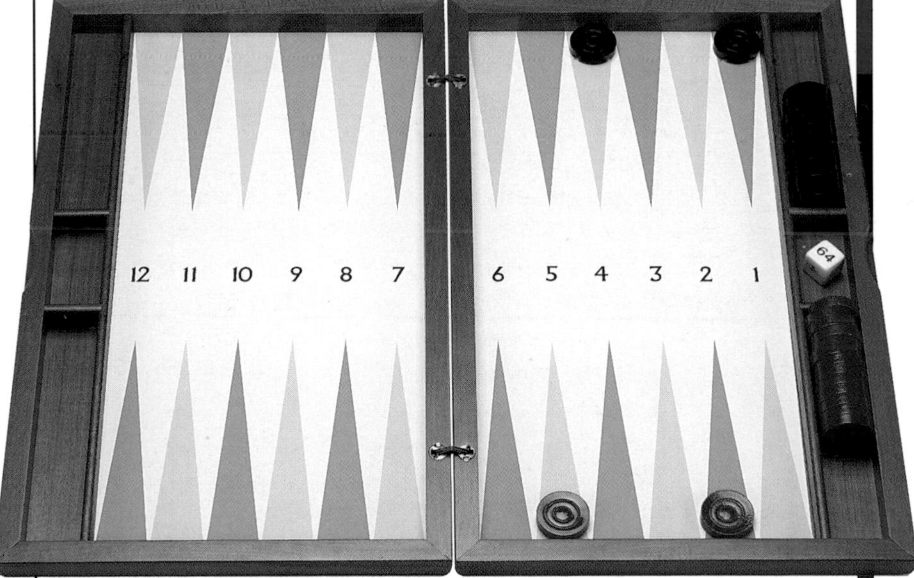

break-even point of 3/1 against, so Black must also go along with this double. Both players are correct.

So remember this rule: If your last two men are in a 5 2 situation (or better) you should double even though your opponent will definitely bear his two remaining men off on his next roll.

Now look at this (**5**). Should Red double? I have already stated that with 5-2 or better this situation calls for a double. And Black is worse off than in my previous illustration. The correct answer, in this case, is that you should *not* double.

Why? Well, by *not* doubling you will be twice as well off! This is because if you fail to bear both men off at your first attempt, you *may* get a second chance because there are seven possible rolls that prevent Black from bearing off first time: 3-2, 2-3, 3-1, 1-3, 2-1, 1-2 and 1-1.

If you had doubled and failed to bear both men off, Black would certainly re-double you and you would have to "drop". His men are *better than 5-2. Twenty-nine* throws will bear both his men off – only seven will cause him trouble. That is odds of slightly over 4/1 in his favour. So all things considered, you will be a lot better off by hanging on to the doubling cube. You are still favourite to win.

THE HUMAN FACTOR

Notwithstanding the mathematics of the doubling cube, the psychology of your opponent should be an important factor in determining whether or not to offer a double. Does he always accept, regardless? Does he show sound judgement? Does he always refuse a double. If your opponent always refuses doubles, you might offer him one against the odds! One man's meat is another man's poison – so be careful. A wrong double given to an expert means suicide.

I now want to state four points that may seem obvious, but which are all too easily forgotten in the excitement of play.

- *Never accept a bad double*. A bad double remember, is when you are worse off than 3/1 against winning.
- *Never give a bad double*. You should be *at least* a 3/2 favourite before doubling and you must be 2/1 or better before you consider parting with the cube by re-doubling.
- *Always accept a good double*. If your opponent offers you a good deal, do not hesitate. Accept with a smile on your face. It is nothing short of criminal to refuse a "gift horse".
- *Always give a good double*. Do not give even a shade of odds away unless you are a far superior player than your opponent or a playing the "psychological field".

BEAVERING

While I remember it, there is one more doubling situation that you must beware of. It is called beavering. This is how a beaver works. Your opponent offers you a double (say from 1 to 2) and you think that his judgement is seriously at fault. Frankly you think that he must have "lost his marbles". You pick up the cube (now showing 2), turn it to 4, and say . . . "I offer you a beaver."

By this action you are intimating that you think he was nuts to offer you the double in the first place and are prepared to back up your opinion by playing for *double* his proposed double! Psychological dynamite!

The real "sting in the tail" when you beaver someone is that you also keep "control" of the cube, even though, by beavering, you offered the last double! In one fell swoop the cube has been turned twice.

Dynamite indeed – but you had better make sure that you are right! If your opponent now backs down and refuses your beaver he loses (in our example) *two points* – not one. If he accepts, and you were right in your assessment of the situation, congratulations – you are now playing for four points.

Beavering is not acceptable practice in tournament play and, frankly, is frowned upon by most players. However, I do not see why you should not profit from the stupidity of your opponent. Do you?

LAYING DOWN THE GROUND RULES

I would advise you to agree the "terms" of play with your opponent before you begin to play. This will save any misunderstanding later. Agree upon the following points:

- Is beavering allowed?
- How much a point are you playing for?
- How many automatic doubles are allowed? As you know, the game is automatically doubled if you both roll the same number at the very outset of the game. Often, when you re-roll, you throw a tie again. The cube now goes to 4. What happens if you tie again? And again? The game could easily get out of hand before you get started. For this reason most players limit automatic doubles to one or, at most, two.
- What colour pieces are you playing?
- Which way round do you want to play? In respect of these last two points, always give first choice to your opponent. Say that you do not mind which way round you play or what colour pieces you play with. Say it with confidence. This is really good psychology!

6

7

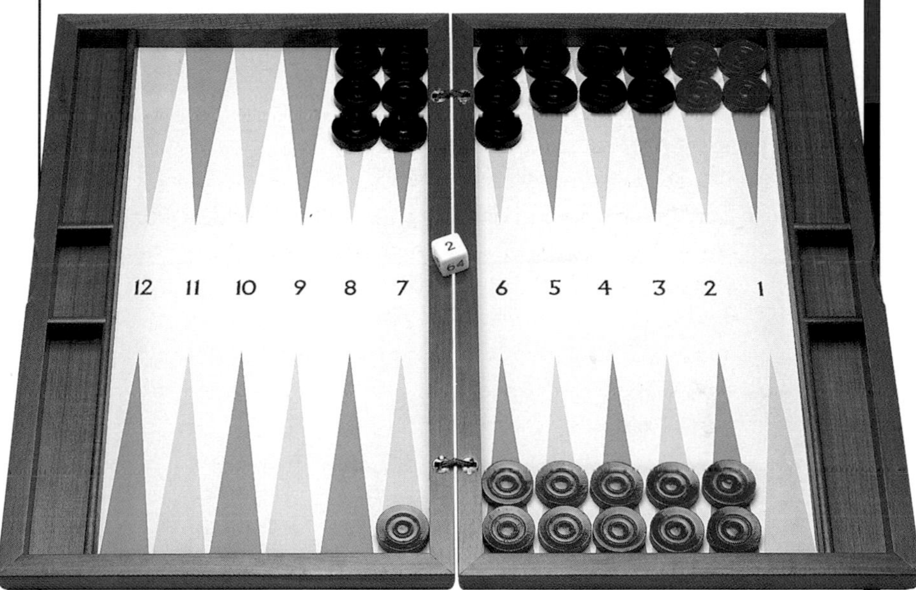

QUIZ QUESTIONS

I shall end the chapter, as always, by giving you a few problems to solve. In this position (**6**) Black doubles. Would Red be correct in accepting?
Here again (**7**) Black doubles. Should Red accept?
Finally, take a good look at this position (**8**). Should Red double? The answers to these problems are on page 125.

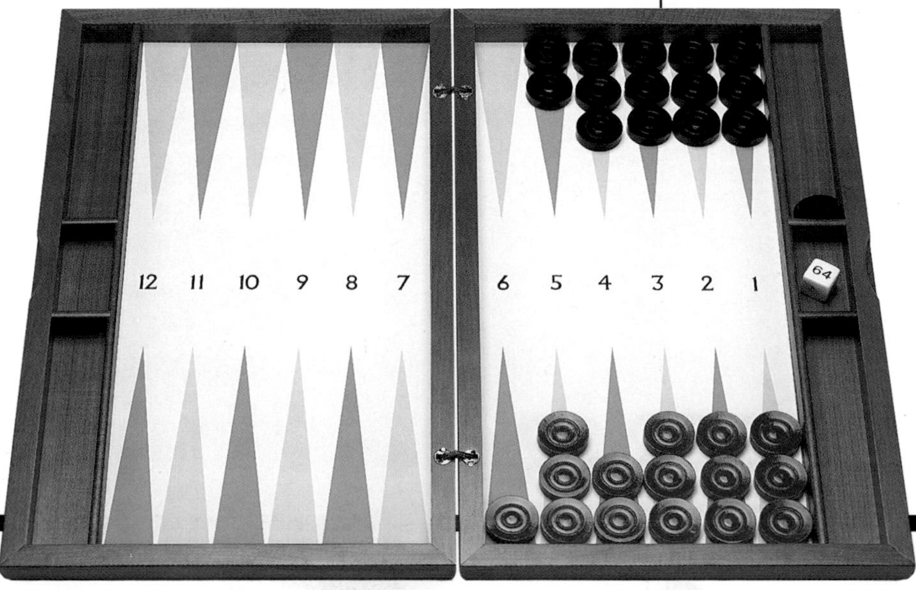

8

CHOUETTE

Wherever backgammon players club together, you will inevitably find games of chouette in progress. Chouette is played by three or more people on the same board. It is a very sociable pastime because even the odd man out gets to play. Nobody is left out in the cold. It is mostly played in backgammon clubs because inevitably in these establishments there are more players wanting to participate than boards to play on.

RULES OF THE GAME

Let us assume that four players decide to play, although any number may do so. This is how they begin. Firstly each player rolls a die to determine an order. Any ties are re-thrown of course. The person throwing the highest number plays against the other three who "gang up" on him. Their highest roller is appointed as their Captain and he or she sits down and plays the "man (or woman) in the box" (**1**).

The team captain can confer and seek advice from his or her partners (C and D) on any question that may arise in the course of the game. However, the captain is the final arbiter and his or her partners must abide by his or her decisions, except when it comes to deciding whether or not to accept a double offered to them by the man in the box.

If the team wins, the man in the box has to pay each team member his full count for the game. If the man in the box wins, each member of the team has to pay him his full count for the game. Furthermore, if the man in the box wins, then the team captain is demoted and becomes the lowest ranking member of the team and (C) now becomes captain and tries *his* luck against (A).

(A) remains in the box until he is beaten. At such a time (A) goes to the foot of the opposing team and becomes its lowest ranking member, while its captain now goes into the box and takes on the other three. It is a very fair way of playing because everyone gets a chance to be the man (or woman) in the box.

Obviously, a very long winning run for the man in the box can be very profitable for him because each win is multiplied by the number of his opponents. Thus, if you are playing against three opponents and you gammon them with the cube at 4, and you are playing for £1 a point, you would win £4 x 2 x 3 = £24!

Extra players can join in on a chouette even after it has begun. The new player becomes the lowest ranking member of the team in the first game in which he participates, and has to advance through the ranks like everyone else.

The man in the box plays alone and scores separately against each one of his opponents because, as already explained, although they are bound by the final decisions of their captain, when it comes to deciding whether or not to accept a double offered them by the man in the box, they are on their own and may make up their own minds. After all it is their own money at stake!

Should the captain decline to accept a double offered by the man in the box, he loses his position and pays the man in the box his due previous to the proposed double. A double that has been declined by the captain may be accepted by any or all of the other team members. The highest ranking of those accepting becomes the captain until the termination of that game.

Accepting or declining a double does not change the rank of any team member when the new captain

loses. If he wins, however, the new captain takes the box. Those players refusing to accept the double are out of that particular game and may not be consulted about it.

The beginner can learn much from playing chouette and this knowledge can come very inexpensively if he handles his money carefully. As a team member he can put forward his suggestions or remain in the background benefiting by noting the moves and listening to the logic expounded by his partners.

The best advice that I can offer a novice backgammon player when playing chouette for the first time and with players whom he considers to be stronger than himself is to follow the play of the person that he thinks is the *strongest* player in the chouette. When, inevitably, he finds himself in the box he should not offer or accept a double unless he is absolutely *certain* that he is right to do so. When in doubt – *drop*.

Many players try to confuse the man in the box by offering very early doubles. Do not be hustled – judge every offer strictly on its merits.

CHOUETTE ETIQUETTE

As a general rule players should not offer advice to their captain unless he or she asks for it, or they violently disagree with the captain's proposed move. Too much discussion slows up the game and detracts from the excitement that usually envelops chouette.

Automatic and fairly obvious moves should, of course, be made by the captain without consultation or comment. However, if the move is somewhat complex, the captain should move the men according to his or her own preference but leave the dice on the table to give the team mates the opportunity to comment. A move is only deemed over when the dice are picked up. If the captain is stumped over a move, he or she should openly ask for suggestions.

If a captain makes a move that is about as good, although not the same, as the move that you would have played were you in his place, it would be rather silly to raise an objection. These situations arise during the opening rolls, where many alternative moves with roughly equal potential abound.

No, save your comments for the situation where your captain has overlooked a far superior move (nobody is perfect – we all make those horrendous bloomers once in a while).

If you have to leave the table during the course of a game, ask the best player present to act on your behalf until you return, otherwise it will be assumed that you abide by the majority decision.

Is it an advantage to be in the box? Most players want it. Winners want it in order to win more. Losers want it in order to recoup their losses. Players who are neither ahead or behind want it in order to get a piece of the action.

I never want it!

The best way to win money at chouette is to keep a low profile – lean towards conservatism and avoid the spotlight at all times. The loser who seeks the box as a means of recouping his losses is doomed to failure. A successful gambler chases his *winning streak*, not his losing one.

If they are ahead, financially speaking, most players seek the box. The argument put forward is that, as you are already winning, the fact that the box is liable to pay out threefold should not concern you, because it is "their money that you are gambling with". This is spurious reasoning. The money is *not* "theirs" – it is "yours" – you have won it fairly and squarely and you should never consider it otherwise.

DEALS

If your partners plan a strategy that you strongly disagree with, you can offer to sell them your game. You may make a profit, break even or lose money on your deal but at least you have the satisfaction of knowing that you have disassociated yourself from what appears to you to be a suicide mission.

In cases like this, the box has the right to intercede and buy the game or games himself. For example, let us assume that the cube is on 4 and your captain has offered to buy your game for 2. You agree to sell. The box can pre-empt and buy your game for the two units agreed upon. He has first option on all sales in such instances.

The box can also instigate offers to the team members. Say the cube is on 4 and you (the box) are not too happy with the way things are going. You can offer to settle for 2. One or all of the team members may accept, or they may haggle and push you up to 3. They may decline your offer and force you to play on. All part of the fun – but be careful! Make sure that you have worked out the odds correctly before offering or accepting such a settlement.

COMING OF AGE

Backgammon, known as the "Game of Kings", is not necessarily the "Game of Gentlemen"! To kick your opponent when he is down is the general rule and to smile while you are doing it is quite normal. The art of "gamesmanship" prevails at all levels of the game. Gamesmanship is the utilization of every crafty dodge that you can think of to unsettle your opponent, force him to lose his concentration and generally "psyche" him out of the game. Many a good player, not versed in the art of gamesmanship, has found himself totally bewildered and confused when confronted with such a psychological onslaught and, as a result, has lost the game. Do not let this happen to you!

FOREWARNED IS FOREARMED

I have always believed that to be forewarned is to be forearmed, so we will here discuss some of these dodges at some length. I am *not* advocating that you adopt these measures, but it is as well that you are able to recognize them when you see them, so that you can avoid being duped or psyched out.

A correct mental approach to your game is essential if you are to aspire to the Hall of Backgammon Fame, but you can be psychologically dynamic in your play without having to resort to underhand methods, such as the ones I am about to expose.

THE BONE SHAKER

The "Bone Shaker" *can* be very irritating if you allow him to be. He sits opposite you and keeps up a monotonous rattling of his dice in the shaker while awaiting his turn (**1**). By shaking the dice in an impatient manner he aims to force you to play faster than you are used to and thus cause you to make mistakes.

I have seen this work successfully on numerous occasions. There are *five* ways to deal with the Bone Shaker:

- Ignore him and play on as normal.
- Start to play even slower and thus irritate *him*.
- Retaliate by shaking your dice too (with a big smile on your face of course)!
- Politely ask him to desist.
- Impolitely ask him to desist!

You take your pick. I tend to favour remedy number two although number three runs a very close second!

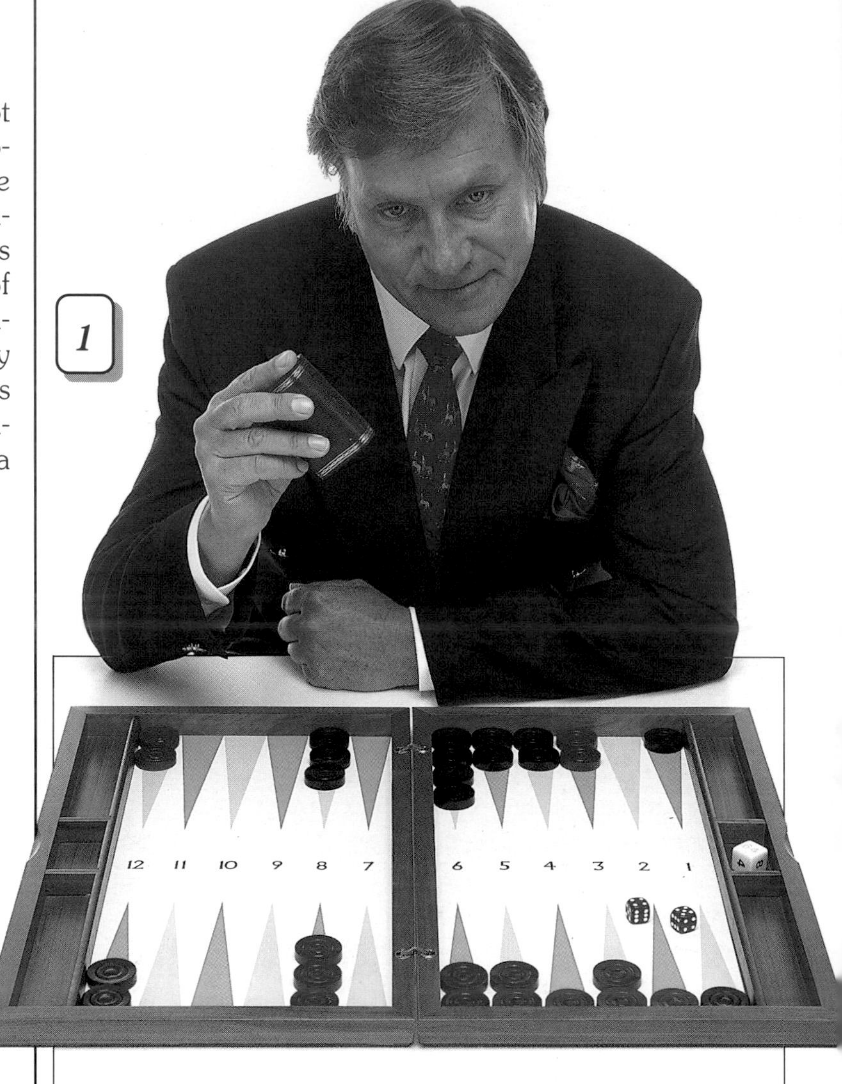

THE TUT-TUTTER

This is very evil! You have must made your move when from across the table you suddenly hear . . . "Tut-tut". You look up and your opponent is slowly shaking his head in apparent disbelief (**2**). He may even add . . ."I *am* surprised!"

Immediately you start imagining all sorts of things. Have you made a wrong move? Have you missed an obvious move? Has he seen something that you have not. The seed of doubt is sown! He will reap a harvest from that seed if you let him. So do not be thrown.

2

THE CHATTERBOX

As his name implies, the "Chatterbox" *never stops talking* (**3**). His verbal onslaught can be devastating. An expert chatterbox can literally "talk" you out of a game! I am not crazy or paranoid and I am not imagining things. I am deadly serious.

Just try to picture *yourself* on the receiving end of the following chatter. It is infuriating. It might well go something like this:

"Well – you stand no chance today, Tremaine. No chance at all. In fact I'm strongly tempted to offer you a double even before we open the set!"

You roll for starters. You win with 6-3.

"It's your first blunder, sorry, move. 6-3! Great roll! Yes, that's good. Very good indeed!"

It's probably the worst opening roll that you can have but, when chatterbox says that it is a good roll, he means good for him. You move B1 to B10. He is now rattling his dice cup furiously.

"A three would be nice . . . double three would be even nicer . . ."

He rolls 3-3 and his face splits with a grin from ear to ear.

"Ah ha! Fantastic! What did I tell you? I knew it was my day today!"

He points on your blot at B10 and also makes his five point with B8 to B5 (two men).

"There we are – it's just a matter of time now! Six and five would be a great roll now!"

3

You roll 6-5 and cannot re-enter. He smacks the doubling cube down in front of you with a resounding crash.

"The day of reckoning is at hand. If I was you I would retire . . ."

And so it goes on . . . and on . . . and on. A relentless barrage of verbal garbage. Be warned! The exponents of this ruse are usually very competent players – hard men to beat even when silent. They become even harder to beat when they use the chatterbox technique because you have to make a conscious effort to ignore them. Effort that you could and should be putting to better use.

There is only one remedy: tell him to shut up! If he persists just pack your bags and refuse to play him.

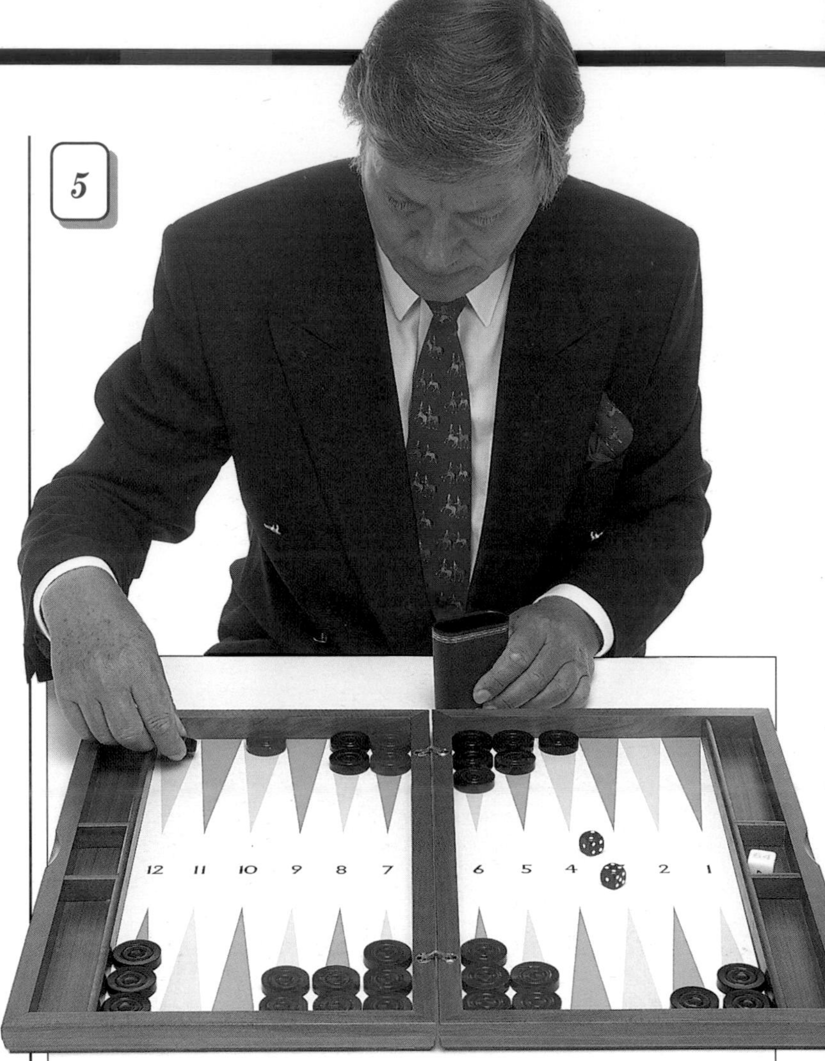

THE BOARD CLEANER

This is very subtle and works more often than you would believe possible. You have just thrown but have not yet moved. Your opponent, the "Board Cleaner", sees that there are two moves open to you – one right and the other wrong. He quickly notes the point on which your man would alight if you made the *wrong* move. He rubs the surface of the board at this point, as if to clean off a speck of dust or a stray hair (**4**). That is all he does!

He does not say a word, nor does he look at you – he just "cleans" the board. For some weird psychological reason an inexperienced player feels drawn to the cleaned point like a duck feels drawn to water.

THE TAKE OFF

One usually encounters the "Take Off" dodge when your opponent is attempting the launch himself into

the back game. He has three men back and would dearly like a fourth. To this end he has opened up and left a couple of blots in your path.

You now roll and could hit his blot if you chose to. *He reaches out, "takes off" his blot* (**5**) *and places it on the bar* (**6**) with a glum expression on his face as if to say that this was the last thing that he wanted you to do!

An inexperienced player may be bluffed into going along with this play; hitting the blot instead of making the move elsewhere on the board as he should. Your opponent's excuse, if you challenge him, is that he was merely being polite and was trying to help you in your play. Help you indeed! Some help!

THE DICE CHANGER

Occasionally found when competing in backgammon tournaments is the "Dice Changer". His luck is out and he seems to be throwing badly. He stops the game and insists on a change of dice (**7**)!

This creates an annoying delay in play. He is insinuating that there is something wrong with his dice and refuses to play on until they are changed. You can lose your rhythm and flow of concentration during such a psychological hold-up.

By far the best way to deal with this situation is to *immediately offer him your own dice to play with* and continue playing your game with his! Psychological dynamite!

THE TOILET TRIPPER

Like the "Dice Changer", the "Toilet Tripper's" aim is to delay the game and disturb your concentration. At the right psychological moment (either when he is a long way behind or a long way ahead), he just excuses himself from the table and vanishes, ostensibly to the toilet.

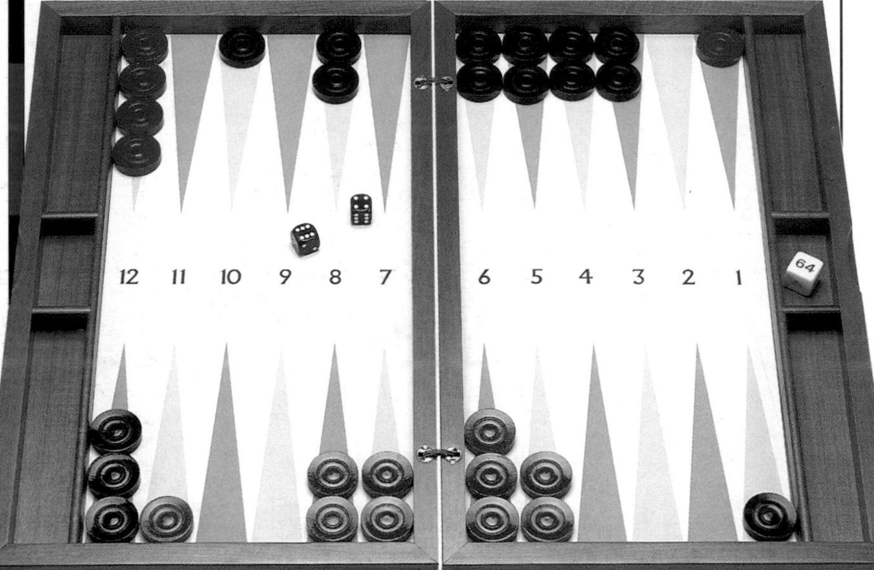

8

I have known players to be absent for as long as twenty minutes! There is nothing you can do about it – although I once saw a player retaliate by leaving the table the moment the offender had returned and absent himself for an additional ten minutes. Quite amusing.

It is a great shame that some players resort to tactics like those I have described. The game is not improved by them. Neither is it improved by out-and-out cheating! The two most common methods of cheating are the "Mis-call" and the "Prime jump". Both are made possible because of the great pace at which expert backgammon is played. I shall explain what they are so that you know what to look out for.

THE MIS-CALL

Exactly as its name implies, this technique involves making a false move. Look at example (**8**). If Black were to roll 6-3 he could make his prime by securing his bar point. however, he rolls 6-4.

Unabashed, he just carries on as if he *had* rolled 6-3, making his bar point (**9**) and quickly picking up his dice. Quite often this blatant move goes unnoticed. If you do notice and challenge him, he will swear blind that he threw 6-3. You are too late. He has picked up his dice. The incriminating evidence has gone.

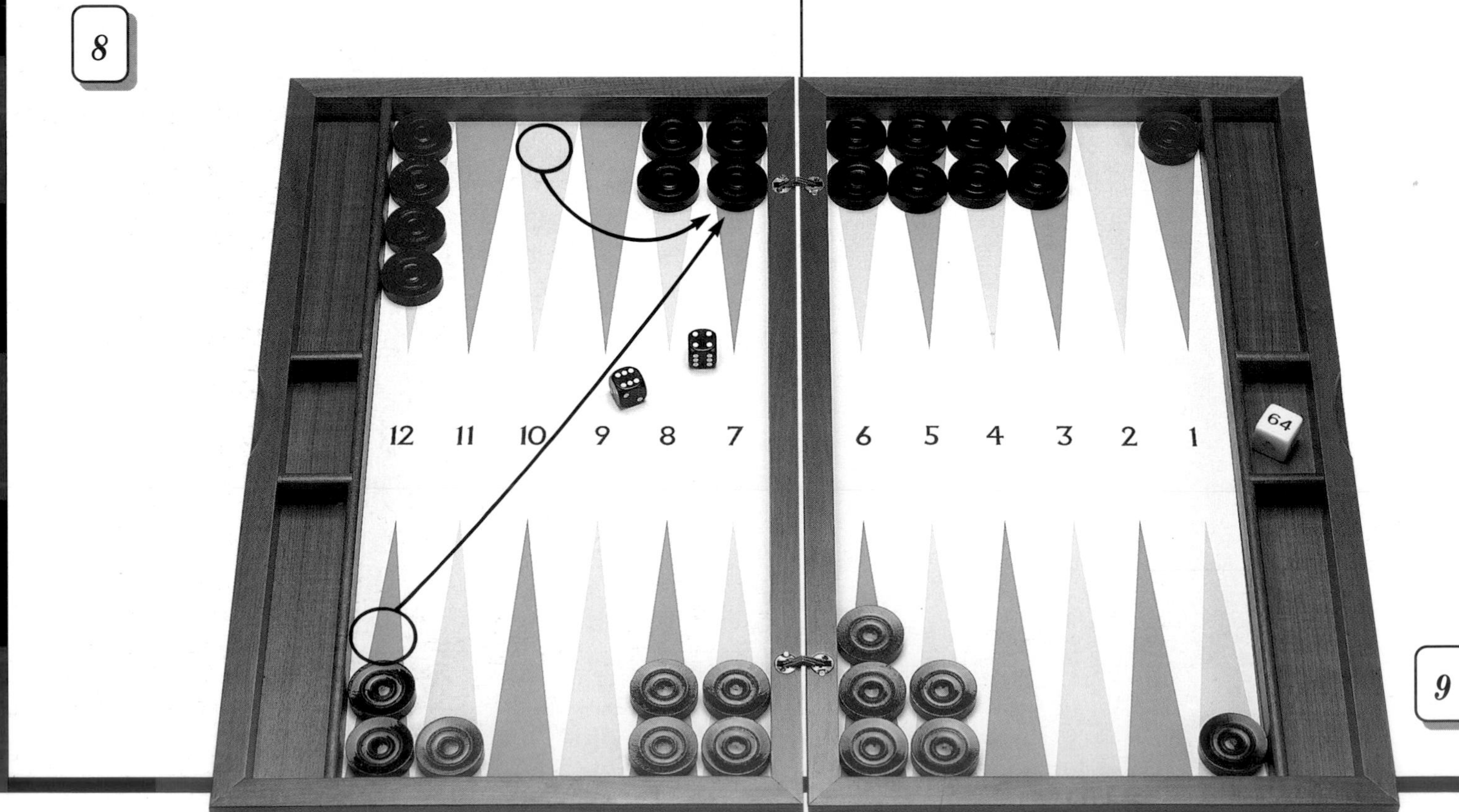

9

THE PRIME JUMPER

Another commonly found cheat is the "Prime Jumper". Look at example (**10**). Here Black rolls 5-1 and moves R3 to R9, moving the one man six places (**11**).

Yes, I know it is an illegal move but I warn you in all sincerity that if the move is played *boldly* enough, the fact that it is illegal will often go unnoticed. Remember that a shoplifter is only a shoplifter when he is caught. A cheat is only a cheat when he is caught cheating. Make sure that you catch the prime jumper in the act.

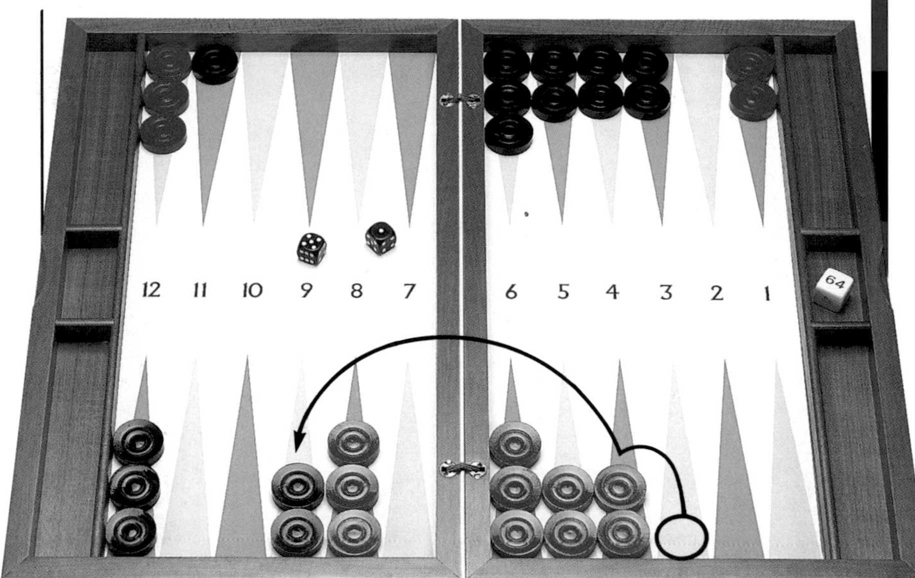

11

10

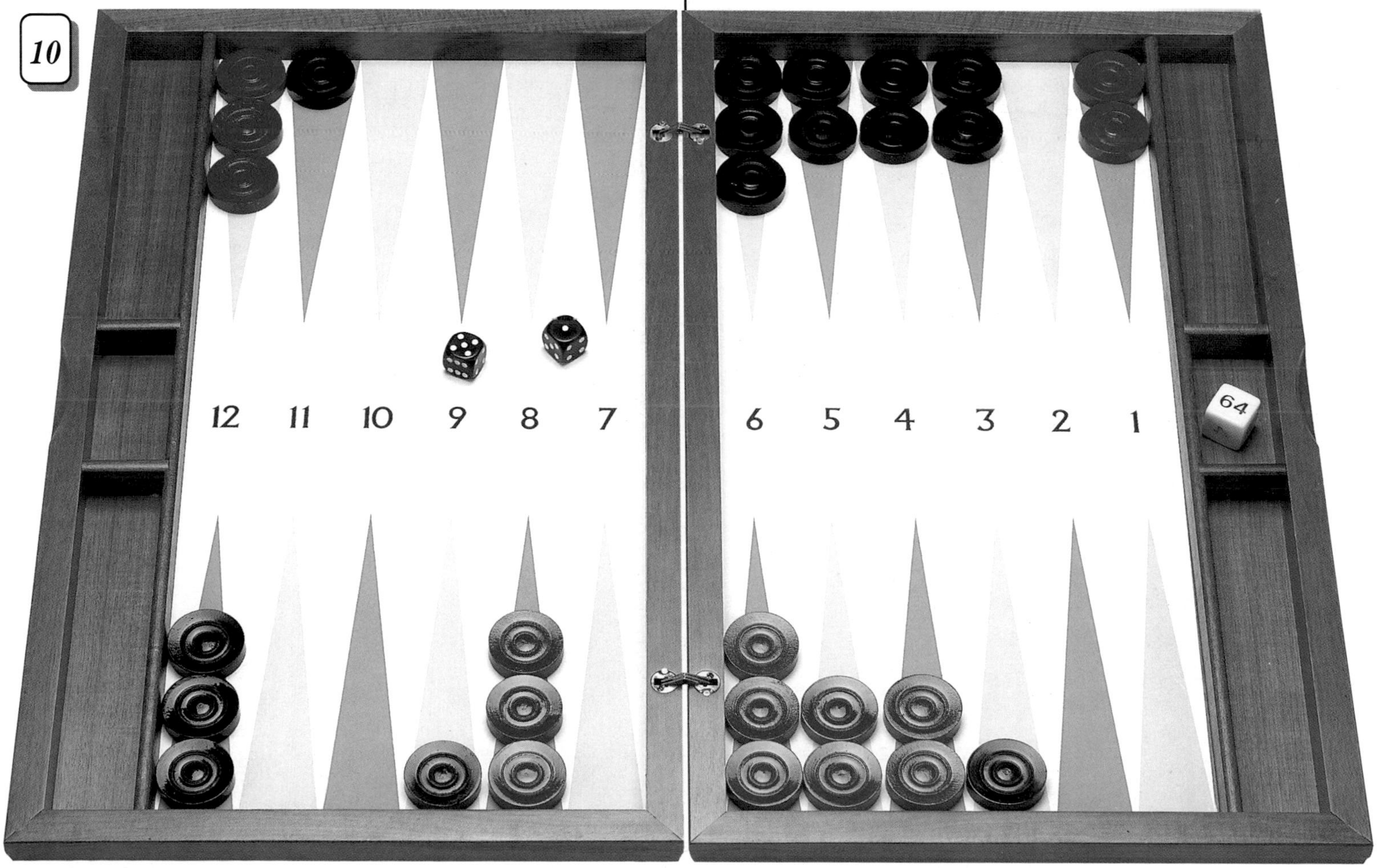

THE COVER UP

I once fell for this one – that is how I found out about it. It cost me money! The game had reached an advanced stage and I was about to begin bearing off. Black had previously doubled me and I owned the cube. It has developed into a running game and it was my roll (**12**).

A position count showed me to be one and a half rolls ahead and, as it was my roll, I reckoned that I was two and a half rolls better off than Black.

With this in mind I offered him the cube, re-doubling him to 4. I figured that he might not accept and thus I would be insuring myself against the eventuality of him throwing "miracle rolls".

12 11 10 9 8 7 6 5 4 3 2 1

12

If he *did* accept, he would have to throw a double or two to make up his two and a half rolls deficit.

He accepted the cube, which did not surprise me, but he accepted it *gleefully,* which did. I rolled 2-1 and began to bear off one man from my two point and another from my one point. Black stopped me immediately.

"Just a minute . . . you can't do that! What about this man over here?"

He was pointing indignantly to his bar point (**13**). My eyes nearly fell out of their sockets with surprise. There, on *his* bar point sat one of *my* own men! How could I have been so stupid? How could I have overlooked this man? Why had I not seen it before?

I will tell you why. Look at (**12**) again. See how Black's right hand is casually draped along the edge of the board? That is why I had not seen it before! Black has been "hiding" it from me!

While bringing the rest of my men round and into my inner table I had stupidly overlooked this "straggler". My opponent had not! Now I always ensure that my opponent keeps his hands and arms well clear of the board when he is not actually in play.

12 11 10 9 8 7 6 5 4 3 2 1

13

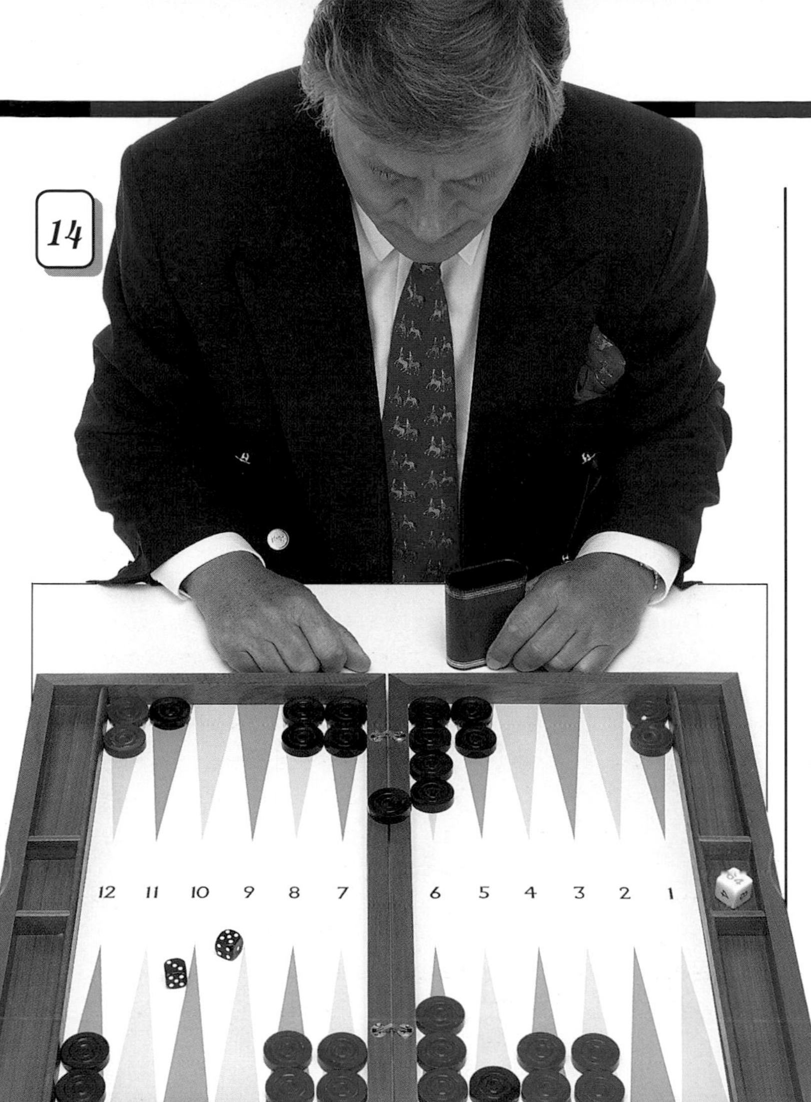

THE KNOCK OFF

Whether you are playing poker, bridge, backgammon or tiddlywinks, the best methods of cheating appear to be no more than accidents and can be passed off as such if they are noticed and challenged by you. What if you *do not* notice? That is the reason why I felt obliged to write this chapter. Prevention is the best policy.

When I first saw the "Knock Off" in action I thought that it, too, was an accident. Unfortunately or fortunately, depending upon the way that you look at it, my opponent tried the same dodge on me again about half an hour later.

We had been playing for about three hours so I had no way of knowing whether he had succeeded with the "Knock Off" as some earlier stage in the game. However, I did know that, this time, it was an intentional attempt to cheat. This was the position (**14**).

It was Black's roll and he threw 4-3. He reached over to his man at R5 and moved it to R12. *At the same time his sleeve brushed against his man on the bar and knocked it off the bar and onto his own six point* (**15**)!

The mis-direction here is good because the greater action of reaching across to move the man at R5 disguises the smaller action of knocking the man off the bar. The eyes always follow the greater movement. Cheeky isn't it! If you are not paying attention, you can be easily fooled by this.

I once played an opponent who, to put it mildly, had "had a few". While making a quite legitimate move he accidently knocked one of *my* men off the bar and onto my own six point! He was too drunk to notice. Never look a gift horse in the mouth!

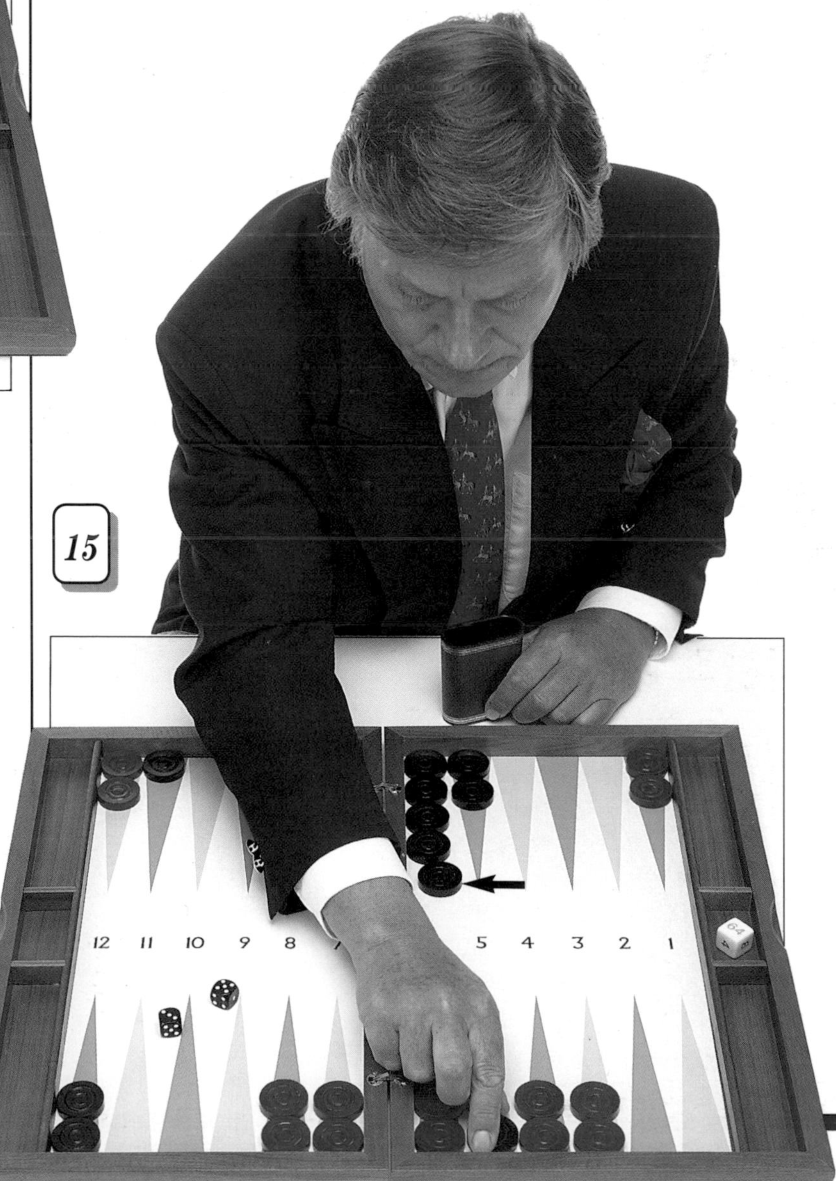

THE CORRECT ATTITUDE

I cannot overestimate the value of having the correct mental approach to your game. Your whole bearing is of the utmost importance. You should appear confident and invincible, smart and alert, clear headed and affluent (if you are playing for money), and assured of victory. Sounds like James Bond doesn't it? Cool as a cucumber – lethal as a man-eating shark. To come second in a game of backgammon is to come last. You must want to win and your bearing must tell your opponent that you probably will. If you can achieve this mental attitude you are half way to victory.

TREMAINE'S GOLDEN RULES

(1) *Learn the Official Rules of backgammon* (see pages 118-119) so thoroughly that you can quote them from memory.
(2) Take time out, before you begin to play, to *ascertain the terms that you will be playing for*: How much a point? How many automatic doubles? Is beavering acceptable? Do this in a matter of fact way.
(3) *Never concede a game unless your downfall is certain*. Note that I have said "certain" not "beyond any reasonable doubt". The unreasonable often happens in backgammon. Miracle rolls do happen. Besides, your opponent might drop dead before he can bear his last man off. You would then win by default!
(4) *Do not say, "Well played" if you mean it*! Keep your appreciation of your opponent's fine play to yourself.
(5) *Never show annoyance,* no matter how infuriating your opponent, his play, or your own bad luck may become.
(6) *Never offer advice to an inferior player* (unless teaching your family or a friend). He may take your advice and use it against you at some future date.
(7) *Do not stand any nonsense from "kibitzers"*. My dictionary defines kibitzer as an onlooker who gives unwanted advice. Unwanted is the operative word here. Tell them to be quiet or leave. Be polite but firm.
(8) *Do not "count out" your moves* by tapping the man you are moving on the board from point to point until it arrives at its final destination. If an expert sees you do that he will know immediately that you are a novice and will go straight for your throat. Practise eye training and co-ordination. The points on most modern boards are designated in two different and alternating colours.

They are coloured in this way purely to help you count, so take advantage of it. If the man that you are moving is on one colour and you throw an *even* number, your man will end up on a point of the same colour. If you throw an *odd* number, your man will end up on a point of a different colour.

Diagonally opposite points in the outer tables are *six* moves apart (**1**). The inside measurement of a table is *five* moves, and outside point (R1) to outside point (R12) is *eleven* moves (**2**).

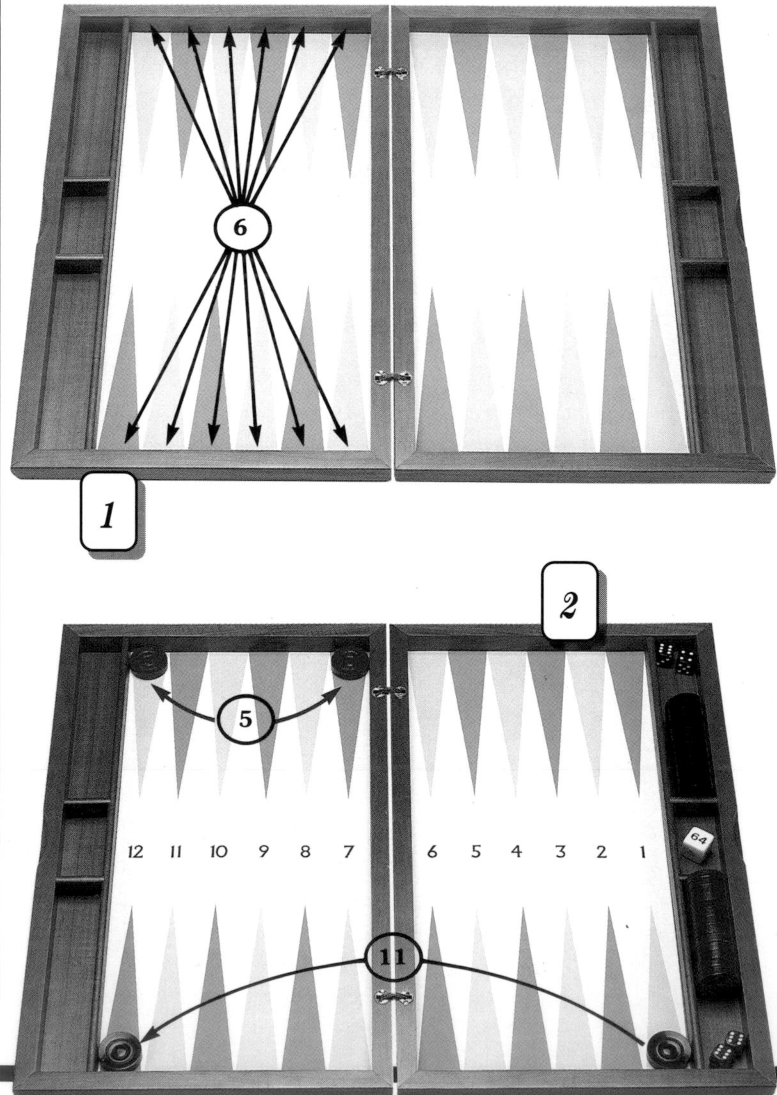

Once you have thrown, work out your move *in your head not on the board*. When you have made up your mind what you are going to do, then (and only then) pick up the man and move it *directly* to its final destination. It is clean and efficient and tells your opponent that you are fully conversant with the board and your game and are not a person to be trifled with.

(*9*) *Do not nod, shake your head or groan* in approval or disapproval at your opponent's moves. Remember that, according to the Rules, a move is only deemed completed when the dice have been picked up. If your opponent sees you shaking your head out of the corner of his eye, or hears you make an exclamation, he may alter his move before picking up his dice. You will have only yourself to blame!

(*10*) *Always play at your own pace* and never let your opponent alter this. Learn to play at a reasonable pace – not too fast – not too slow.

(*11*) *Make sure that you are sitting comfortably*. You are likely to remain seated for quite some time so it is important that you feel at ease.

(*12*) *The board should be well lit*. The size of board is important too.

(*13*) *Try not to play on a board that is smaller than 18" (45 cm) from one side to the other*. Smaller sets are really "toys" and play on them becomes rather fiddly. However, it is advisable also to own a small travelling set. I used to travel about 80,000 miles every year and my small set has helped me while away many a pleasant hour during the inevitable delays that the seasoned traveller encounters.

(*14*) Remember my warnings regarding the *size of dice and the type of shakers* to use? Turn back to Chapter Two and recap.

(*15*) *Be ambidextrous*. All the illustrations in this book are taken from Red's point of view and to him the board looks like this (**3**). From Black's point of view the board looks like this (**4**). As you will have to play Black as often as you are called upon to play Red, it is absolutely imperative that you learn to play both ways. Some players are only really happy playing one way. You must become indifferent to the direction of play and equally adept at both.

(*16*) *Correct an opponent's incorrect move if it is disadvantageous for you to let it stand*. If you want to practise a little gamesmanship, do so with an injured air – a "You'll have to do better than that" attitude!

(*17*) *Never correct an opponent's incorrect move if it is to your advantage to let it stand*. You are not obliged to.

(*18*) *Never play for more money than you can comfortably afford to lose*. You cannot expect to play well if you are worrying about money.

(*19*) Make sure that your opponent realizes that you regard a win as no more than your rightful due, and a loss as a travesty of justice!

(*20*) Let justice prevail!

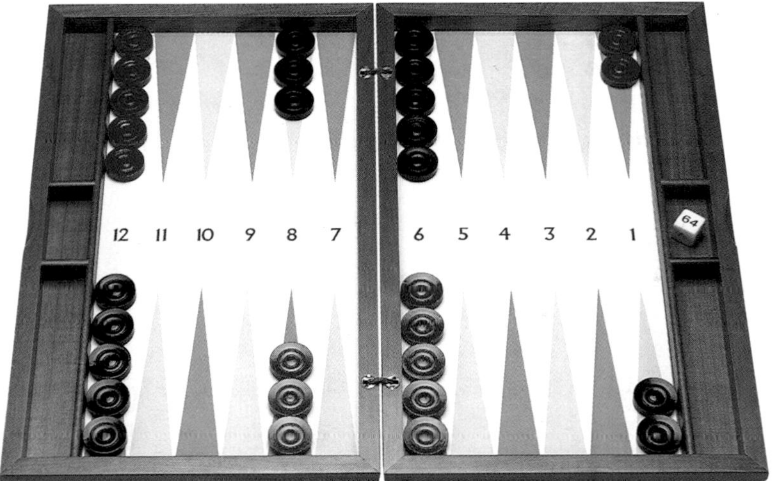

3

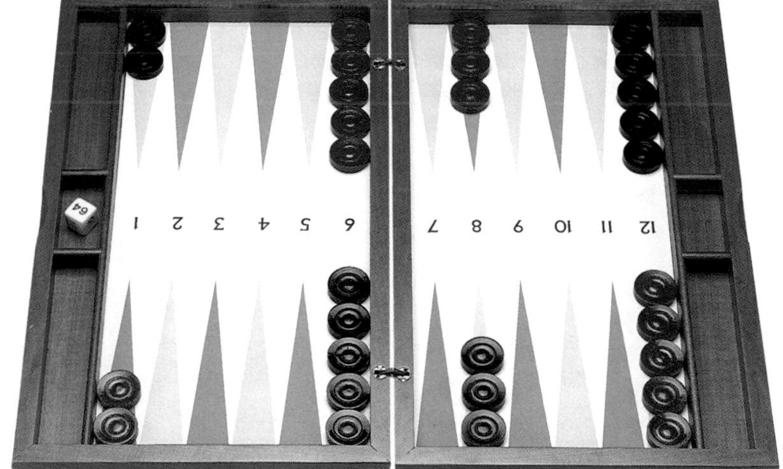

4

THE OFFICIAL RULES OF BACKGAMMON

These rules were laid down in 1931 by the Backgammon and Cards Committee of the Racquet and Tennis Club of New York, and have been adopted by players and clubs throughout the world.

THE GAME

(*1*) The game of backgammon is played by two persons.
(*2*) Thirty men, fifteen of one colour and fifteen of another, are set up as shown (**1**) on a standard board of four quarters or tables each having six points. In illustration (**1**) the players' inner tables are shown to the right. This means that Red's inner table is opposite his right hand, and Black's inner table opposite his left hand. In actual play it is customary to have the inner tables nearest the light.
(*3*) For entering and bearing off, the points in both inner tables are considered as numbered from one to six, beginning with the point nearest the edge of the board.
(*4*) Direction of play is from the opponent's inner table to the opponent's outer table, to your outer table, and then to your inner table.
(*5*) Play of the men is governed by two dice, thrown from a cup in which the dice are shaken before being thrown.
(*6*)(*a*) For the first game either player may ask to roll for choice of seats, men, or dice. Alternatively they may just sit down, set up the men and play.
(*b*) At the start of any later game either player may ask to mix the dice. In this case he shakes the four dice together in one cup and rolls them out. The opponent selects a die, then the roller, then the opponent, with the roller taking the last one.

THE THROWS

(*7*) For the opening throw, each player throws a single die. A tie requires another opening throw. Whoever throws the higher number wins, and for his

1

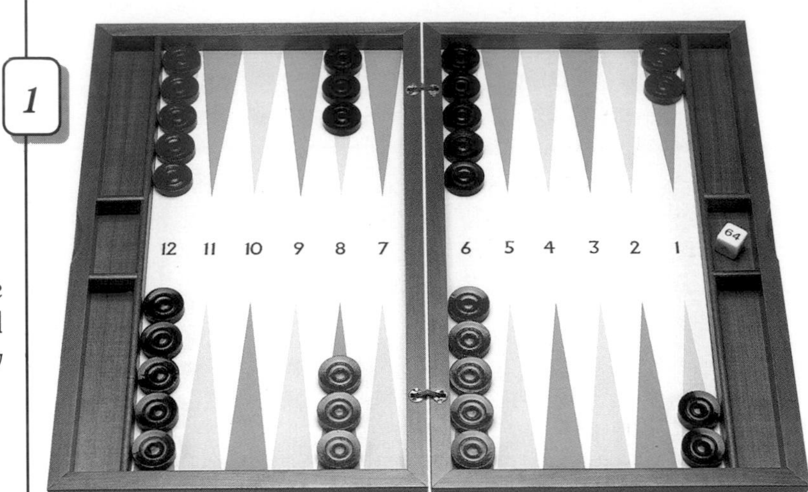

first move plays the numbers upon both dice. After that each player in turn throws two dice.
(*8*) The dice must be shaken thoroughly, rolled together, and come to rest flat (i.e. not "cocked") upon the table to the player's right. Otherwise they must be thrown again.
(*9*) There must be a rethrow if a throw is made before an opponent's play is completed.
(*10*) A play is deemed completed when a player has moved his men and starts to pick up his dice. If he starts to pick them up before playing all numbers he is legally allowed to, his opponent has the right to compel him to complete or not to complete his play. A roll by the opponent is considered an acceptance of the play as made (*see* Rule 19).

THE PLAY

(*11*) The play of the men consists of:
(*a*) Moving a man (or men) the exact number of points indicated by the number on each of the two dice thrown. One man may be moved the total of the two dice, or one man may be moved the number shown on one die, and an entirely different man the number shown on the other die.
(*b*) Entering a man from the bar, in the opponent's inner table, on a point corresponding to the number on a die thrown.
(*c*) Bearing off a man in the player's inner table, when no man is left outside that table or on the bar, in accordance with Rule 17.
(*12*) Doubles require four plays of the number on the dice.

(*13*) Plays must be made for both dice if possible. Either number may be played first. If either number may be played, but not both, then the higher number must be played.
(*14*) No play may be made which lands, or touches down, on a point held by two or more of the opponent's men.
(*15*) When a play lands on a point occupied by a single man (blot) of the opponent's, such a man is "hit" and must be lifted from the board by the hitter and placed on the bar in the centre of the playing board, to await entry in accordance with Rule 11(b).
(*16*) A player having a man on the bar may not play any other man until that man has been re-entered.
(*17*) When in position to bear off, you may bear off a man from a point corresponding to the number on a die thrown, or from the highest occupied point which is lower than the number indicated by a die. If the number is thrown for an unoccupied point, no man below can be borne off using this number, while any man remains on a higher point. You are not required to bear off a man if you are able to move forward on the board. Rule 13 applies here as in all other situations.

For example, look at (**2**). Your roll is 5-1. You may use the "1" to move from your five point to your four point, and then use the "5" to bear off a man from the four point; thus, you do not leave a man (a blot) exposed to a hit by Black's men positioned on your one point. In other words, Rule 13, stating that as long as you play both numbers you may play either one first, applies in bearing off as well as at all other times.

2

ERRORS

(*18*) If an error has been made in the set-up, it must be corrected if either player notices it before the second play of a game has been completed.
(*19*) If an error in play has been made, either player may require its correction before a subsequent throw, but not thereafter. The man played in error must be correctly played if possible.

SCORING

(*20*) A game is won by the player who first bears off all of his men. A gammon (double game) is won if the opponent has not borne off a single man. This doubles the count for a single game. A backgammon (triple game) is won if the opponent has not borne off a single man and has one or more men still in the winner's inner table or upon the bar. This triples the count for a single game.

DOUBLING GAME

(*21*) The count is raised (i.e. the doubling cube comes into play):
(*a*) *Automatically*: Each tie that occurs on the opening throw of a game doubles the previous count. Automatic doubles are not played unless the players have agreed to use them and an understanding has been reached as to the method and limitations of such doubles.
(*b*) *Voluntarily*: Either player may offer the first optional double of the previous count. After that the right to double the previous count alternates, being always with the player who accepted the last double.

A double or re-double may be offered only when it is the player's turn to play and before he has thrown the dice. He shall be deemed to have thrown the dice even if he rolls cocked dice. A double may be accepted or declined. The refusal of a double terminates the game, and the player refusing loses whatever the count may amount to before the double was offered.
(*22*) Gammons and backgammons double and treble the last doubling count respectively.

These, then, are the rules by which modern backgammon is played. Learn these rules thoroughly and quote them only if and when a dispute arises.

QUIZ QUESTION ANSWERS

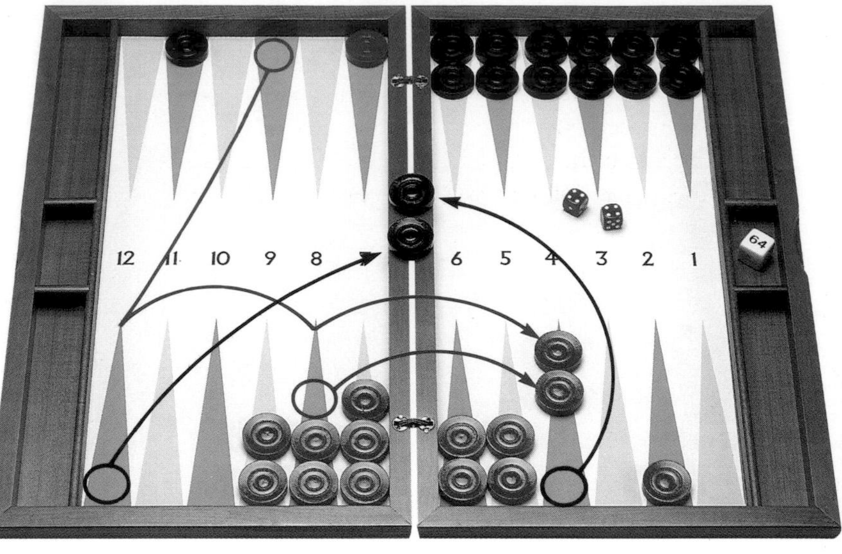

Page 57 (**11**):
B9 to R4 for three of the fours and R8 to R4 for the remaining four. You create a prime *and* hit two blots at the same time. It does not matter that you have a blot on R2. While you have a prime you can leave as many blots as you like.

Page 57 (**12**):
One man B8 to R8 and one man R11 to R8. This completes a prime for you. What about the blot on B8? Black has a closed board. Red is shut out. Good! Red is hoping that Black will hit this blot. He will have to break his shutout before Red can enter and all this time Black's back men have to remain captive behind Red's prime.

Page 57 (**13**):
B4 to B11. The obvious step of establishing a prime with R7 to R2, R4 to R2 would be quite wrong here. No – first you must get your back men free – then go for a prime.

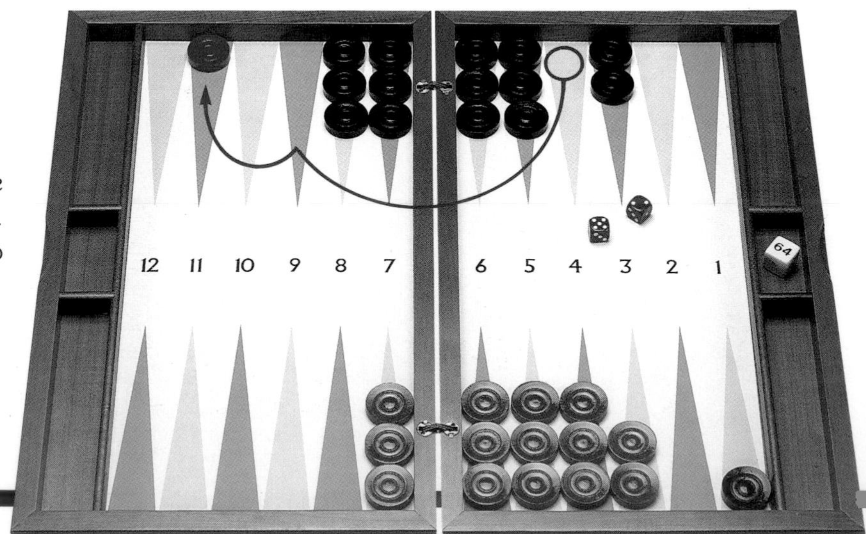

Page 65 (**17**):
Move two men B8 to R9. Before this roll both position counts total 46. After the roll, if you play it the way I recommend, Red's position count is 42 for a difference of *two throws*. Now, given an equal share of luck, Red will win and is, therefore, right in running.

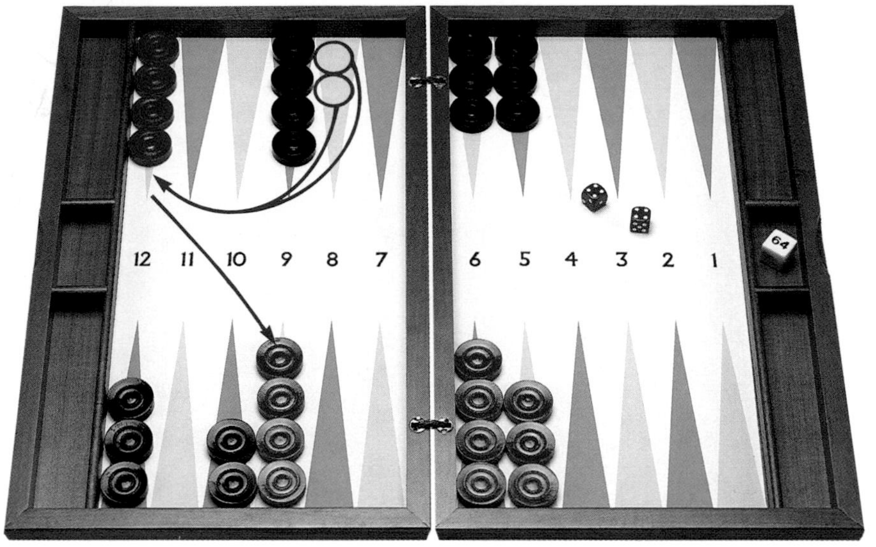

Page 65 (**18**):
Do not play B4 to B12 taking your back man to safety. If you do, your count will be 49 to your opponent's 39 – that is *five throws behind*. Your only hope is to stay back, hoping that Black will leave you a blot to aim at while coming round. So the correct move is R10 to R4, R6 to R4, making a strong point in your inner table. You should now aim to improve your inner table by securing more points if you can.

Page 65 (**19**):
A position count gives Red 44, Black 37. Therefore, Black is seven dice ahead. That is three and a half throws. But it is Red's roll – so Black is two and a half throws ahead.

Page 83 (**47**):
B12 to R7, B12 to R12. Timing is the problem again. Black may well get her two back men (on R9) past your block at B12 and home safely. This means that she may not have to leave a blot for several throws yet. This could be disastrous for you and would result in you having to break your semi-prime. Therefore you must be hit again in order to slow your game down. My recommendation gives you the best chances.

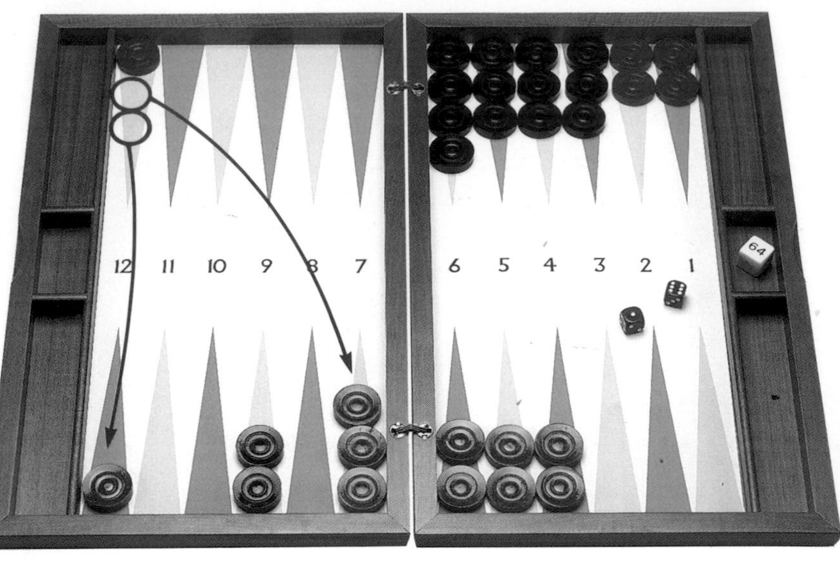

Page 83 (**48**):
R7 to R1, R10 to R5. If Black secures the R1 point she will have all the necessary ingredients for a good back game. Her man on the bar threatens to do this. You must stop her at all costs. R7 to R1 half secures the point for you and sends Black to the bar. If she now hits your blot, it is not serious because her inner table is wide open for you to re-enter. If she fails to hit you, the R10 to R5 move gives you the most combinations to close off the R1 point.

Page 83 (**49**):
B9 to B12, B12 to R7. *Do not hit* Black's blot on R10. By not hitting the blot you will probably force Black to break up the block in *her* inner table and also vacate her points in *your* inner table sooner than she would otherwise have to.

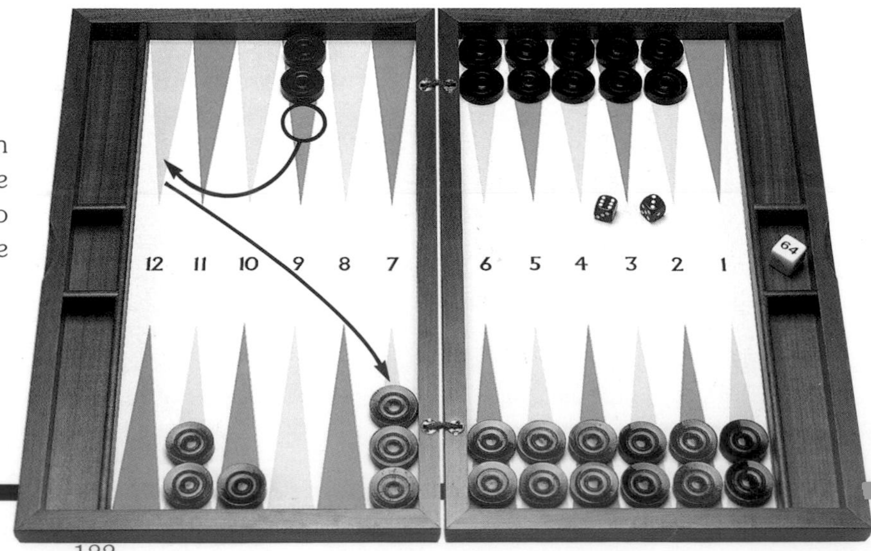

Page 83 (**50**):
Bar to B3, B3 to B9. Entering at B3 is pretty obvious but why B3 to B9 for the six? Unless you do this, a roll of 4-4 for Black would more than likely win the game. Now, a 4-4 roll hits your blot at B9 giving you a shot at Black's other blot at B2.

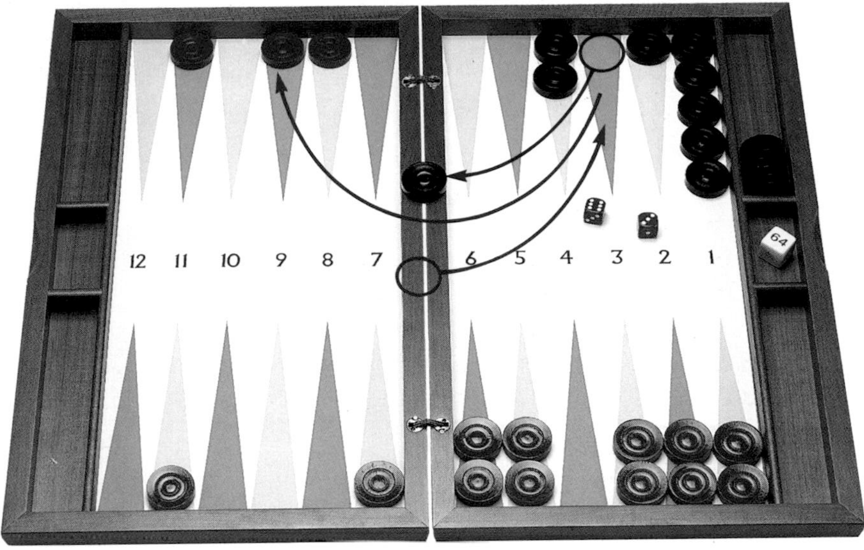

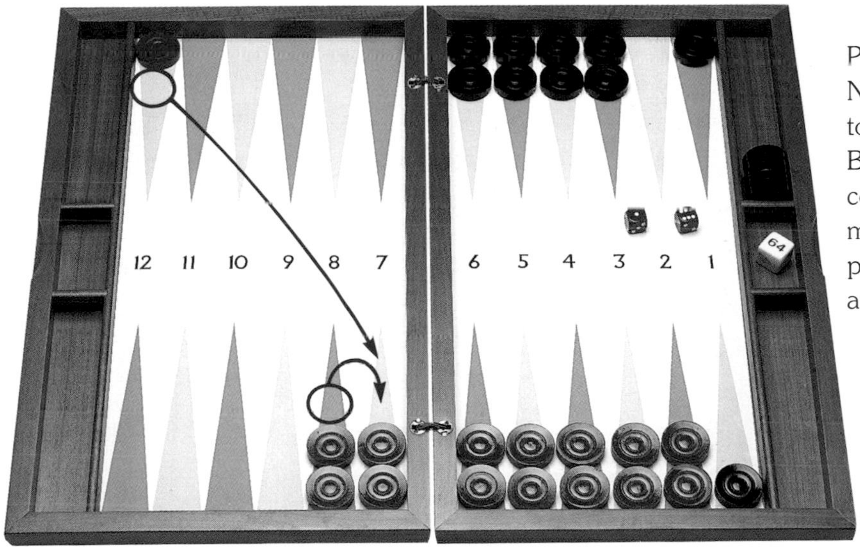

Page 85 (**5**):
No, this is not a "return play" situation. To play R8 to R1 would not just be wrong, it would be criminal! Black has only five men borne off and a position count shows the players fairly even. The correct move here is B12 to R7, R8 to R7 making your bar point and completing a prime. The stranglehold is on and a shutout is on the way.

Page 85 (**6**):
In this position R8 to R1 is correct. Black has already borne off eleven men and will almost certainly win this game unless you round up one of Black's blots at B1 and B3 with a return play.

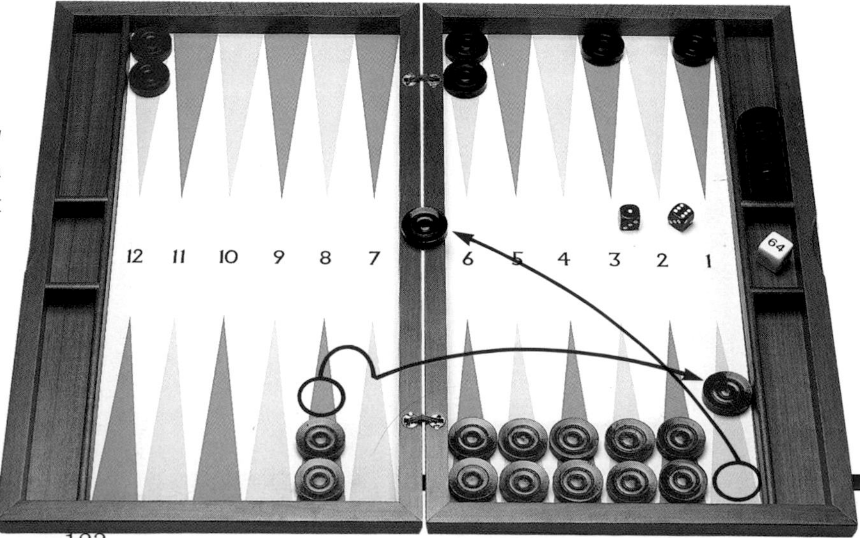

Page 94 (**24**):
Bear off at R6, R3 to R2 obeying the "closest-closer" rule. You now have a *greater* than even chance of bearing both men off on your next roll. You have also observed the "5-2" rule. On no account should you play the one by moving R5 to R4. The odds are 19/17 against you bearing both men off on your next roll as opposed to 17/19 with my recommendation. Avail yourself of the two extra chances!

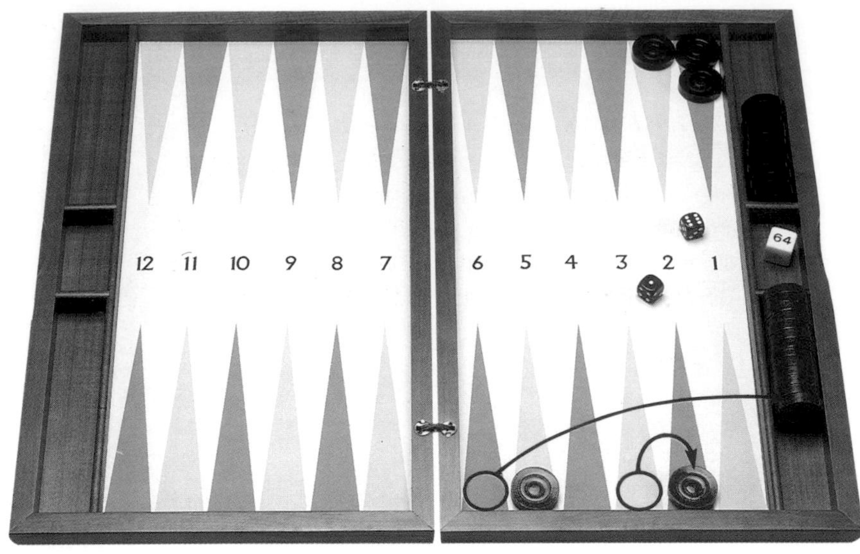

Page 94 (**25**):
R9 to R5 and bear off at R5. You play the four *first* and then bear the same man off the five point for the six. This is a simple problem but one that is often mis-played through negligence. The only bad roll for you now is 6-5, a 17/1 shot. The usual error is to play R9 to R3 and bear off at R4. This exposes you to four and a half times the danger of leaving a blot for Black's man on the bar to hit on re-entering.

Page 95 (**26**):
Bear one off R5 and hit the blot with R5 to R1. If Black re-enters at R1, he will hit your blot. There are eleven ways of doing this, seven of which also cause Black to begin breaking up his closed board. Nine other rolls will force him to re-enter on your six point and be out of your hair forever. Or he may fail to re-enter at all (sixteen ways). If, however, you bear men off from R5 and R4 you leave Black a three shot. The odds of him hitting you are the same – still eleven ways – but now only *two* of the hits also cause him to break up his closed board. Not so good!

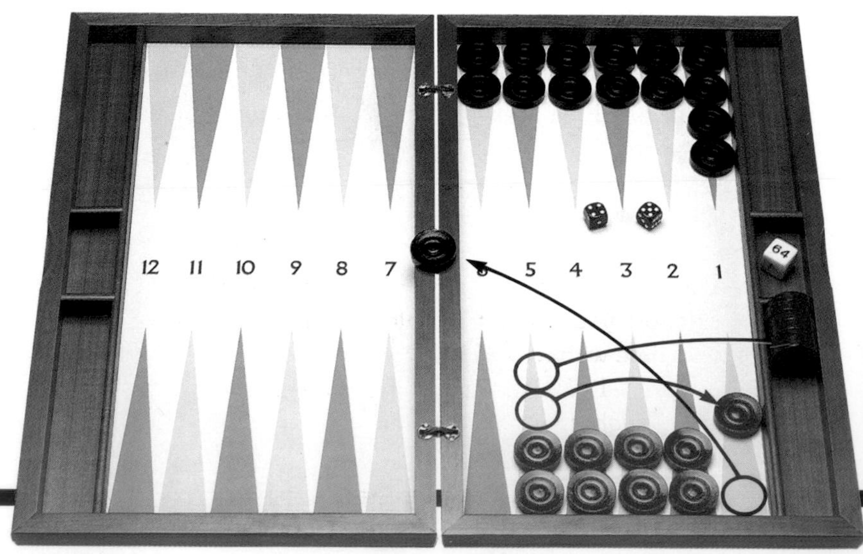

Page 95 (**27**):
Bear off at R4 and one off at R3. Black has two open points in the inner table so you can afford to go all out for a gammon. If Black hits you, it is not serious. You should still be able to re-enter, come round, and win the game without too much trouble. If he fails to hit you . . . go for the throat!

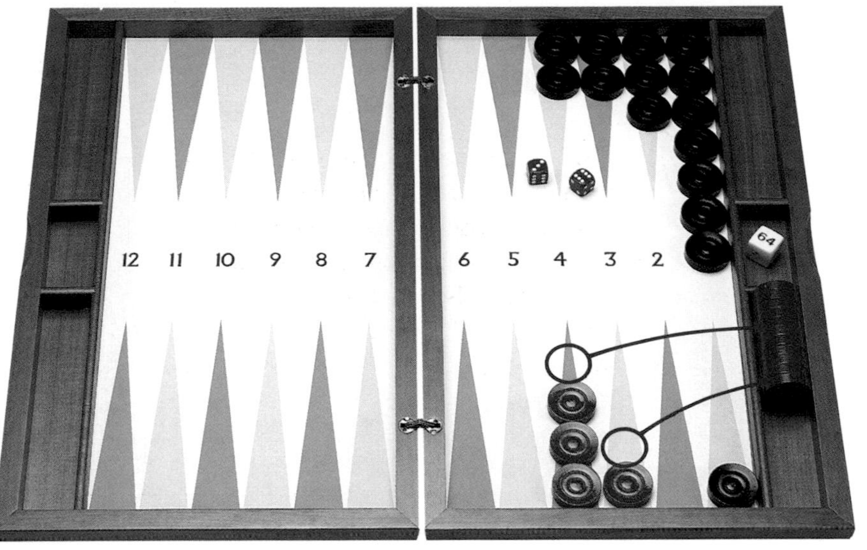

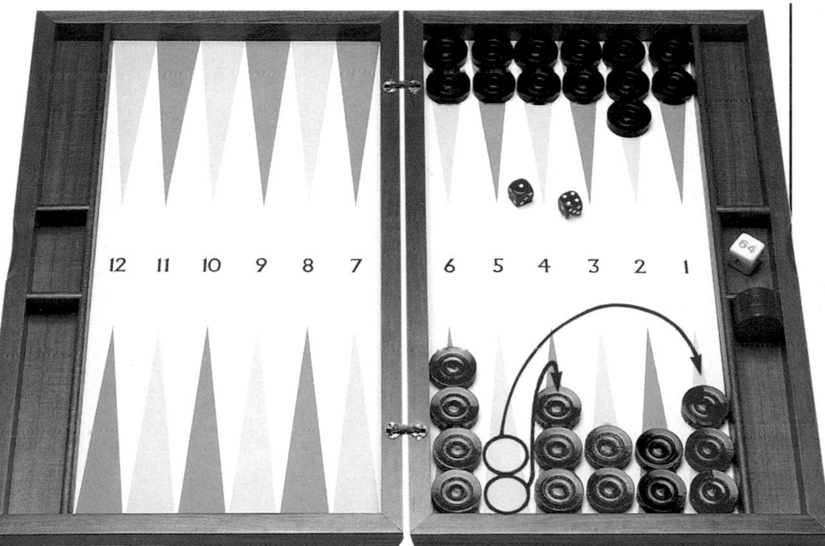

Page 95 (**28**):
R5 to R4, R5 to R1. Now, no matter what your next roll is, you will not have to leave a blot. If you had played R6 to R1, a dozen different rolls can cause you problems.

Page 99 (**4**):
28/8 or 7/2 against. You can re-enter on B5, B3 or B1; therefore you can only re-enter and hit the blot at the same time with rolls of 5-3, 3-5, 5-1, 1-5, 3-3, 3-1, 1-3, and 1-1. That is a total of eight rolls that hit, and twenty-eight that do not.

Page 105 (**6**):
Yes. Black will fail to bear off 11 times out of 36 if the law of probabilities runs true. Thus you will
lose 25 (x 2) = 50 points
win 11 (x 2) = 22 points
for a net loss of 28 points.
If you refuse all 36 games, you lose 36 points. So, in the long run, you will be a full 8 points better off if you accept.

Page 105 (**7**):
No. Red is too far advanced to think of mounting a successful back game and will have to begin breaking up the points in his inner table very soon, thus ruining his board. There is no doubt that Red would win sometimes were this same position played out say fifty times but I doubt if his odds are any better than 4/1 against.

Page 105 (**8**):
No. Black has already borne off one man and, therefore, needs seven rolls to remove all his men (providing he does not throw a double, 5/1 against). So he is ahead. He has a better position than Red also. Red will need eight rolls to bear off (barring doubles) because of his fifteenth man. If Black offers you the cube, you should refuse because you cannot win unless you throw a double. Black stands as much chance of doing this as you do.